# Innovation, Technology, and Knowledge Management

**Series Editor**

Elias G. Carayannis, George Washington University, Washington, WA, USA

This series highlights emerging research and practice at the dynamic intersection of innovation, technology, and knowledge management, where individuals, organizations, industries, regions, and nations are harnessing creativity and invention to achieve and sustain growth. Volumes in the series explore the impact of innovation at the "macro" (economies, markets), "meso" (industries, firms), and "micro" levels (teams, individuals), drawing from such related disciplines as finance, organizational psychology, R&D, science policy, information systems, and strategy, with the underlying theme that in order for innovation to be useful it must involve the sharing and application of knowledge.

This book series is indexed in Scopus.

Shuai Li

# Bridging the Innovation Gap

## From Technological Breakthroughs to Market Integration

Springer

Shuai Li
University of Oulu
Oulu, Finland

ISSN 2197-5698 ISSN 2197-5701 (electronic)
Innovation, Technology, and Knowledge Management
ISBN 978-3-032-22651-8 ISBN 978-3-032-22652-5 (eBook)
https://doi.org/10.1007/978-3-032-22652-5



This Springer imprint is published by the registered company Springer Nature Switzerland AG
The registered company address is: Gewerbestrasse 11, 6330 Cham, Switzerland

《Scandinavian Reflections: From Scientific Invention to Technology Transfer》

## *If You Find Someday Juha Suddenly Disappear*

At latitude 25° below the Arctic, where Juha lives, and where my friends are

*If you find someday Juha suddenly disappear, it must because the lingonberry is ripe. In Oulu's fields, the autumn's near, and mist rolls slow through northern light.*

*The ravens know, they circle low, their wings hum songs of long ago. He leaves his tools, his pipe, his chair—if you find someday Juha suddenly disappear.*

*He's the one they trust when storms arise, who mends the nets, who tells no lies. The children wait for his steady hand, the old ones smile—"He'll understand."*

*For in the hush where red fruit gleams, he gathers silence, breathes in dreams. The forest keeps what hearts confide, where rivers hum and stars abide.*

*So do not call, nor shed a tear—if you find someday Juha suddenly disappear. He'll return when snows begin to creep, for Oulu rests in the faith he keeps.*

# Preface

In every leap of human civilization, the power of technology has always played a central role. From the sharpening of stone tools to the roar of the steam engine, and to the vast waves of the information age, inventors have repeatedly expanded the boundaries of human understanding and reshaped our world through extraordinary intelligence and tireless exploration.

Yet, a thought-provoking phenomenon has long troubled countless ambitious technologists: why do brilliant inventions in laboratories often struggle to reach the market? Why are the groundbreaking theoretical breakthroughs of university professors so difficult to transform into commercial value accessible to the public?

This is not due to a lack of intelligence or creativity. Rather, it is because there exists an apparently invisible yet profound gap between technological invention and commercial success. Invention pursues pure creation—from nothing to something—it is about breakthroughs in principles and the perfection of performance. Business, on the other hand, is a complex system of going from "existing" to "excellent"; it requires a delicate balance and integration of markets, users, operations, supply chains, and even finance. Many technologists excel at "doing the right thing," yet often struggle with "doing things right."

This book was born to bridge that gap. We begin with a familiar yet often misunderstood legendary figure: Thomas Edison. We will analyze in depth his transformation from a pure inventor to an outstanding entrepreneur. Edison was not just the "King of Inventors"; he was a master of business operations, skilled in resource integration, and deeply market-oriented. His success was far from a stroke of luck—it was rooted in precise insights into market demand, unique understanding of supply chain management, and the optimal use of information transmission and sharing.

We also draw lessons from the fate of ancient Neanderthals to warn modern technology entrepreneurs. Despite their robust physiques and exceptional intelligence, Neanderthals lacked effective mechanisms for information transmission and sharing, forcing each generation to "reinvent the wheel," eventually disappearing in the tide of evolution. This serves as a vital warning for today's tech entrepreneurs: in an era of knowledge explosion and rapidly changing information, avoiding "reinventing the wheel," efficiently leveraging existing resources, and breaking down information silos are critical to success.

This book does more than recount the stories of Edison, the Neanderthals, British merchants' thinking, German meticulous technical approaches, the decisive strategies of chess, the long-term planning of Go, and the survival strategies of living fossil species like horseshoe crabs. Most importantly, it is a practical guide tailored for entrepreneurs from all technical backgrounds. It will guide you to step beyond purely technical thinking and consider the broader business landscape. It will help you understand how to transform technological invention into substantial commercial value. It will teach you how to integrate resources, manage supply chains, and effectively communicate your innovative ideas.

If you are a technologist with dreams, poised to embark on your entrepreneurial journey; if you are a technologist navigating obstacles and confusion along the path of entrepreneurship—then open this book. Edison's wisdom, the lessons of the Neanderthals, and the entrepreneurial principles revealed within will illuminate your way forward, helping you achieve steady, far-reaching success in the world of technological entrepreneurship.

Oulu, Finland
October 2025

Shuai Li

# Contents


**1 The Entrepreneurial Journey of a Successful Inventor and Businessman: Thomas Edison** ..... 1

1 Introduction: The Inventor's Dilemma and Edison's Breakthrough ..... 1

2 Technology cannot Move to Market on its Own: The "Valley of Death" on the Path of Invention ..... 2

3 The Edison Model: A Strategic Paradigm for Systematically "Building Companies" ..... 4

3.1 Organizational Invention as a Model beyond Individual Heroism ..... 4

3.2 The Company Incubator Model: Transforming Technological Achievements into Commercial Entities ..... 5

3.3 Invention as an Investment: Commercial Success as the Ultimate Goal ..... 6

4 Pain Points for University Professors: The Conflict between Research Diversity and Entrepreneurial Focus ..... 7

5 How to Replicate Edison: Designing Paths and Strategic Choices for Professors' Entrepreneurship ..... 9

5.1 Model 1: Lab-as-a-Venture-Studio ..... 9

5.2 Model 2: Linking Technology Portfolios with Specialized Incubation Funds ..... 10

5.3 Model 3: Collaborative Cross-Disciplinary Incubation Platforms ..... 11

6 Coordination Mechanism: Building a "Scientist + Entrepreneur" Dual-Drive Model ..... 11

7 Risks and Countermeasures: Challenges and Strategies of the Edison Model ..... 12

7.1 Market Validation Difficulties ..... 12

7.2 Slow Management System Development ..... 13

7.3 Challenges in Capital Coordination ..... 13
8 Conclusion: Organizing Creativity for Scalable Brilliance ..... 13
Further Reading ..... 15

**2 From a "Makeshift Troupe" to "Grand Accomplishment": The "Seven Dragon Balls" Strategy on the Entrepreneurial Journey ..... 17**
1 Introduction ..... 17
2 The "Seven Dragon Balls" Theory: Assembling and Coordinating Core Success Elements ..... 17
3 When the "Dragon Balls" Are Not all Gathered, where to Seek Them? ..... 21
4 When the "Dragon Balls" Are Not all Gathered: Wait or Act Immediately? ..... 22
4.1 Considerations for Acting Immediately without Waiting ..... 22
4.2 Considerations for Waiting and Exploring ..... 24
5 Conclusion ..... 24
Further Reading ..... 25

**3 From Crawling to Upright: Was this Humanity's Once-and-for-all Choice?: Humankind Has Been Restless about it for Millions of Years ..... 27**
1 Introduction ..... 27
2 The Duality of Evolution: The Costs of Upright Posture and the Wisdom of Adaptation ..... 27
3 The Inevitability of Survival: No Turning Back ..... 31
4 Lessons for Entrepreneurship: Nothing Is Ever Final; "Moving Under Load" Is the Norm ..... 32
5 Conclusion ..... 33
Further Reading ..... 33

**4 Learning Entrepreneurship Through Academic Writing: Refining Core Elements ..... 35**
1 A Good Idea Alone is not Enough: Invention + Feasibility + Relative Advantage ..... 35
2 Theoretical Analysis and Validation: The Entrepreneurial Business Model Must Be Self-Consistent ..... 37
3 Experimental Validation and Prototype Iteration: The Critical Leap from PPT to Product ..... 39
4 The Art of Writing a Good Paper: Entrepreneurship also Requires "Communication" Skills ..... 41
5 Choosing the Right Battlefield: Identifying Platforms and Channels is the Premise of Success ..... 43

6 Revision and Feedback: Feedback is not a Blow, but a Ladder to Progress ... 44
7 Leveraging Legacy: Standing on Shoulders Beats Closed-Door Reinvention ... 46
8 Conclusion ... 49
Further Reading ... 50

**5 Prioritizing R&D or Sales—A Reflection from the British Merchant Mindset vs. The German Rigorous Approach** ... 51
1 Introduction ... 51
2 The Transformation of Britain: From Invention Furnace to Commercial Hub ... 51
3 The Rise of Germany: The "Engineer Gene" Forged in Latecomer Advantage ... 53
4 Lessons for Entrepreneurs: Which "Historical Stage" is Your Company at? ... 56
5 Conclusion: Business Wisdom Beyond Technology ... 57

**6 Winning Through Strategic Positioning: Insights from the Comparison Between Go and Chess on the Long-Term Value of Corporate Strategy** ... 59
1 Introduction ... 59
2 Strategic Positioning: Building Enterprise Resilience and Sustained Growth Across Cycles ... 60
3 Avoiding the "Tactical Busyness" Trap: Returning to Strategic Essence and Top-Level Design ... 62
4 Implementing Long-Term Strategic Layouts: Challenges, Pathways, and the Critical Role of Leadership ... 63
5 Conclusion ... 65
Further Reading ... 66

**7 Asymmetric Advantage: Transforming Technical Depth into Commercial Moats** ... 69
1 Introduction ... 69
2 Anticipating the "End-State" in Technology Integration ... 70
3 From "What Others Have, I Have" to "What Others Don't Have, I Have" ... 70
4 The Data Flywheel Effect: Symbiotic Evolution of Technology and Data—Building Exclusive "Veins" ... 71

5 Network Effects: Exponential Value Growth with User Expansion—Weaving an Inescapable "Web of Value" ............ 73
6 High Switching Costs: The Invisible Chain of User Stickiness—Making Users "Willing to Stay" .................... 74
7 Brand and Trust: The Intangible Asset of Technical Strength—Forging an Impregnable "Mental High Ground" ........ 76
8 Conclusion ............................................... 77
Further Reading ............................................. 77

**8 Differentiation and Homogenization in Team Building ............ 79**
1 Introduction ............................................... 79
2 What Truly Holds a Team Together Is Not Shared Beliefs ......... 79
3 The Challenge of Complementarity—The Necessity of Management, Division of Labor, and System Design ........... 82
4 Culture as the Adhesive—Building a Hidden Mechanism for Sustainable Collaboration ................................ 84
5 Designing a Win-Win Structure—Binding the Team's Fate through Incentive Mechanisms ............................... 86
6 Corporate Culture and Regulations—The Lubricant for Cohesion in Differentiated Teams .......................... 88
7 Conclusion: Strategic Balance between Differentiation and Homogeneity—Building an Efficient and Stable Team System ..................................................... 89
Further Reading ............................................. 90

**9 Automation Vs. Centralization: The Hidden "Marginal Cost" of Centralization ............................................. 91**
1 Introduction ............................................... 91
2 Automation: The Allure of the Stars and the Reality of Reefs ...... 91
3 Centralization: The Infinite Magic of Marginal Cost Dividends .... 93
4 Dual-Engine Drive: How Automation Empowers Centralization ............................................. 96
5 Navigating for Entrepreneurs: Centralize First, Automate Later .... 97
6 Conclusion: Humans and Machines in Harmony, Navigating toward Shared Prosperity ................................... 100
Further Reading ............................................. 101

**10 Supply Chains: The Cornerstone of Corporate Strategy—with a Discussion on the Boundaries of Independent R&D ......................................... 103**
1 Introduction ............................................... 103
2 The Strategic Anchor of Supply Chains: Near-100% Reliability .... 103

3 The Risk Boundaries of Independent R&D: Natural Constraints on Success Probability ... 106
4 Strategic Choice: If You Can Leverage the Supply Chain, Don't Pursue Independent R&D ... 108
5 Conclusion and Outlook: Building a Strategic System of Resilience and Efficiency ... 111
Further Reading ... 112

**11 Paradigm Shift in Business Logic: From Products to Scenarios, from Industries to Ecosystems** ... 115
1 Introduction ... 115
2 Lessons from the History of Computer Programming: From "Adapting to Machines" to "Adapting to Humans" ... 116
3 Mapping to the Business World: The Paradigm Shift from "Producer-Centric" to "Consumer-Centric" ... 117
4 Industry Disintegration and the Rise of Ecosystems: The Inevitability of Breaking Traditional Boundaries ... 120
5 Conclusion: Survival Rules in the New Business Era ... 121
Further Reading ... 122

**12 Adapting to Change Vs. Responding to Change from Constancy** ... 123
1 Introduction ... 123
2 Origins: The "Atomic" Pursuit in Western Scientific Thought ... 123
3 The Entrepreneurial Misstep: When "Adaptability" Loses its Foundation ... 125
4 The "Atomic Theory" of Entrepreneurship: Building an Immutable Inner Drive ... 127
5 Conclusion: Anchoring the Unchanging amid Change, Embracing Change within the Unchanging ... 129
Further Reading ... 130

**13 Monetization Breakthroughs for Researchers: Turned: Entrepreneurs** ... 131
1 Introduction ... 131
2 The Essence of Sales: A Deep Analysis of Brand and Market Forces beyond Rational Consumption ... 133
3 Selecting the Ideal Battlefield: The Intersection of Market Forces, Competition, and Supply-Demand Imbalance ... 135
3.1 Highly Market-Driven and Sales-Competitive Industries: The Case of Quantitative Investing ... 136

3.2 "Boom" Industries: Where Demand Overwhelms Supply .... 136
4 Strategic Essence: Combining Fully Marketized Demand with Scarce Supply Advantages .... 138
5 Conclusion and Outlook: Cognitive Transformation and Ecosystem Building for Research Entrepreneurs .... 141
Further Reading .... 142

**14 Scientific Thinking Vs. Engineering Thinking: The Twin Wings of Corporate Strategic Planning** .... 143
1 Introduction .... 143
2 Scientific Thinking: Deep Insight and Long-Term Consideration .... 143
2.1 The Relentless Pursuit of Truth and Fundamentals .... 144
2.2 Deep Manifestations in Corporate Strategy .... 145
2.3 Resisting Short-Termism: Lessons From Chinese and Western Medicine .... 147
3 Engineering Thinking: Efficiency and Pragmatic Practice .... 148
3.1 Problem-Solving and Pragmatism .... 148
3.2 Efficient Implementation in Business Operations .... 149
3.3 Emphasizing Efficiency and Risk Control: Calculating the "Economic Equation" .... 150
4 Scientific and Engineering Thinking: Dialectical Unity and Integrated Application .... 151
4.1 Complementary Strategic Wings .... 151
4.2 Task Layering and Matching Thinking Modes .... 153
4.3 The Art of Dynamic Balance Between Depth and Speed .... 154
4.4 The Key Role of Organizational Culture and Leadership .... 155
5 Practical Pathways to Building an Outstanding Enterprise .... 157
5.1 Scientific Construction of Strategic Framework .... 157
5.2 Engineering Implementation of Execution Systems .... 157
5.3 Knowledge Management and Experience Accumulation Loops .... 158
5.4 Talent Development and Internalization of Thinking .... 159
6 Conclusion .... 160
Further Reading .... 160

**15 Persist or Adapt: How to Choose When Direction is Unclear** .... 161
1 Are You Upholding Your Beliefs, or just Being Stubborn? .... 161
2 Is Great Persistence Really About Willpower? .... 163
3 True Adaptability is Far from Simply Giving up .... 164
4 The Analogy of Choice Mechanisms—a Robot in a Maze .... 166
5 Cognition Determines the Path—How to Build Your Judgment System .... 168
6 Conclusion .... 170
Further Reading .... 170

**16 The Wisdom of Maritime Civilization—Complementary Balance and the Survival Laws of Modern Entrepreneurial Teams** ... 173
1 Introduction ... 173
2 Learning Management Wisdom from the Waves of Ancient Greece: How Geography Shapes Civilization ... 174
3 The "Island" Ecology of Startup Teams: Division of Roles and the Risk of Imbalance ... 175
4 Building a "Maritime Order" for Startups: The Practice of Complementary Balance ... 178
4.1 Clarifying Boundaries and Empowering Roles: Granting Sovereignty to Each "Island" ... 178
4.2 Building Multidimensional Communication and Collaboration Mechanisms: Constructing "Bridges Between Islands" ... 179
4.3 Equity and Incentive Design: Building a "Community of Interests" ... 179
4.4 The Role of Leaders: The Art of Balance ... 181
5 Beware of "Continental Thinking" in Startup Teams ... 183
6 Toward a "New Marine Civilization": Continuous Self-Evolution ... 184
7 Conclusion ... 185
Further Reading ... 186

**17 The Death of the Neanderthals: Why Strength and Intelligence Could Not Save Them** ... 187
1 Introduction ... 187
2 The Strong and Intelligent Neanderthals ... 187
3 Homo Sapiens and Neanderthals: A Contest of Information Sharing ... 189
4 Archaeological Evidence: Differences in Cultural Transmission and Technological Invention ... 192
5 The Pitfall of "Reinventing the Wheel": The Neanderthals' "Island Effect" ... 193
6 Modern Lessons: How Can we Avoid Becoming "Information Islands"? ... 194
6.1 Rejecting Closed-Door Reinvention: Leveraging Existing Knowledge—Learning and Transmission as the Foundation of Invention ... 195
6.2 Actively Socialize: Proactively Share and Learn ... 195
6.3 Ensuring Information Flow and an Inclusive Culture ... 197
6.4 Coordination of Supply Chains and R&D: Leveraging Existing Resources for Invention ... 198
7 Conclusion ... 200
Further Reading ... 202

**18 The First Principles of Success: Imitate those Who Have Achieved Results** ..... 205
1 Introduction ..... 205
2 The Paradox of Success: The Limits of Diligence and Intelligence ..... 205
3 Imitating those Who Have Achieved Results: The Shortcut to Success ..... 207
4 Observation and Immersion: From Information Acquisition to Cognitive Upgrade ..... 208
5 Imitation and Invention: First Imitate, Then Surpass ..... 210
6 Implications for Entrepreneurs ..... 211
7 Conclusion ..... 212
Further Reading ..... 212

**19 From Evolutionary Strategies to Business Wisdom: Navigating the Survival Rules of an Uncertain Era** ..... 215
1 Introduction ..... 215
2 The Echo of Evolution—Human Origins and Strategic Choices of Civilization ..... 216
2.1 Africa: The r-Selection Cradle—Exploring Genetic Breadth ..... 216
2.2 The K-Selection Stage of Eurasia: Deep Accumulation of Civilization ..... 217
3 The Commercial Jungle—The Evolutionary Laws of Business Strategy ..... 218
3.1 R-Selection: Explosive Growth in Chaos ..... 219
3.2 K-Selection: Forging Excellence in Stability ..... 219
3.3 Strategic Evolution and Switching ..... 219
4 Personal Growth: The Dynamic Balance of Breadth and Depth ..... 220
4.1 Exploration Phase: The r-Selection Model ..... 220
4.2 Advancement Phase: The K-Selection Model ..... 220
4.3 The Dynamic Balance of Personal Development ..... 221
5 Conclusion: The Wisdom of Timing and Judgment ..... 221

**20 From "Paper Publication" to "Product Endorsement": How to Win Public Trust** ..... 223
1 Introduction ..... 223
2 Paper Publication in the Scientific Community ..... 223
3 From "Lab Prototype" to "Market Success": Crossing the Trust Gap ..... 225
4 The New "Journals" of Public Trust: Traffic and Word-of-Mouth as Social Consensus ..... 225
5 Case Study: When the "Influencer Strategy" Becomes the New Product Launch ..... 227
6 From Lab to Market: Marketing as the Reproduction of Trust ..... 228
Further Reading ..... 229

**21 From Tulips to Bitcoin: How to Give a Product Lasting Monetary Value** .... 231
1 Introduction .... 231
2 The Feast of the Bubble: The "Pseudo-Scarcity" of Tulips .... 231
3 The Eternal Moat: Gold, Art, and the Secret of "True Scarcity" .... 232
4 The Value Amplifier: How Monetary Attributes Transform Product Destiny .... 233
5 Modern Case Studies: Who Plays with Scarcity and Monetary Attributes .... 233
6 The Complete Logic of Value and Insights for Entrepreneurs .... 234
7 Insights for Entrepreneurs .... 234
8 Conclusion .... 236
Further Reading .... 236

**22 Perseverance and Adaptability—Understanding the Choices of Modern Youth through Agrarian and Nomadic Civilizations** .... 237
1 Introduction: An Ancient Paradox .... 237
2 The Same Predicament, Yet Opposite Optimal Solutions .... 237
3 The Logic of Environment: The Distinct Survival Genes of Agrarian and Nomadic Civilizations .... 238
3.1 Nomadic Civilization: The Spirit of Adventure in Migration .... 238
3.2 Agrarian Civilization: The Logic of Perseverance in Settlement .... 240
3.3 Reward Mechanisms and Cultural Genetic Differences .... 241
4 The Cultural and Behavioral Extensions .... 242
4.1 The Extensions of Nomadic Culture: Invention and Expansion .... 242
4.2 The Extensions of Agrarian Culture: Stability and Order .... 242
4.3 Cultural Conflict and Complementarity .... 243
4.4 The Shaping of Individual Behavior .... 244
5 Cases from History and Reality .... 244
5.1 Successful Cases of "Nomadic Thinking" .... 244
5.2 Successful Cases of "Agrarian Thinking" .... 245
5.3 The Cost of Wrong Choices .... 246
5.4 Lessons from the Cases .... 246
6 Implications for Contemporary Entrepreneurs and Young People .... 247
7 Conclusion: The Environment Determines the Answer .... 248
Further Reading .... 249

**23 Respecting the Weak, Embracing Diversity: Long-Term Survival Principles in an Uncertain World** ..... 251
1 Introduction ..... 251
2 Cognitive Limitations: The Trap of Local Optima ..... 251
3 Environmental Dynamism: Today's Optimum, Tomorrow's Poison ..... 253
4 Implications for Entrepreneurship and the Future: Strategic Portfolios ..... 254
5 Conclusion ..... 255
Further Reading ..... 256

**24 The Cognitive Dilemma of Entrepreneurship—Why Grand Visions Often Stall at the Details** ..... 257
1 Introduction ..... 257
2 Modularity Thinking—The Key to Managing Complexity ..... 258
3 The Choice Between "Build" and "Buy" ..... 260
4 The Essence of the Supply Chain—Humanity's Collective Wisdom Across Time and Space ..... 261
5 The Pioneer's Dilemma and the Later Entrant's Opportunity—Lessons from History ..... 262
5.1 Pioneering Alone in a Technological Wasteland ..... 263
5.2 Supply Chain Integration of Core Modules: From "Build" to "Commodity" ..... 263
5.3 The Later Entrant's "Aggregated Advantage" ..... 263
6 Profound Lessons for Entrepreneurs ..... 264
6.1 The Primary Imperative of Risk Management: Survival ..... 264
6.2 Timing of Entrepreneurship: Beyond Market Trends to Supply Chain Maturity ..... 264
6.3 The Essence of Teams: Modular Organizational Structure ..... 265
6.4 The Golden Rule for Launching Projects: Map Module Risks ..... 265
7 Conclusion: Evaluating Projects Means Evaluating the Number of "Self-Developed" Modules ..... 265
Further Reading ..... 266

**25 End-State Thinking: Foreseeing the Inevitable, Strategizing the Present** ..... 267
1 Introduction ..... 267
2 Darwin and Malthus: Revealing the Inevitable of Natural Selection ..... 267
3 Mao Zedong's *on Protracted War*: Insights into the Terminal Victory of War ..... 270
4 Computational Algorithm Complexity: Anticipating End-State Performance with Large-Scale Data ..... 271
5 The Essence and Practical Value of End-State Thinking ..... 273

5.1 The Essence of End-State Thinking: Insight from Inevitability ..... 273
5.2 The Practical Value of End-State Thinking: Begin with the End, Strategize the Present ..... 274
6 Implications for Entrepreneurs ..... 275
7 Conclusion: Anchoring Certainty Amid Uncertainty ..... 277
Further Reading ..... 277

**26 Terminal Cost—Understanding the Evolutionary Logic of Business** ..... 279
1 Introduction ..... 279
2 Your Business Compass: What is Terminal Cost? ..... 279
3 Act I: The Endless Linear Trap (O(N)) ..... 280
4 Act II: The Magical Leap to Zero Marginal Cost (O(1)) ..... 281
4.1 Virtual Information Products: The Miracle of Replication ..... 281
4.2 Shared Infrastructure: The Power of One-Time Investment ..... 282
5 Act III: The Ultimate Evolution of Platforms and the "Winner-Takes-All" Dynamic ..... 283
6 Seeing Beyond the Numbers: The Ultimate Link Between Terminal Cost and Profit ..... 284
7 Your Business Compass: Applying Terminal Cost Thinking ..... 285
8 Conclusion ..... 285
Further Reading ..... 286

**27 The Secret to Longevity Is "Petrification": Survival Strategies from the Horseshoe Crab** ..... 287
1 Introduction ..... 287
2 The "Petrified" Survival Rules of the Horseshoe Crab: The Underlying Logic of Longevity ..... 287
2.1 The Life Philosophy of "Minimal Appetite": Low-Cost Survival through Minimalism ..... 288
2.2 "Indestructible" Defense System: The Wisdom of Stability amid Change ..... 289
3 The Universality of "Petrification" Wisdom: Comparing Lifespans of Living and Non-living Entities ..... 290
3.1 Animals: High Activity and High Consumption Lead to Shorter Lifespans ..... 291
3.2 Plants: Relatively Stationary and Self-Sufficient, Living Longer than Animals ..... 291
3.3 Non-living Entities Have the Longest Lifespans: The Ultimate Manifestation of "Petrification" ..... 291
4 The Boundaries of Expansion and the Reevaluation of Defense Value ..... 293
5 Balancing Offense and Defense in Invention and Development: Practicing "Petrification" Wisdom ..... 293

5.1 Strategic Defense: Building the Foundation for Survival ..... 293
5.2 Precision Offense: Expanding Boundaries Judiciously ....... 294
5.3 Continuous Learning and Adaptation: The Art of Dynamic Balance ..... 295
6 Conclusion ..... 295
Further Reading ..... 295

**28 Constancy in Evolution: The Survival Wisdom of Living Fossils ... 297**
1 Introduction ..... 297
2 Universal Traits: The Conservative Beauty and Extreme Efficiency at Life's Core ..... 298
3 The Art of Survival for Living Fossils: Responding to Change Through Constancy ..... 299
3.1 Coelacanth: A Time Refuge in the Deep Sea and a Conservative Life Philosophy ..... 299
3.2 Horseshoe Crab: Multi-Layered "Biological Insurance" and Robust Defense ..... 301
3.3 Nautilus: The "Technological Monopoly" and Niche Competition in the Deep Sea ..... 302
4 The Wisdom of "Living Fossils": Profound Lessons for Modern Entrepreneurship ..... 303
5 Conclusion: The Enduring Wisdom of Living Fossils and the Future of Entrepreneurship ..... 304
Further Reading ..... 305

# Chapter 1
# The Entrepreneurial Journey of a Successful Inventor and Businessman: Thomas Edison

## 1 Introduction: The Inventor's Dilemma and Edison's Breakthrough

In today's wave of technology-driven entrepreneurship, there exists a seemingly paradoxical yet awkward reality—a vast chasm that stretches before countless scientists and university professors. Among them are top talents capable of solving world-class technical problems, even nurturing technological prototypes in their laboratories that could change the world. Yet, when these brilliant creations attempt to reach the broader market, they often encounter barriers, struggling to convert into tangible commercial value.

This is especially true for university professors. They possess deep academic foundations and unparalleled creativity, yet often falter on the rugged path of entrepreneurship. This is not due to a lack of intelligence or creativity, but rather because the intrinsic logic and operational patterns of scientific research and commercial practice are fundamentally different (Fig. 1).

In addition to founding the well-known General Electric Company, he established numerous other notable enterprises, including the Edison Electric Light Company, the Edison Phonograph Company, and the Edison Storage Battery Company. Understanding how Edison transformed from a technical specialist into a successful entrepreneurial businessman provides valuable lessons for technologists seeking to venture into entrepreneurship.

Technological invention, at its core, is pure creation—from nothing to something. It pursues breakthroughs in principles, the perfection of performance, and the expansion of cognitive boundaries. Commercial success, on the other hand, is a complex system of moving from "existing" to "excellent." It requires meticulous refinement and balance across multiple dimensions: market demand, user experience, operational efficiency, supply chain management, financial health, and more.

Technologists are more adept at "doing the right thing"—achieving technical perfection supported by rigorous logic and data. The business world, however, is far



S. Li, *Bridging the Innovation Gap*, Innovation, Technology, and Knowledge Management, https://doi.org/10.1007/978-3-032-22652-5_1

**Fig. 1** Edison is a familiar name as an inventor, but he was also an outstanding entrepreneur.

harsher, demanding "doing profitable things"—identifying and realizing commercial value within complex and ever-changing market environments. Between these two realms, Thomas Edison stands out as a quintessential example of successfully bridging the gap. He was not the first inventor in human history; indeed, countless flashes of genius before him had propelled societal progress.

What truly set Edison apart was that he was the first to systematically "mass-produce inventions" and to convert these inventions into large-scale industries. His model reveals the deeper logic of how technological achievements move from the laboratory to the market.

## 2 Technology cannot Move to Market on its Own: The "Valley of Death" on the Path of Invention

Between a promising technological prototype in the laboratory and a mature product widely accepted by consumers and generating stable revenue lies a long and perilous stretch known as the "Valley of Death." Successfully crossing this valley often requires navigating a series of complex and high-risk stages: technology must advance from theoretical validation to engineering maturity; prototypes must be productized to meet user experience requirements; critical financing must be secured to support subsequent investment; complex supply chains and production management must be established; distribution channels and market promotion must be built across regions; and ongoing customer education and maintenance must be conducted.

**Fig. 2** University professors typically face significant challenges in the process of technology commercialization, as technologies must navigate the "Valley of Death" when moving from the laboratory to the market

Each stage entails substantial financial investment, significant time consumption, and unpredictable risk. Most technologists, relying solely on their expertise and resources in their specialized fields, often find it difficult to independently manage any of these critical stages (Fig. 2).

This challenge is particularly pronounced for university professors. They spend years immersed in an academic environment centered on research, with their careers focused on exploring the mysteries of science, emphasizing technical precision, elegant principles, and the boundaries of theory. In their mindset, "invention" is often synonymous with "breakthrough research," while market considerations receive relatively little attention.

In stark contrast, the business world defines "invention" in a far more pragmatic and utilitarian way: it focuses on whether demand is real and strong—that is, whether users truly need the product and are willing to pay for it; it concerns whether users will actually buy—the ability of the product to translate into tangible sales; and it emphasizes whether competitors might reach the market first, highlighting the brutal reality of fleeting market windows.

If a university professor, fueled by passion, attempts to personally establish and operate a company, they are likely to fall into the dilemma of "being both general and soldier." They must dive deep into cutting-edge research while simultaneously managing teams, expanding markets, coordinating supply chains, and handling finances—tasks that often pull them in conflicting directions, leaving them overwhelmed.

Moreover, professors typically explore multiple research directions throughout their academic careers, each of which may contain potential commercial breakthroughs. This raises a fundamental question: how can they achieve "scalable commercialization" of their research outcomes, rather than relying on chance for isolated successes? This inherent structural contradiction creates enormous challenges when translating a single scientific achievement into a sustainable commercial entity.

## 3 The Edison Model: A Strategic Paradigm for Systematically "Building Companies"

Thomas Edison is widely recognized as the "King of Inventors," but defining him merely as an inventor undoubtedly underestimates his strategic vision. His most remarkable achievement was not a single light bulb, but his success in transforming his patents into an industrial giant—General Electric (GE)—while simultaneously creating a comprehensive and effective process for technological commercialization. Edison was the first to propose the concept of the "invention factory," which was not a simple laboratory but an organized system capable of continuously generating commercially viable inventions. Even as inventions were being created, he systematically considered how to build markets around them (Fig. 3).

Edison's success stemmed from his profound insight into the relationship between invention and commercialization, which he translated into three core strategic approaches:

### *3.1 Organizational Invention as a Model beyond Individual Heroism*

Edison understood that in the face of complex inventions, the capabilities of a single individual were limited. He broke away from the traditional model of the solitary inventor and built an interdisciplinary R&D team. This team brought together top talents from physics, engineering, chemistry, and other fields to collectively tackle technical challenges.

He was no longer a lone genius locked away in a laboratory, but rather a visionary project manager or CTO (Chief Technology Officer), guiding the overall direction while efficiently coordinating team resources and systematizing and standardizing the invention process. This organizational approach to invention laid the foundation for

**Fig. 3** Edison successfully explored an integrated process combining research, industrialization, management, and leadership, which guided the success of both his R&D and entrepreneurial ventures

Edison's ability to "mass-produce" inventions and greatly increased both the success rate of his inventions and their potential for commercial transformation (Fig. 4).

## 3.2 *The Company Incubator Model: Transforming Technological Achievements into Commercial Entities*

One of Edison's most remarkable strategies was the establishment of nearly independent commercial companies for each of his major inventions. For example, the development of the light bulb ultimately gave rise to the Edison Electric Company (the predecessor of General Electric); battery technology led to the creation of the Edison Storage Battery Company; and the phonograph resulted in a separate phonograph company. These companies were not merely technical licensing entities; they were

**Fig. 4** Organizational invention is far more than individual heroism; it requires effective team collaboration

founded on technological inventions and equipped with independent management teams and fully functional commercial operations.

This meant that beyond pure technical invention, these companies had professional teams to optimize market strategies, manage daily operations, and handle finances effectively. This "company incubator" model allowed Edison to isolate risks between different businesses and ensure that each invention received professional commercial management and market cultivation, greatly increasing the likelihood of commercial success.

## *3.3 Invention as an Investment: Commercial Success as the Ultimate Goal*

Unlike many scientists who view research papers as the final product, Edison from the outset considered "commercial success" the ultimate goal of his inventions. For him, an invention was merely the first step, the starting point of an "investment project." The subsequent steps included finding suitable business partners, securing effective financing, assembling professional operational teams, packaging the technology into market-competitive products, and ultimately bringing them successfully to market.

Edison's role was never that of a laboratory-bound gatekeeper of research; he was an industry pioneer and organizer. Through a process-oriented, organized, and structured approach, he closely connected technological R&D with commercial realization, achieving systematic "mass production" and commercialization of his inventions (Fig. 5).

**Fig. 5** Edison adopted the "company incubator" model, establishing an independent company for each of his major inventions, such as the Electric Light Company, the Phonograph Company, and the Battery Company

## 4 Pain Points for University Professors: The Conflict between Research Diversity and Entrepreneurial Focus

In their academic careers, university professors typically explore multiple research directions. This diversity in research is an inherent requirement for academic development. For example, a professor in the field of electrical engineering may be deeply interested in optimizing smart grids, while also conducting in-depth research on high-efficiency electric vehicle motors, and even maintaining a keen focus on cutting-edge wireless energy transfer technologies. This multi-track approach, balancing both breadth and depth, is a defining characteristic of academic accumulation and knowledge invention (Fig. 6).

However, the logic of running a business is entirely different. Commercial success often requires extreme focus and specialization. A company must concentrate its

**Fig. 6** Invention is not the endpoint but merely the starting point for commercial success. Edison continually presented his inventions to entrepreneurs and bankers, actively seeking opportunities for commercialization

limited resources and energy on a core product or service, refine it to perfection, and continuously invest in R&D, marketing, and operations to secure a position in fierce market competition. This "focused approach" inherently conflicts with the "dispersed research" style that professors are accustomed to.

As a result, many professors face a critical strategic fork when considering entrepreneurship: If a professor chooses to personally serve as the core manager of a company and devotes all their energy to founding it, they inevitably must abandon most of their research directions, concentrating years of academic accumulation on a single focus, and sustain this effort for a decade or more before seeing significant results. For those used to the freedom of academic exploration, this represents a tremendous shift.

Conversely, if a professor chooses to maintain their existing research path and continue exploring multiple frontiers, it becomes extremely difficult to genuinely focus on and deeply manage a company. Daily operations and market competition demand full engagement from management, creating an almost irreconcilable conflict with academic responsibilities.

Consequently, we often observe professors entering entrepreneurship with high enthusiasm, only to see their companies overwhelmed by market forces within three to five years. Simultaneously, they may find it difficult to return to their original research state after being detached from the academic frontier for so long. This is not a matter of individual ability but a structural mismatch between scientific research and commercial practice. Resolving this deep-seated contradiction is key to successful professor-led entrepreneurship.

## 5 How to Replicate Edison: Designing Paths and Strategic Choices for Professors' Entrepreneurship

Since professors find it difficult to personally immerse themselves in a commercial project, can we learn from Edison's "platform-based entrepreneurship" model? The answer is yes. With clever path design and strategic choices, professors can fully leverage their technical advantages while avoiding areas of commercial weakness, achieving scalable commercialization of their research outcomes.

### *5.1 Model 1: Lab-as-a-Venture-Studio (Fig. 7)*

Viewing a professor's laboratory as an organically operating "technology incubation platform" is a modern interpretation of Edison's "invention factory" concept. In this model, the professor's role is no longer that of the company's day-to-day manager but resembles that of a "chief scientist" or "chair of a technical advisory board." Their primary responsibilities are to maintain leadership over technical direction, plan forward-looking research, and tackle key technical challenges. Specific commercial technology development tasks can be undertaken by research teams such as graduate students and postdoctoral fellows, while the company's core business functions—operations, market expansion, financing, and management—are handled by externally recruited professional teams. Whenever a research project validates its technological maturity and commercial potential in the lab, an independent incubation process can be initiated, spinning it off into a startup with independent legal status and a dedicated management team. This clear division of roles allows professors to focus on their core strengths while avoiding the distractions of daily business operations.

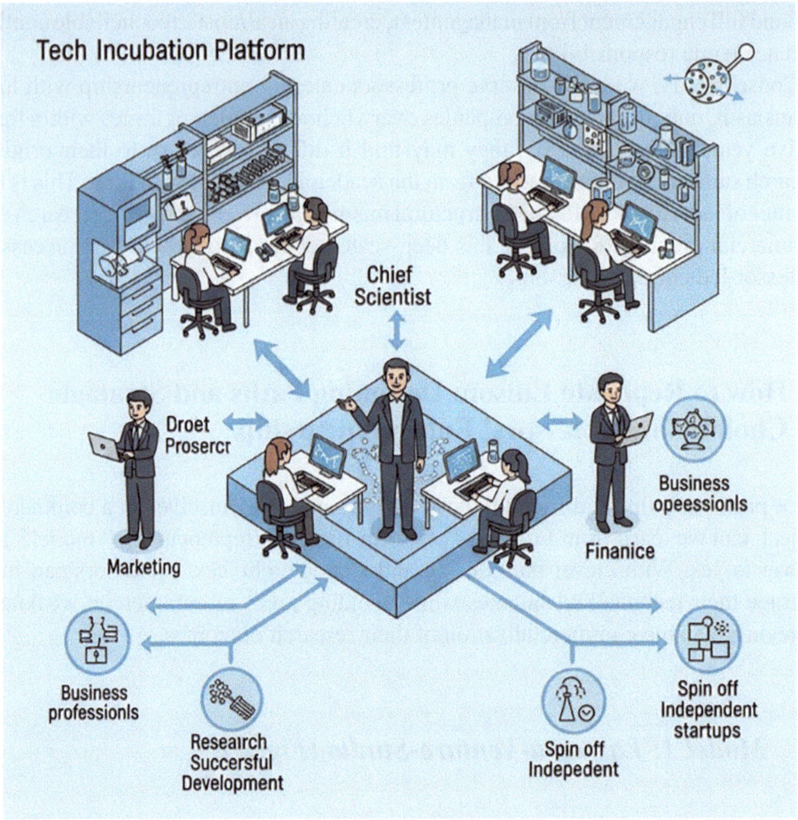


**Fig. 7** The model of transforming a professor's laboratory into a "technology incubation platform"

### *5.2 Model 2: Linking Technology Portfolios with Specialized Incubation Funds*

Professors can also draw inspiration from Edison's use of patents and company equity, treating their technological outputs as an "investment portfolio." In this model, a professor may consider establishing—or partnering with the university to establish—a technology achievement foundation or tech investment fund. This fund can accept applications from research projects with commercial potential both inside and outside the university, using the lab's outcomes as early-stage investment targets for incubation. Professors themselves or the fund's professional investment team can screen projects from an investor's perspective, assign dedicated operational teams, provide seed funding, and organize necessary external resources. This approach parallels Edison's use of capital to manage a portfolio of technologies, incubating and scaling multiple companies, and enables diversified and capitalized operations of research outputs.

### 5.3 *Model 3: Collaborative Cross-Disciplinary Incubation Platforms*

Edison's early R&D teams were exemplary in their cross-disciplinary nature. Today, universities can similarly organize cross-departmental incubation platforms. For example, a professor with deep expertise in AI algorithms could collaborate with another professor skilled in embedded hardware design, and combine efforts with a business professor or external expert with strong market insight. Together, they can incubate disruptive startup projects. This diverse combination of knowledge and skills can significantly increase the success rate of technology commercialization, as a successful commercial project typically requires seamless integration across technology, product, market, and operations. This model encourages breaking down academic silos, promotes knowledge cross-pollination, and fosters inventions with greater market competitiveness.

## 6 Coordination Mechanism: Building a "Scientist + Entrepreneur" Dual-Drive Model

A technology project requires capabilities far beyond the technology itself to move from lab research to market launch. It is like a high-performance car: it needs a powerful engine (technology), a responsive steering system (market), an efficient transmission (operations), and a stable fuel tank (finance). Thus, establishing an effective "scientist + entrepreneur" dual-drive coordination mechanism is key to invention success.

In this mechanism, roles are clearly defined:

- **Technical Decision-Maker (Scientist):** Typically the university professor, responsible for defining the frontier of technology, ensuring the product's uniqueness and advancement, and serving as the source of invention. They continuously monitor technological trends and provide long-term strategic guidance for the enterprise.
- **Business Architect (Entrepreneur):** A crucial complementary role in tech entrepreneurship. They design business models, secure external financing, build sales channels, and establish the company's initial organizational structure. They bridge technology and market, transforming abstract technical value into concrete business opportunities.
- **Operations Executor (Manager):** Responsible for turning the business architect's vision into reality, ensuring product production and delivery, optimizing daily operations, and guaranteeing efficient resource utilization—the foundation of a healthy company.

Edison's genius lay in instinctively establishing this clear, efficient, collaborative mechanism in the early stages of tech commercialization. He understood that his strength was technology and his weakness business, so he actively recruited and trusted professional business talent. Today, professor-entrepreneurs should similarly reflect: "Which part am I best suited for, and who will handle the remaining business and operational responsibilities?"

Moreover, universities can proactively construct a systematic collaborative ecosystem—for example, "Professor + Entrepreneurial CEO + Alumni Fund + Incubator." The professor provides the technological source, the CEO manages daily operations, the alumni fund supplies early capital, and the professional incubator offers comprehensive mentorship and resource integration. Such institutionalized, platform-based mechanisms effectively promote technology commercialization and create a virtuous cycle of invention.

## 7 Risks and Countermeasures: Challenges and Strategies of the Edison Model

While Edison's model is highly instructive, directly replicating it in today's complex tech entrepreneurship environment faces significant challenges. Market competition is fiercer, technology evolves faster, and capital markets are more demanding. The three main risks and strategies are:

### *7.1 Market Validation Difficulties*

A laboratory-tested, high-performance product does not automatically guarantee market acceptance. Tech teams often overestimate technological value while underestimating the diversity, complexity, and volatility of customer needs. Insufficient market validation is a core reason many tech startups fail in the "Valley of Death." Even Edison had failed inventions, but he could quickly pivot.

*Countermeasure:* Encourage professors and tech teams to participate in entrepreneurship bootcamps or market validation courses to strengthen their understanding of business logic and market dynamics. Promote early-stage MVP iterations and user testing to validate demand and adjust direction rather than developing in isolation. Leverage third-party market consulting for objective analysis and user profiling to enhance technology-market fit.

### 7.2 *Slow Management System Development*

University professors, accustomed to loose collaboration in small research teams, often lack experience in building rigorous company systems, standardized processes, and efficient team management, which may lead to chaos and inefficiency as the company scales.

*Countermeasure:* Establish a university-led entrepreneurial mentor system, inviting alumni or entrepreneurs with successful startup or management experience to advise professor-led teams. In early-stage companies, bring in experienced professional managers as COO or VP to build operational systems. Encourage team members to attend professional management courses to improve organizational and leadership skills.

### 7.3 *Challenges in Capital Coordination*

Early-stage tech projects often involve heavy assets, long cycles, and high risk, making them unattractive to traditional venture capital. Finding angel investors willing to assume early risks and understand technology invention is a major challenge.

*Countermeasure:* Universities can establish or guide the creation of angel funds led by internal or alumni networks, focused on early-stage commercialization of faculty research, lowering the barrier to initial financing. They can also actively collaborate with incubators, accelerators, or government-guided funds, which are more inclined to support early tech projects and provide incubation services and resource integration, refining business models and enhancing investment appeal. Participation in startup competitions and pitch events also provides early capital and visibility.

## 8 Conclusion: Organizing Creativity for Scalable Brilliance

It is better to organize a team to invent a hundred light bulbs than for one person to invent just one. Thomas Edison not only invented the light bulb but also organized teams to produce numerous innovative technological products across multiple fields. This transcends the glory of a single invention and strikes at the core of true technology commercialization: success does not rely on the flash of a single genius, but on structural organizational design and strategic coordination, systematically aggregating dispersed creativity and guiding it toward the market (Fig. 8).

For today's university professors, the most critical strategic decision is not simply whether to start a business, but rather to deeply consider what kind of structure to use for entrepreneurship. Instead of personally plunging into the commercial

**Fig. 8** Moving from the laboratory to industrialization requires a shift from individual heroism to organized invention

frontlines and consuming precious research time on areas outside their expertise, it is wiser to become the one who builds the platform, integrates resources, and guides direction. Professors can be the soul of a company's "technological engine," but they should more importantly serve as the mind of a "systems designer." By using Edison's model as a mirror, they can maintain their research leadership while, through sophisticated organization and collaboration, transforming academic achievements into a continuous stream of commercial value.

Edison's model serves as a practical guide for professors to achieve the "mass production" of research outcomes. It outlines a clear path: from a single breakthrough in the laboratory to a systematic invention factory; from individual flashes of inspiration to cross-disciplinary team collaboration; from pure technological pursuit to value creation driven by commercial success. In the future of technological competition, those who best understand and implement this model will be able to convert limitless creativity into boundless commercial potential, ultimately achieving industrial brilliance of their own in the tide of the times.

## Further Reading


1. X. Cao, *Modern Business Management*, Palgrave Macmillan, 2025a.
2. X. Cao, *Strategic Management and Organizational Development*, Springer, 2025b.
3. T. Hughes, *Networks of Power: Electrification in Western Society, 1880–1930*, Johns Hopkins Univ. Press, 1983.
4. A. Pacey, *The Maze of Ingenuity: Ideas and Idealism in the Development of Technology*, MIT Press, 1992.
5. P. Israel, *Edison: A Life of Invention*, Wiley, 1998.
6. D. Nye, *American Technological Sublime*, MIT Press, 1994.
7. J. Schumpeter, *The Theory of Economic Development*, Harvard Univ. Press, 1934.
8. H. Etzkowitz, *The Triple Helix: University–Industry–Government Invention in Action*, Routledge, 2008.
9. R. Nelson and S. Winter, *An Evolutionary Theory of Economic Change*, Harvard Univ. Press, 1982.
10. C. Christensen, *The Innovator's Dilemma: When New Technologies Cause Great Firms to Fail*, Harvard Business School Press, 1997.
11. E. G. Carayannis, Ed., *Encyclopedia of Creativity, Invention, Innovation and Entrepreneurship.* New York, NY: Springer, 2013. doi:https://doi.org/10.1007/978-1-4614-6616-1.

# Chapter 2
# From a "Makeshift Troupe" to "Grand Accomplishment": The "Seven Dragon Balls" Strategy on the Entrepreneurial Journey

## 1 Introduction

Amid the vast and turbulent waves of the business world, countless entrepreneurs start from zero, endure countless hardships, and ultimately achieve remarkable success. The journey from a seemingly modest "makeshift troupe" to a brilliant "grand accomplishment" is not a simple linear progression. Rather, it resembles a challenging and opportunity-filled quest to "gather the Seven Dragon Balls." This journey requires entrepreneurs to possess the strategic wisdom to identify, collect, and effectively integrate core elements, thereby laying a solid and unshakable foundation for the success of their enterprise (Fig. 1).

## 2 The "Seven Dragon Balls" Theory: Assembling and Coordinating Core Success Elements

Any grand and complex endeavor, no matter how intricate or multifaceted it may appear on the surface, ultimately relies on the completeness and efficient coordination of a series of critical core elements. Just like a modern automobile, which consists of thousands of precision components, each performing a unique function, yet only when properly organized and integrated under a precise control system can the vehicle operate efficiently, travel great distances, and fulfill its intended mission. In this seemingly complex but inherently structured process, the fundamental condition for success is the assembly of all these essential core elements. This mirrors the premise in the classic Japanese manga *Dragon Ball*, where collecting all seven Dragon Balls summons the dragon to grant a wish—symbolizing that only by gathering all key elements can one unlock the "divine power" of success.

In the entrepreneurial context, building a company from scratch is essentially a challenging and intelligent quest to find and assemble these "Seven Dragon

 
S. Li, *Bridging the Innovation Gap*, Innovation, Technology, and Knowledge Management, https://doi.org/10.1007/978-3-032-22652-5_2

**Fig. 1** Each Dragon Ball represents a core element of success. The process of achieving entrepreneurial success is essentially the process of gathering all these core elements—in other words, the quest to collect all seven Dragon Balls

Balls." These "Dragon Balls" may be scattered across different fields, reside within different individuals, or sometimes a "chosen one" may simultaneously hold more than one "Dragon Ball," possessing multiple key abilities. Historical examples of legendary successful team formations consistently validate the profound wisdom of this "Dragon Ball assembly."

Take, for example, the Tang Sanzang expedition team from the Chinese classic *Journey to the West*. The "Dragon Balls" they needed to collect on their journey to the West clearly included: a Dragon Ball representing formidable execution and problem-solving abilities, capable of defeating demons, clearing obstacles, and opening paths forward, embodied by the powerful Sun Wukong; a Dragon Ball representing steadfast diligence, loyal execution, and the unwavering implementation of leadership principles, embodied by the reliable Sha Wujing; and a Dragon Ball representing team cohesion and emotional bonding, acting as a lubricant to ease the long and monotonous journey while mediating internal conflicts, embodied by the optimistic and affable Zhu Bajie. Together, these abilities constituted the essential core elements for the success of the expedition—none could be omitted. Similarly, whether it was Liu Bei's "Three Visits to the Thatched Cottage" to secure Zhuge Liang's strategic wisdom during the Three Kingdoms period, or Emperor Gaozu Liu Bang's wide recruitment of talent after the Hongmen Banquet, culminating in great achievements, they were all, consciously or unconsciously, engaging in "Seven Dragon Ball" assemblies, gathering top talent from diverse fields to build strong teams capable of supporting ambitious goals.

Since "Dragon Balls" are the foundation of success, which "Dragon Balls" are the most critical and indispensable for entrepreneurship? While specific industries, business models, and development stages may bring differentiated needs, the following seven "Dragon Balls" are generally recognized as universal and essential, collectively forming the "golden combination" for entrepreneurial success:

- **Vision and Strategic Foresight**: This Dragon Ball is the soul and steering wheel of entrepreneurship. It encompasses not only the entrepreneur's or team's deep insight into future market trends, industry direction, and enterprise positioning but also the ability to translate such insight into a clear, inspiring vision and executable strategy. It determines the enterprise's course, guides resource allocation, and maximally unites the team around shared goals and motivation. Without this Dragon Ball, even the strongest execution could end up on the wrong path, heading toward failure.
- **Core Tech/Product Invention**: In today's increasingly competitive market, unique technological barriers or disruptive product inventions form the foundation for an enterprise's survival and the key to sustaining competitive advantage. This Dragon Ball ensures that the enterprise can deliver solutions that are rare in the market, address deep user pain points, or significantly enhance user experience, creating a hard-to-replicate differentiation. Whether tech-driven or business model-innovative, every enterprise must possess its own "killer feature."
- **Market Insight and User Connection**: This Dragon Ball represents the enterprise's ability to understand true market needs, capture deep user psychology, and establish effective channels for user engagement and feedback. It ensures that products or services precisely hit market pain points and can rapidly iterate and optimize as user demands and market conditions evolve. Without this Dragon Ball, even superior technology or products may go unnoticed.
- **Operational Excellence and Execution**: No matter how grand the strategy or inspiring the vision, strong execution is required for realization. This Dragon Ball encompasses efficient process management, rigorous cost control, flexible supply chain optimization, and responsive operational capability. It serves as the bridge from strategic blueprint to tangible results, ensuring that objectives are achieved with maximum efficiency and minimal cost.
- **Funding and Capital Management**: Especially in the early stages of a startup, sufficient and sustainable funding is the lifeblood of the enterprise. This Dragon Ball represents the entrepreneur's ability to secure external investment (such as angel investors or VC funds), manage cash flow effectively, and allocate capital wisely to support business growth. Insufficient funding or poor financial management is often a critical cause of failure.
- **Talent Acquisition and Team Building**: A successful enterprise cannot exist without a high-quality, cohesive team aligned toward common goals. This Dragon Ball reflects the entrepreneur's ability to attract top talent, build a sound organizational structure, unlock team potential, and cultivate a positive, dynamic corporate culture. Talent is the enterprise's most valuable asset; without the right team, even the best ideas cannot succeed.
- **Risk Management and Agility**: The entrepreneurial journey is full of uncertainty. The ability to identify potential risks (market, technical, policy, managerial), formulate contingency plans, and swiftly adjust strategies and tactics in

crises is vital. This Dragon Ball ensures that the enterprise can navigate unforeseen challenges, maintain resilience, and even discover new opportunities amid adversity (Fig. 2).

Of course, these seven "Dragon Balls" do not exist in isolation; they are interrelated and mutually supportive, collectively forming an organic whole. A successful startup team is often the product of these "Dragon Balls" being effectively combined and synergized.

**Fig. 2** The key core elements required for entrepreneurship—the "dragon balls" of startup success

## 3 When the "Dragon Balls" Are Not all Gathered, where to Seek Them?

If entrepreneurs or teams find, after self-assessment, that one or several of the "Dragon Balls" are still missing or show significant gaps, how should they effectively search for and fill these deficiencies? This requires a systematic "Dragon Ball-seeking" strategy—sharp like a detective, patient like a hunter.

First, conduct a thorough self-inventory and objective assessment. Startup teams should regularly and honestly examine the capabilities and resources they already possess, clarifying which "Dragon Balls" are already in hand and at an advantage, and which remain blank or have significant gaps. This requires a high degree of self-awareness, avoiding blind optimism or overconfidence, and encourages open communication among team members to jointly identify capability gaps.

Second, regarding the missing "Dragon Balls," there are several main avenues to pursue, each with its own advantages and disadvantages, requiring flexible selection based on the specific situation:

1. **Internal Development and Capability Enhancement**: For skills that can be acquired through learning, practice, and experience accumulation (such as refined operations, basic technical development, project management), team members can improve through self-study, internal training, external professional courses, or industry workshops. This is a relatively low-cost but longer-term way to fill gaps, suitable for non-core but important and malleable capabilities.
2. **External Recruitment and Talent Acquisition**: This is the most direct and fastest way to supplement critical "Dragon Balls." For especially rare skills that are difficult to cultivate in the short term and are crucial to the company's success (such as top-tier scientists, experienced marketing experts, or senior CFOs), bringing in top talent from outside—through competitive compensation, equity incentives, an attractive corporate culture, and growth opportunities—is a common practice among successful enterprises. This approach requires entrepreneurs to have the ability to identify, utilize, and retain talent.
3. **Strategic Partnerships and Resource Integration**: If a company cannot acquire a certain "Dragon Ball" quickly, or if the cost of acquisition is too high, it can consider deep cooperation with external organizations or companies that already possess the "Dragon Ball" through strategic alliances, joint ventures, outsourcing, technology licensing, or even mergers and acquisitions. For example, partnering with an entity that has a strong distribution network to compensate for lacking market channels, or collaborating with a research institution or startup with core technology to accelerate product development and commercialization. This method enables complementary advantages and quickly generates synergistic effects.
4. **Consulting and Advisory Support**: In some specialized fields, short-term professional consulting services can help a company quickly access the necessary knowledge, experience, and guidance—essentially "borrowing a temporary Dragon Ball" to support business decisions. For instance, hiring advisors in legal,

financial, or market strategy areas can provide critical advice at key moments, preventing major mistakes.
5. **Mentorship and Experience Transfer**: Seeking senior mentors or successful entrepreneurs within the industry, and benefiting from their experience sharing, regular guidance, and network resources, can help entrepreneurs avoid common pitfalls and accelerate the understanding and mastery of certain "Dragon Balls." This informal learning and growth approach often yields unexpected rewards.
6. **Community and Ecosystem Participation**: Actively participating in industry communities, incubators, accelerators, or related ecosystems can broaden the channels for "Dragon Ball" acquisition. In these platforms, entrepreneurs have opportunities to meet potential partners, investors, and talent, and gain inspiration and support from peer exchanges.

The process of seeking "Dragon Balls" is, at its core, a continual cycle of learning, adaptation, and evolution for entrepreneurs and their teams. It demands an open mindset, keen insight, strong learning ability, relentless perseverance, and, when necessary, the humility to seek guidance.

## 4 When the "Dragon Balls" Are Not all Gathered: Wait or Act Immediately?

This is a question that frequently challenges entrepreneurs at a deep strategic level, concerning the very survival of their venture: "If the 'Dragon Balls' are not fully gathered, should one wait and explore until everything is in place, or should one act immediately, even with some elements missing?" The answer is not one-size-fits-all; it requires careful consideration based on the specific circumstances (Fig. 3).

### *4.1 Considerations for Acting Immediately without Waiting*

In the following situations, even if the "Dragon Balls" are not fully gathered, it may be necessary to act decisively and seize the opportunity:

- **Ephemeral Market Opportunities (First-Mover Advantage)**: If facing a market window that is extremely short and where first-mover advantage is critical—such as the early stages of emerging technologies or the onset of policy incentives—excessive waiting could mean losing the entire market to competitors. In such cases, even with some capability gaps, it is necessary to enter quickly and learn or fill the gaps during the process, advancing in a "learn and fix along the way" approach.
- **Urgent Need to Validate Core Assumptions (MVP and Validation)**: Sometimes, the most critical "Dragon Ball" is the market's genuine feedback and user

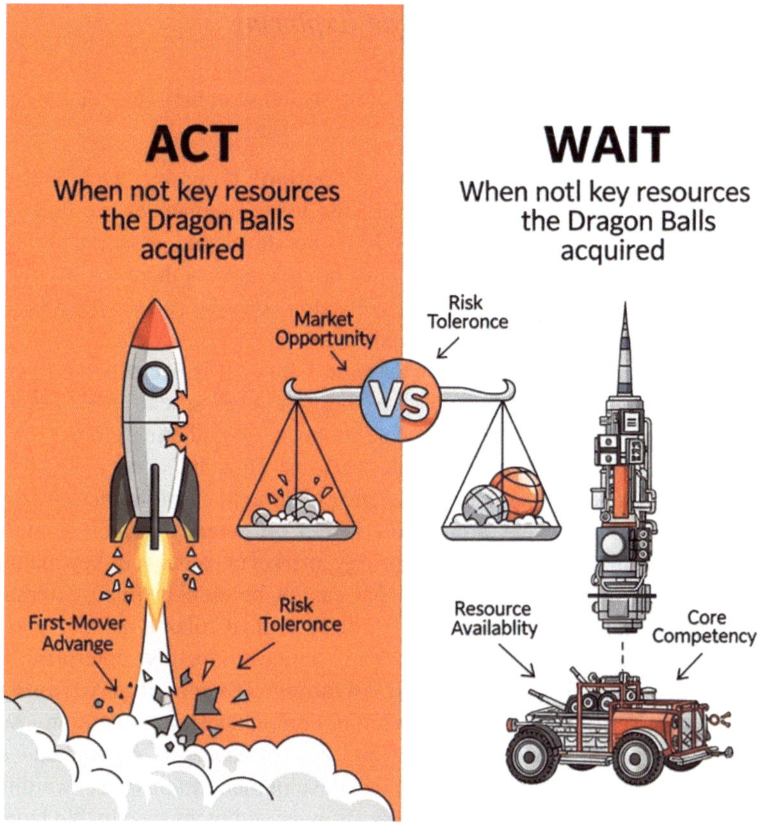


Fig. 3 When the "Dragon Balls" are not all gathered, should you wait or take immediate action?

demand for the product. Even if the team is incomplete and the product is not fully functional, it is necessary to launch a minimum viable product (MVP) promptly to validate key business hypotheses and collect user data, avoiding excessive investment in the wrong direction. This rapid iteration strategy itself is an important method of "Dragon Ball" acquisition.

- **Learning and Iteration as Core Competency (Learning by Doing)**: In certain industries, the ability to rapidly experiment, learn from failures, and continuously iterate is itself a crucial "Dragon Ball." Rather than waiting for perfection, it is better to refine the team and capabilities through practice, viewing action as part of the "Dragon Ball" acquisition process.
- **Scarce and Hard-to-Obtain Resources (Resource Constraints)**: If acquiring certain "Dragon Balls" is extremely costly or time-consuming, waiting could lead to cash flow problems or team morale depletion. In such cases, it may be necessary to start with partial capabilities and gradually fill the gaps through operational progress, using business growth to attract more resources.

### 4.2 Considerations for Waiting and Exploring

However, in other circumstances, strategic waiting and searching may be the wiser choice, helping to avoid greater risks:

1. **Unbearable Core Risks (Critical Risk Mitigation)**: If missing "Dragon Balls" directly impact the enterprise's survival, and the consequences are unacceptable—for instance, core technologies are not yet developed, essential certifications are unavailable, the product has major safety issues, or there are unsolvable legal or compliance problems—premature action could be catastrophic. In such cases, these core issues must be resolved first.
2. **Ambiguous Strategic Direction (Strategic Clarity)**: If even the "Vision & Strategic Foresight Dragon Ball" is missing, leaving the team unclear about direction, target customers, or core value proposition, gathering other "Dragon Balls" may result in inefficient or aimless efforts. Time and energy should first be invested in market research and strategic planning to clarify direction.
3. **Severe Gaps in Core Team Capabilities (Core Competency Gap)**: If the startup team lacks essential skills in core technology, market expansion, or key management roles (e.g., CEO, CTO, CMO) that cannot be quickly filled externally, waiting to find partners or talent to fill these critical roles is a safer choice. Without core capabilities, the team cannot sustain a competitive enterprise.
4. **Full Preparation Brings Exponential Advantage (Exponential Advantage)**: In certain complex or high-investment sectors, comprehensive preparation—such as patent layouts, key talent in place, and market education completed—can deliver exponential benefits for subsequent development. In this case, waiting is not passive but a deliberate strategy for a stronger and more sustainable launch.

Ultimately, entrepreneurs must weigh the costs of waiting (opportunity, time, morale) against the risks of immediate action (failure, wasted resources, misdirection). There is no absolute right or wrong; the key is a deep understanding of the team's resources, market conditions, industry characteristics, and the importance of missing "Dragon Balls." A wise entrepreneur, like an experienced chess player, applies tactics flexibly within a macro-level strategic perspective, neither losing sight of the bigger picture nor remaining rigid, but dynamically balancing to gather "Dragon Balls" and achieve business success.

## 5 Conclusion

From a "makeshift troupe" to a "grand accomplishment," the entrepreneurial journey is filled with challenges yet brimming with possibilities. Understanding and actively gathering the "Seven Dragon Balls" is a necessary path to success. This requires not only recognizing the core elements of success but also possessing the wisdom and courage to find, supplement, and integrate them. In rapidly changing markets, knowing when to act decisively and when to patiently prepare is key to ultimately summoning your own “Shenlong” and achieving your grand vision. Each collection of a “Dragon Ball” tests the entrepreneur’s intelligence, perseverance, and decisiveness, marking milestones in the growth and evolution of the enterprise.

## Further Reading


1. X. Cao, *Modern Business Management*, Palgrave Macmillan, 2025.
2. X. Cao, *Strategic Management and Organizational Development*, Springer, 2025.
3. J. Collins, *Good to Great: Why Some Companies Make the Leap and Others Don’t*, Harper Business, 2001.
4. H. Mintzberg, *The Rise and Fall of Strategic Planning*, Free Press, 1994.
4. E. Teece, *Dynamic Capabilities and Strategic Management*, Oxford Univ. Press, 2009.
5. M. Porter, *Competitive Strategy: Techniques for Analyzing Industries and Competitors*, Free Press, 1980.
6. P. Drucker, *Invention and Entrepreneurship*, Harper & Row, 1985.
7. S. Blank, *The Startup Owner’s Manual*, K & S Ranch, 2012.
8. E. Ries, *The Lean Startup*, Crown Business, 2011.
9. R. Katz and T. Allen, “Investigating the Not-Invented-Here (NIH) syndrome: A look at the performance, tenure, and communication patterns of 50 R & D project groups,” *R&D Management*, vol. 12, no. 1, pp. 7–19, 1982.
10. E. G. Carayannis, Ed., *Encyclopedia of Creativity, Invention, Innovation and Entrepreneurship*. New York, NY: Springer, 2013. doi:https://doi.org/10.1007/978-1-4614-6616-1.

# Chapter 3
# From Crawling to Upright: Was this Humanity's Once-and-for-all Choice? : Humankind Has Been Restless about it for Millions of Years

## 1 Introduction

When we discuss human evolution, bipedalism undoubtedly stands as a milestone leap. It liberated our hands, opening the door to tool-making and fine manipulation, which in turn accelerated the development of the brain, ultimately enabling humans to become the rulers of the Earth. We tend to regard this remarkable achievement as a divinely granted, perfect choice, assuming its benefits are pure and limitless. However, a closer examination of millions of years of human evolutionary history reveals that the path to upright walking was fraught with hardship and trade-offs. Humans are still paying the price to adapt to this posture and continue to engage in a long and profound "struggle" with the accompanying negative consequences. This was far from a once-and-for-all decision; rather, it is an ongoing, dynamic process that continues to this day.

## 2 The Duality of Evolution: The Costs of Upright Posture and the Wisdom of Adaptation

Around six million years ago, the environment in the eastern African Rift Valley began to undergo dramatic changes. Dense forests gradually gave way to savannahs, forcing tree-dwelling apes to adapt to life on the ground. This environmental pressure is believed to have been the key driver behind our ancestors' adoption of upright walking. Archaeological evidence, such as the 3.7-million-year-old hominin footprints discovered at Laetoli in Tanzania, clearly illustrates that early hominins (like *Australopithecus afarensis*) were already capable of bipedal locomotion—long before the emergence of the earliest stone tools (Fig. 3.1).

However, the evolutionary process of humans descending from the trees to the ground was far from a one-time achievement. The transition from ape-like crawling

 
S. Li, *Bridging the Innovation Gap*, Innovation, Technology, and Knowledge Management, https://doi.org/10.1007/978-3-032-22652-5_3

**Fig. 3.1** The Laetoli footprints reveal well-preserved hominin tracks embedded in volcanic ash, illustrating the arduous steps from ape-like crawling to upright walking. However, what appears to be a "one-step" evolutionary leap was in fact a series of complex physiological trade-offs; our body was not "designed" for long-term bipedalism

to upright walking involved arduous steps. What appears to be a "one-step" leap in evolution was actually a series of complex physiological trade-offs; our bodies were not "designed" for long-term bipedalism.

The most immediate cost is reflected in the difficulty of childbirth. Human infants are born with relatively large heads—about 25% of body weight—which is crucial evolutionarily, as it accommodates a larger brain. Yet, upright walking, necessary to support the weight of the torso, narrowed the female pelvis, creating a relatively tight birth canal. This conflict between a "big head and small body" and a "narrow birth canal" makes human childbirth among the most difficult, prolonged, and dangerous of all mammals.

In stark contrast, the vast majority of other animals' offspring can stand or run shortly after birth. Human babies, however, are effectively "premature" at birth: their nervous systems are underdeveloped, muscle strength is insufficient, and they are completely incapable of independent survival. This extreme vulnerability undoubtedly increased survival risks for early human groups, requiring adults to invest considerable energy in prolonged and meticulous caregiving. Yet, this very challenge also fostered a high degree of social cooperation, deepened parental care, and strengthened emotional bonds, laying the foundation for the emergence of complex social structures (Fig. 3.2).

Secondly, the upright posture has imposed unprecedented stress on our skeletal and circulatory systems. The spine, originally curved like an arch, evolved into an S-shaped curve to accommodate upright walking, but this structure also makes it more susceptible to vertical pressure-related injuries. This helps explain why modern humans commonly suffer from cervical spondylosis, lumbar disc herniation, and sciatica—conditions that are rare among quadrupeds. Under gravity, the return of

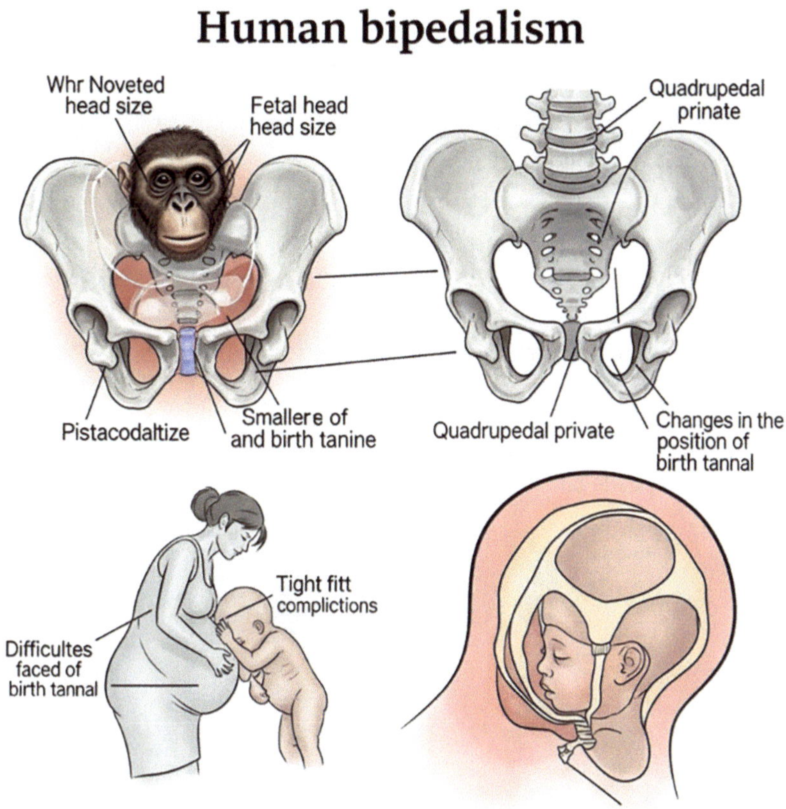


**Fig. 3.2** As human brains grew larger over time, combined with the narrowing of the female pelvis caused by upright walking, an evolutionary dilemma in childbirth emerged, effectively making every human a "premature infant." Unlike other animals, whose offspring can walk shortly after birth, humans must endure a prolonged period before being able to stand and walk independently

blood from the lower limbs to the heart becomes more difficult, increasing pressure in the venous system and making hemorrhoids and varicose veins common in humans, whereas the horizontal torso of four-legged animals greatly alleviates such pressure. Additionally, the repositioning of the digestive system may contribute to gastroesophageal reflux (Fig. 3.3).

Furthermore, bipedalism altered the structure of our feet. To support the weight of the entire body, the arches of the feet evolved, but this also made them more prone to injuries, such as flat feet, plantar fasciitis, and hallux valgus—issues rarely encountered in quadrupedal animals. Human knees and hips also bear significantly greater loads, making osteoarthritis particularly common in the elderly. In short, while bipedalism conferred advantages, it also embedded numerous "hidden risks" in our bodies, giving rise to many "human-exclusive" ailments seldom seen in other animals.

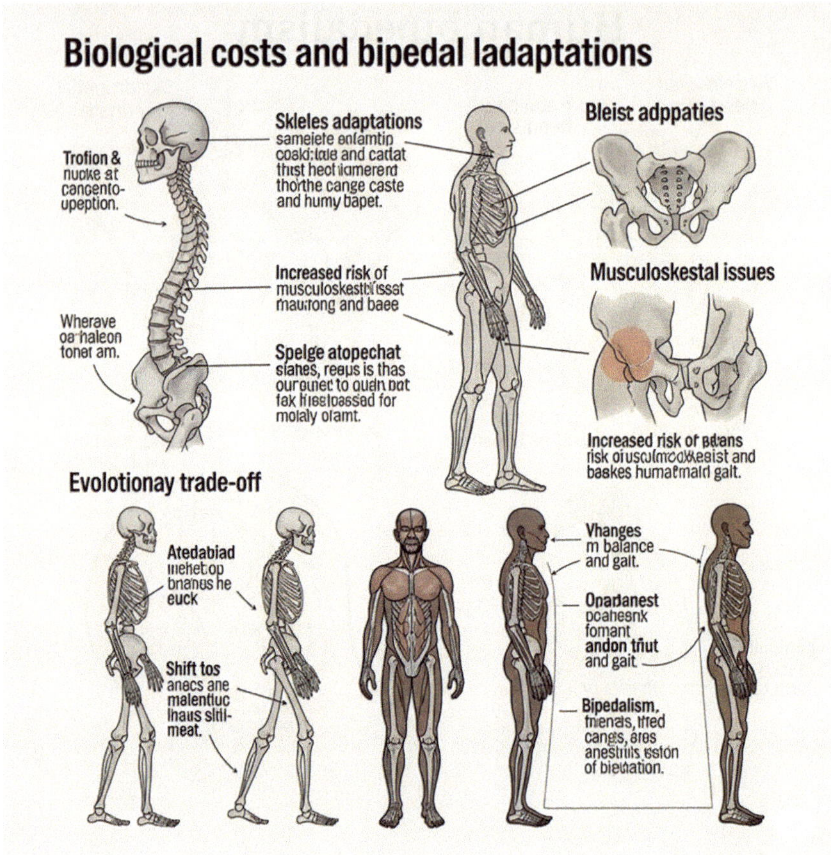


Fig. 3.3 The biological costs and adaptations of bipedal walking in humans

Yet human evolution did not passively endure these challenges. To counteract the hazards brought by upright walking, our bodies evolved corresponding adaptations:

**S-shaped spine:** Though it carries stress, the S-shaped curvature of the spine is a clever design, functioning like a spring to absorb and dissipate shocks, cushioning the brain from impacts during walking and running.

**Developed gluteus maximus:** Humans possess the most developed gluteus maximus among primates, crucial for maintaining an upright posture and providing powerful propulsion during walking and running.

**Medially angled knees:** Our knees bend slightly inward while walking, positioning the legs beneath the body's center of gravity, reducing sway and improving efficiency.

**Foot arch structure:** Despite the increase in foot problems, the arch itself acts as a sophisticated shock absorber and spring, effectively absorbing ground impact and converting it into forward propulsion.

**Adaptive genetic variations:** As previously mentioned, the human genome contains roughly 100,000 gene variants, many of which arose to meet the physiological challenges of bipedalism. Genes related to bone density, joint cartilage repair, and vascular elasticity, for example, may have undergone adaptive changes over millions of years to mitigate the negative effects of upright walking.

These ingenious evolutionary adaptations reveal the principle of "nature counters nature's advances." Humans did not merely "adapt" to upright walking; we engaged in continuous, millions-of-years-long "repairs" and adjustments at both the genetic and anatomical levels, striving to maximize advantages while minimizing disadvantages.

## 3 The Inevitability of Survival: No Turning Back

Some may wonder: if upright walking brought so many "troubles," why not simply remain quadrupedal? This hypothetical overlooks the harshness and inevitability of evolutionary selection.

Between roughly three million and two million years ago, as the climate continued to change, African forests further shrank and open savannas expanded. Our ancestors were forced to leave the gradually vanishing forest shelter and move into open terrain. In such environments, crawling on all fours was inefficient and perilous. At this point, the unique advantages of bipedalism became evident:

**Elevated vision and early warning:** In dense grasslands, quadrupedal vision is limited, making it difficult to detect distant predators (like saber-toothed cats or hyenas) or potential prey. Upright walking allowed humans a higher vantage point, improving detection of threats and opportunities, buying precious time for escape or pursuit, and greatly increasing survival odds.

**Energy efficiency and long-distance travel:** Studies show that bipedalism is more energy-efficient than quadrupedal crawling over long distances in open terrain. For early humans needing to forage, find water, or migrate, energy-efficient locomotion provided a crucial survival advantage.

**Freeing the hands and tool-making:** This is perhaps the most important "by-product" of bipedalism. Free hands enabled early humans to gather more food and transport more resources. More importantly, it allowed for tool manufacture. Archaeological evidence traces the earliest stone tools back roughly 2.6 a. These tools enabled cutting meat, breaking bones for marrow, and processing plants, greatly expanding food sources and ensuring access to high-calorie, high-protein nutrition essential for sustaining large brains. Without upright walking, fine tool-making—and thus effective food processing—would not have been possible, making it harder to meet the brain's nutritional demands.

**Weapons and defense:** Freed hands allowed early humans to pick up stones or branches as defensive weapons, and even throw them, providing extra protection against formidable predators and altering their position in the food chain.

Thus, bipedalism was not a "choice" in the casual sense but a crucial, and even inevitable, adaptation to environmental pressures. Its emergence gave our ancestors unique competitive advantages, enabling them to survive, reproduce, and ultimately dominate the planet. Had they not taken this arduous path, humans might have quietly vanished from the evolutionary stage, replaced by species better suited to the environment. This underscores the principle: "There is no idyllic calm; only burdened progress." Human survival and development have always been a continuous struggle and adaptation.

## 4 Lessons for Entrepreneurship: Nothing Is Ever Final; "Moving Under Load" Is the Norm

The protracted evolution of human bipedalism offers profound and practical insights for entrepreneurship. It reveals a universal truth: any seemingly great advancement or advantage inevitably comes with costs and challenges, often long-term and recurring.

Just as upright walking brought humans enormous evolutionary benefits but also innumerable physiological costs, every entrepreneurial decision, action, or strategy carries dual effects. There is rarely a purely correct or perfect choice. A seemingly successful market strategy might create production bottlenecks; a disruptive technological invention might introduce unforeseen compliance risks. Entrepreneurs must recognize the complexity of consequences, understanding that few outcomes are entirely positive or negative, and must learn to weigh and manage them effectively (Fig. 3.4).

Humans did not adapt to upright walking in a single leap; rather, it involved millions of years of continuous adjustments and refinements at both physiological and genetic levels. Entrepreneurship is no different. Every attempt and invention may bring new challenges and problems. Entrepreneurs must maintain clear awareness and a proactive mindset to cope with these "side effects" and continually manage the aftermath of prior decisions. This is not an incidental phenomenon—it is the inevitable norm of entrepreneurship. Rather than chasing "perfect decisions," the focus should be on "effective responses."

Our ancestors chose upright walking because it offered the greatest survival advantage in their environment. For entrepreneurs, market conditions, technological trends, and user demands change at lightning speed. Only by embracing change courageously, adapting actively, and even evolving proactively—just as our ancestors did—can one carve out new survival space amid fierce competition and continually surpass oneself. Clinging to old patterns and refusing to confront challenges leads only to being left behind by the times.

Faced with the myriad physiological challenges brought by upright walking, humans did not give up; they adapted and overcame over millions of years. Entrepreneurship, likewise, is a marathon, not a sprint. It is full of uncertainty,

**Fig. 3.4** Human evolution is not a one-time accomplishment; it requires long-term efforts to enhance strengths and mitigate weaknesses

setbacks, and repetitions. Products that seem successful today may be obsolete tomorrow; teams that inspire pride today may face reorganization tomorrow. Entrepreneurs need strong resilience, an absence of fear of failure, the ability to learn from each "side effect," and sufficient patience to tackle every emerging challenge.

## 5 Conclusion

When we admire the upright posture of humans, we should not romanticize it as flawless perfection. On the contrary, it serves as a warning: there is no effortless "quiet life," and there is no decision that yields permanent results. Whether in human evolution or the entrepreneurial journey, the essence is an endless process of adaptation and trade-offs—a continual struggle against negative consequences. Only with this clear awareness and enduring resilience can one truly go further.

## Further Reading

1. X. Cao, *Modern Business Management*, Palgrave Macmillan, 2025.
2. X. Cao, *Strategic Management and Organizational Development*, Springer, 2025.
3. R. Leakey and R. Lewin, *Origins Reconsidered: In Search of What Makes Us Human*, Doubleday, 1992.

4. D. Lieberman, *The Story of the Human Body: Evolution, Health, and Disease*, Pantheon Books, 2013.
5. S. Gould, *The Structure of Evolutionary Theory*, Harvard Univ. Press, 2002.
6. J. Diamond, *Guns, Germs, and Steel: The Fates of Human Societies*, Norton, 1997.
7. R. Dawkins, *The Selfish Gene*, Oxford Univ. Press, 1976.
8. N. Tinbergen, "On aims and methods of ethology," *Zeitschrift für Tierpsychologie*, vol. 20, pp. 410–433, 1963.
9. D. Dennett, *Darwin's Dangerous Idea*, Simon & Schuster, 1995.
10. C. Waddington, *The Strategy of the Genes*, Macmillan, 1957.

# Chapter 4
# Learning Entrepreneurship Through Academic Writing: Refining Core Elements

## 1 A Good Idea Alone is not Enough: Invention + Feasibility + Relative Advantage

The starting point of an academic paper is an "idea"—a seemingly dazzling concept. However, a "good" idea is never just a product of spontaneous inspiration; it must satisfy three criteria simultaneously: first, clear invention that pushes beyond existing work; second, practical feasibility, meaning it can be validated and implemented using available tools and techniques; third, relative advantage, signifying that it outperforms current mainstream solutions in a specific context. The logic of entrepreneurship mirrors this precisely.

In reality, too many entrepreneurs enter the market brimming with passion for their "first great product," proclaiming they will "disrupt the industry," only to be quickly humbled by the market (Fig. 1). They often overlook three crucial questions: how is this idea actually better than existing solutions? Can this product truly be built? Do customers have sufficient pain points and willingness to pay for it?

In academic research, an outstanding researcher never starts writing without preparation. They spend a significant amount of time conducting a literature review, investigating what the most advanced work in the field is, which problems remain unsolved, and where existing methods fall short. For example, a PhD student working on image recognition algorithms cannot propose a valuable improvement without understanding mainstream frameworks like ResNet or Transformer. Similarly, an entrepreneur who is unaware of existing solutions in their industry—unfamiliar with competitors' features, pricing, user feedback, and pain points—cannot claim true "invention"; at best, they are merely reinventing the wheel.

Take the smart home industry as an example: many startups claim, "We can control everything with voice," yet fail in the market. Why? Because Amazon's Alexa and Google Home had already perfected such solutions years ago; these so-called new ideas were merely designs others had tried—and even abandoned—three years earlier. In the electric vehicle sector, NIO stood out from a sea of imitators not



S. Li, *Bridging the Innovation Gap*, Innovation, Technology, and Knowledge Management, https://doi.org/10.1007/978-3-032-22652-5_4

**Fig. 1** There are many similarities between writing a paper and launching a startup. Teaching entrepreneurship can draw valuable insights by reflecting on the process of academic writing

merely by making cars, but by systematically building a differentiated value curve combining "user operations + service experience." NIO did not start from scratch; it carefully studied the strengths and weaknesses of Tesla, XPeng, and BYD, and found a niche breakthrough focused on premium user experience.

Therefore, before "thinking up ideas," the most important task for an entrepreneur is not to doodle on a whiteboard, but to systematically study the market and competitors: What are the real pain points of customers? To what extent do existing solutions address them? How are they being solved? How effective are they? Where are the gaps? Ignorance of these factors means that even the flashiest idea may amount to "pseudo-invention."

Moreover, entrepreneurship involves practical feasibility. In academic writing, this manifests as "can the algorithm run?" or "can the theory be derived?" In entrepreneurship, it translates to "can the product truly be built?" and "can it be implemented within reasonable cost, time, and team capacity?" For example, many entrepreneurs present dazzling slides during fundraising, only to stall during execution: technical difficulties are underestimated, development timelines misjudged, and team capabilities mismatched, leading to project failure. Experienced entrepreneurs, from the outset, involve engineering leads and technical co-founders to repeatedly refine and assess feasibility—much like ensuring a paper closes the loop between theory and experiment.

Finally, and often most overlooked, even if the idea is innovative and the solution feasible, it must possess relative advantage. Academically, if a new algorithm performs only slightly better than existing methods but has three times the complexity and ten times the training time, reviewers will still reject it. Entrepreneurship is no different. A product must not only outperform competitors but do so convincingly enough to justify the user's switching cost. In many industries, user switching costs are high. A SaaS service that is marginally better may still lose users if the transition process is complicated, compatibility is poor, or training costs are high. This dimension of "relative advantage" ultimately determines market acceptance.

In summary, a "good idea" is never the starting point of entrepreneurship; it is merely the first step in a systematic process. It must be grounded in deep understanding of the market, technology, and competitors, be feasible, and present clear advantages to target customers. Just like in academic research, blind "invention" is often mere self-entertainment; only by seeking breakthroughs on the foundation of existing knowledge and ecosystems can one truly carve out a unique blue ocean.

## 2 Theoretical Analysis and Validation: The Entrepreneurial Business Model Must Be Self-Consistent

In academic research, theoretical analysis is indispensable. Its role is to use rigorous logic and tools to demonstrate to reviewers that an idea is not only novel but also theoretically feasible—it "makes sense." This may involve analyzing algorithmic complexity, proving model stability, or deriving convergence and boundary conditions. In other words, it is the "underlying logic verification" of a research plan (Fig. 2).

Entrepreneurship is no different. The "theoretical analysis" in entrepreneurship is not built from formulas but from rigorous reasoning that connects business models, market assumptions, resource allocation, and growth logic. How will you make

**Fig. 2** Conducting "theoretical analysis" in entrepreneurship—through rigorous reasoning among business models, market assumptions, resource allocation, and growth logic—can safeguard the success of a startup

money? Can your revenue model be sustained? Does your growth logic hold up? Does the value you promise your users truly address their pain points? The answers to these questions constitute an entrepreneur's "theoretical analysis system."

Many startups appear to be thriving: products are launched, early users are acquired, and momentum seems high. Yet, they are often still in the "experimental validation" stage—similar to a research paper that only has simulations but lacks theoretical support. Such projects often run into trouble after the first round of funding. Once investors start asking questions like, "How will you scale? How will you reduce marginal costs? Will customer lifetime value cover acquisition costs? What will your cash flow look like in five years?" the project's underlying weakness becomes apparent—there is no internal logic, only intuition.

This problem is particularly common during market hype. Take the O2O (online-to-offline) startup wave around 2015. Many companies assumed that burning capital on subsidies would secure eternal users. Their logic was: "As long as we quickly capture market share, we will monetize later." However, few seriously analyzed whether low-margin, high-frequency, essential local services could actually generate customer stickiness, or whether inherent price wars could emerge. Once subsidies ended and capital dried up, users quickly switched to cheaper platforms, causing many projects to collapse instantly. This is akin to submitting a paper with only a few simulation experiments, only to have reviewers reject it for lack of theoretical foundation.

A successful startup always has a self-consistent "theoretical backbone." For example, SaaS companies typically adopt a subscription model. The underlying logic is clear: continuously deliver value, secure recurring purchases, and optimize products through user data. The model works in theory as long as customer acquisition costs remain below lifetime value and retention rates are sufficient. This mirrors the role of a theoretical framework in research, which supports the validity of experimental results.

Another example is Tesla. In its early days, it did not target the mass market directly but followed a staged strategy: high-end sports cars → luxury vehicles → mainstream models. This created a complete "high-margin first, then scale" path. Elon Musk repeatedly emphasized the self-consistency of this strategy during early fundraising: high-end models generate profit, which is reinvested into developing and scaling more affordable models. Even if large-scale profitability was not immediately visible, investors were willing to back Tesla because the growth path was logically coherent.

Theoretical analysis also plays a critical role in risk anticipation and contingency planning. In research, theoretical analysis identifies scenarios in which an algorithm may fail and proposes improvements. Similarly, a mature business plan must include strategies for different market conditions. A cash flow projection that only assumes "optimistic linear growth" without accounting for demand fluctuations, policy changes, or increased competition constitutes an incomplete theoretical framework. Investors seeing such a plan will naturally question whether the team truly understands the industry.

This is why effective startups often combine "theory" with "practice." The theorists build clear business logic and revenue models, while the practitioners drive rapid product testing and iteration. Both are indispensable. Just as a paper cannot rely solely on experiments without theoretical support, a startup cannot survive without verifiable, replicable, and sustainable business logic, no matter how polished the product is.

Therefore, before rushing to build prototypes, launch websites, or run marketing campaigns, entrepreneurs should first ask themselves: How will I actually make money? Why would customers choose my product? Is my cost structure healthy? Can this model scale? If I receive ten million in funding today, do I know exactly how to spend it? If these questions cannot be answered clearly, the plan is still in the "idea" stage, not yet at the "solution" stage.

The value of theoretical analysis lies not in creating illusions but in validating logic. Only projects with self-consistent logic can withstand the pressures of entrepreneurship, navigate market bubbles, and achieve long-term sustainability. Just as a paper must endure rigorous derivation and argumentation, every business decision in a startup must be grounded in careful, solid analysis.

## 3 Experimental Validation and Prototype Iteration: The Critical Leap from PPT to Product

In academic research, even if you propose a seemingly perfect theoretical model, it is difficult to convince reviewers without supporting experiments or simulation data. The reason is simple: theory represents potential, but practice provides actual validation. The same logic applies to entrepreneurship, forming the decisive leap from a PPT presentation to a real product. Many startups in the early fundraising stage remain at the demonstration level: a polished PPT, a carefully edited concept video, or a few visually appealing UI designs, all used to "sell" their vision. The problem is that a vision cannot operate, a concept cannot be clicked by users, and demonstrations cannot account for the complexities of real-world conditions.

Clients and investors ultimately ask a crucial question: "Do you have a product that actually works?" Once serious flaws emerge during real-world testing—especially for consumer-facing applications—user experience suffers, and reputation and word-of-mouth can collapse rapidly. Such setbacks often occur when the founding team lacks a sufficient respect for the principle of "validation."

Mature entrepreneurs, particularly those with engineering backgrounds or experience across multiple product development cycles, rarely pursue a "perfect product" from the outset. Instead, they tend to build a Minimum Viable Product (MVP). The goal of an MVP is not to please customers but to test hypotheses—for example: Do users really have this need? Which features are they willing to pay for? Is your solution truly more efficient or convenient than existing alternatives? This mirrors the research approach of first constructing a prototype system, testing core mechanisms, and running controlled comparisons before committing extensive resources to full-scale implementation.

For instance, Dropbox's founders did not initially build a complete file synchronization system. They recorded a demonstration video to clearly present the idea and gauge early user interest. This was a low-cost "experimental design." Only when user registrations exceeded expectations did the team invest technical resources to formally develop the product prototype. In research terms, this is akin to building a functional demo to verify basic assumptions before committing to a system-level implementation.

In contrast, many failed startups follow a different pattern: teams aim for a "perfect product" from the start, continually adding features and pursuing visual impact. As a result, upon launch, critical bugs emerge, even basic functions fail, user confidence collapses, and investor trust erodes. This is comparable to submitting a research paper to *Nature* without prior experimental validation—the core experiments fail, simulation parameters are wrong, and the paper is ultimately rejected.

Prototype testing is not only about verifying "can it be built?" but also about understanding "what happens once it exists?" This includes user behavior feedback, bug reports, system load testing, response speed and reliability, and user acceptance from a psychological perspective. Tool selection and methodology are critical. Just as researchers need familiarity with simulation platforms like COMSOL, MATLAB, or ANSYS, entrepreneurs must be adept with tools like Figma (interactive prototyping), Firebase (rapid deployment and testing), Mixpanel (user behavior analytics), and Product Hunt (early exposure testing) to enable rapid iteration.

During product iteration, understanding the "feedback → learning → improvement" flywheel is essential. After the first-generation prototype is released and user feedback is collected, the team must respond quickly and roll out updates. This requires a highly responsive and learning-oriented organizational structure. Products like Slack and Notion became market leaders in part because they established comprehensive early user feedback channels—each piece of feedback became an input variable driving continuous optimization.

It is also crucial to emphasize the authenticity of prototype testing—tests must closely mimic real usage scenarios, not idealized "laboratory conditions." In research, we know that algorithms performing well in the lab can fail in the real world when faced with noise, missing data, or edge cases. Similarly, a startup product that runs perfectly on a founder's MacBook but frequently crashes on ordinary Android devices is analogous to a research algorithm tested only on a specific dataset without generalization ability; reviewers will naturally judge it as lacking practicality.

Thus, prototype validation and iterative experimentation serve as the bridge for entrepreneurs to move from "idea" to "reality." This is not merely a technical process but also a cognitive upgrade. Entrepreneurs must shift from "I think this idea is good" to "users have validated that this feature works"; from "I think we are fast enough" to "data shows we need to better meet demand"; from "we are the first to do this" to "we are the first to truly solve the problem and gain user approval."

In summary, moving from PPT to product is a leap from abstraction to concreteness. It requires the rigor of an engineer, the curiosity of an experimental scientist, the sensitivity of a product manager, and the pacing of a skilled manager. A startup that has never undergone prototype testing is like an unvalidated academic paper—no matter how elegant the theory, it cannot withstand practical scrutiny. Every aspiring entrepreneur must respect "experimentation," embrace "iteration," and treat "hypothesis validation" as the most important early-stage mission.

## 4 The Art of Writing a Good Paper: Entrepreneurship also Requires "Communication" Skills

The final stage of academic writing is transforming a complex research idea and experimental results into a clear, logical, well-structured, and persuasive paper. This is not merely about compiling data; it is an art of "storytelling." Entrepreneurship follows the same principle. Even if you have excellent technology, a mature product, and deep market insights, if you cannot convey these effectively to investors, customers, or potential partners in a short period, you are likely to be misunderstood, overlooked, or even eliminated.

A business plan that is structurally chaotic, visually rough, or written in rambling language is like a patchwork paper with poor grammar and disorganized logic. Even if the core content has value, failing this "communication" stage can result in immediate rejection. In a world of limited resources and information overload, readers' patience and attention are scarce. Whether you can quickly establish credibility and interest largely determines whether your project will receive the next opportunity.

In academia, communication emphasizes clarity, rigor, and logic; LaTeX is often chosen for polished typesetting and precise formula presentation. In business, communication focuses on structure, conciseness, and visualization. A competent pitch deck typically contains around ten slides: problem statement, solution, market size, business model, competitive landscape, team background, financial projections, and funding requirements. It is akin to condensing a paper into the abstract and introduction—designed to spark investors' curiosity for deeper exploration within minutes. Just as writing an abstract requires careful word choice and highlighting contributions, a pitch deck must convey maximum value in limited space.

Experienced entrepreneurs understand that communication is not just about transmitting information; it is about guiding perception. They do not merely pile up facts; they weave logic: starting from "here is an unsolved problem in the world," moving to "I have a unique solution," and then "this solution has been preliminarily validated, with market demand, a capable team, and a path to profitability." This mirrors the structure of a strong academic paper: from research motivation, to method design, to experimental results, ultimately pointing to future work and theoretical significance. In other words, the pitch itself embodies a narrative logic.

The art of communication goes far beyond words. Chart design, color selection, slide titles, information layout, and even the storytelling sequence all affect audience reception. For example, Airbnb's early fundraising presentation is celebrated as a classic template due to its clear structure, strong problem awareness, and concise, direct data support. They defined the user pain point in one sentence: "Travelers cannot find affordable, comfortable accommodation," followed immediately by a concrete, differentiated solution: "A platform that lets you stay in someone else's living room." Such clear, visual, and emotionally resonant communication greatly enhanced persuasiveness.

It is not only investors who are observing your "paper"; users, partners, and even regulators are evaluating it. A team with strong communication skills can quickly explain what they are doing to different audiences, build trust, and mobilize resources. Many failed startups do not collapse because of product or technology failures but because of poor communication, which leads to team breakdowns, interrupted resources, and missed opportunities—this is particularly common in tech startups.

Beyond external communication, there is a deeper layer: team alignment in communication. Academic writing is often a collaborative effort—the lead author must coordinate with co-authors to avoid inconsistent arguments, formatting chaos, and style conflicts. In entrepreneurship, this "coordinated expression" is even more critical: How does the CEO convey strategic vision externally? How does the CTO explain the technical path? How does the COO present the operational plan? Do these narratives form a coherent ensemble rather than separate voices? Ultimately, communication reflects structured thinking, orderly execution, and strategic alignment.

It is worth noting that communication skills can be trained. Just as a new graduate student learns to write effective "Introduction" and "Related Work" sections, entrepreneurs need to become familiar with pitch structure, business plan writing, media communication, and public speaking. Studying classic cases, simulating pitch presentations, or seeking guidance from experienced mentors can greatly enhance communication effectiveness. Rather than agonizing over being "misunderstood," it is more productive to cultivate the ability to be understood.

Ultimately, entrepreneurship, like academic writing, is not only about content—it is about expression. A truly effective startup team should resemble an excellent research team: capable of producing solid content while presenting it clearly and elegantly, earning the recognition of reviewers—investors, customers, and the market alike.

## 5 Choosing the Right Battlefield: Identifying Platforms and Channels is the Premise of Success

In academic research, even a high-quality paper can be rejected if submitted to the wrong journal, simply due to "mismatch," no matter how solid or innovative the content. The cost of choosing the wrong battlefield exists equally in entrepreneurship, often with even greater consequences. A technically strong startup can fail to gain traction—or even collapse entirely—if it enters the market at the wrong point or launches its product through the wrong channels. Choosing the right battlefield is a prerequisite for entrepreneurial success.

Many novice entrepreneurs approach the market from the perspective of "what I can do" or "what I want to do," brimming with enthusiasm but lacking broad vision. They may be intimately familiar with their product's features but know little about market demand, user scenarios, or channel strategies. This is akin to a graduate student writing an excellent paper that completely misses the journal's thematic focus, wasting submission opportunities, and losing the chance to build connections with suitable reviewers.

Mature entrepreneurs think in reverse: "What is missing in the market?" "Which needs are users genuinely willing to pay for?" "In which scenario does my solution have the greatest advantage?" They do not blindly pursue "big and comprehensive" solutions. Instead, they precisely match market pain points and user psychology, concentrating resources on high-impact niche areas. This positioning ability is analogous to a scholar evaluating a journal's impact factor, review cycle, rejection rate, and research scope—a judgment built on data, experience, and strategic insight.

Selecting platforms and channels is the "art of choosing a journal" in entrepreneurship. Are you targeting consumers (B2C) or businesses (B2B)? Will your sales path be direct, e-commerce, or through distribution partners? Do you plan to start with a high-end niche to build your brand, or adopt a low-price strategy for rapid expansion? Each path implies a distinct business model, team structure, and capital allocation. Choosing the wrong channel is like submitting a paper to a completely irrelevant research field—no matter how hard you try, you will not get meaningful feedback.

For example, many hardware startups initially target consumers, dreaming of overnight success through online crowdfunding. They underestimate consumer dependence on brand, aesthetics, word-of-mouth, and the complexity of after-sales service. The product launches to poor reviews such as "too complicated to use," and sales quickly decline. Other entrepreneurs succeed by applying the same technology in B2B contexts, such as factory automation or enterprise services, achieving stable revenue and opportunities for continuous improvement at lower marketing costs. This "scenario reconfiguration" often determines a project's survival.

Channel selection is similarly critical. In the Chinese market, WeChat ecosystem, e-commerce platforms, short-video livestreaming, offline promotion teams, and telemarketing are suited for different products and user groups. Entrepreneurs who lack a deep understanding of these channels may spend heavily on promotion with minimal return—just as a paper intended for a top computer vision journal might be rejected if mistakenly submitted to an applied machine learning journal, where reviewers cannot accurately assess its value. To avoid this, entrepreneurs need a "market map" comparable to a researcher's "journal map," understanding user behavior, acceptance thresholds, price sensitivity, and conversion mechanisms in each segment.

Timing and pace must also be considered. In academia, some conferences and journals have strict cycles and stable acceptance rates; experienced researchers avoid peak submission periods, use rolling review windows, and plan around hot topics. Similarly, in entrepreneurship, market entry timing is crucial. Should you enter early to capture first-mover advantages before standards form, or wait until technology matures and enter as a "fast follower"? In industries like new energy vehicles or AI-assisted writing, differences in timing often translate into dramatic disparities in resource access and competitive advantage.

It is important to note that this "battlefield selection" ability depends not on talent alone but on learning, accumulation, and reflection. Entrepreneurs, like researchers, must actively study the market, analyze competitors, attend industry forums, gather user feedback, and identify trends. Synthesizing this information allows the creation of a personal "battlefield map." Just as top scholars are familiar with the review styles and trending topics of major journals, successful entrepreneurs must know major market platforms, funding channels, distribution routes, and customer pathways inside out.

Ultimately, entrepreneurship is not about building in isolation; it is a strategic game of positioning. Successful projects succeed not necessarily because of superior technology, but because they are in the right place—facing the right market, embracing the right users, using the right channels, and telling the right story at the right time. Submitting the right paper to the right journal can trigger citations and dissemination; selecting the right channels for your product can generate conversion and growth.

## 6 Revision and Feedback: Feedback is not a Blow, but a Ladder to Progress

No outstanding paper is ever completed in a single draft. Even top researchers often undergo multiple rounds of revision and resubmission, sometimes encountering "reject but resubmit" decisions. The key is not just *how* to revise, but *how* to interpret feedback, absorb it, and create breakthroughs from it. The entrepreneurial process mirrors this, often in a harsher form: while academic reviewers may offer suggestions politely, market feedback is blunt, intense, and sometimes merciless—user churn, negative reviews, and declining sales are all raw evaluations of a startup's performance.

Yet, feedback itself is not a setback—it is the starting point for growth and iteration. Whether it comes from a reviewer's comments or a user's critique, feedback provides an essential "external perspective." Founders often become trapped within their own logic and blind spots; feedback represents the reality outside the system. Just as a reviewer might point out a hidden variable control problem in your experiment, a user comment like "I have no idea how to use this product" may reveal a critical flaw in your onboarding or guidance flow. If you can abstract the core issue from such signals and adjust your product or processes accordingly, you move one step closer to success.

How one treats feedback marks the maturity of an entrepreneur. Novices often perceive negative feedback as rejection, react emotionally, and may even doubt themselves. Mature entrepreneurs behave more like seasoned academics: they understand that "rejection does not equal failure" but is a catalyst for growth. They do not merely defend themselves; instead, they dissect the problem, trace its root causes, identify actionable improvements, and plan the next iteration deliberately.

This leads to a crucial skill: the ability to *convert feedback into actionable change*. In academia, crafting a strong response letter to reviewers is often key to a paper's acceptance. You must respond to each comment professionally, humbly, and logically, demonstrating respect for the feedback and your willingness to act. In entrepreneurship, the same skill is vital. Can you respond gracefully to negative user reviews? Can you promptly reassure customers and provide solutions when defects arise? Can you answer investors' questions about your business model with compelling data and logic after careful reflection? These acts of "expressing and correcting" determine whether an apparent crisis can be transformed into customer trust and product evolution.

There is a frequently underestimated variable: the importance of mentors and experience transfer. Many early-career researchers struggle during revisions not because of lack of ability, but due to insufficient guidance. A mentor may explain: "A rejection like this actually indicates the journal values your research direction; only certain details need polishing." They may also show how to craft a strategic response letter—what to acknowledge positively, what to explain politely, and where to provide stronger evidence (Fig. 3). Similarly, in entrepreneurship, founders who appear "responsive and composed" often benefit from at least one experienced mentor who has taught them how to "diffuse user frustration in a sentence" or "highlight turning points to investors rather than dwelling on difficulties."

These coping strategies are not innate instincts but learnable and trainable "professional expression skills." In fact, different contexts often require different "communication templates": standard phrases for customer service responses, brand tone on social media, and presentation structures in investor meetings—all are distilled collective wisdom accumulated from countless entrepreneurs' trial and error. Just as academia has widely circulated templates for efficient reply letters or rebuttals, entrepreneurship has its own set of implicit norms for interacting with feedback. Truly outstanding entrepreneurs don't know how to respond gracefully from the outset; they gradually acquire these "socialized repair skills."

More importantly, feedback in entrepreneurship doesn't only come from customers or investors—it also comes from within the team. Disputes between product managers and engineers, critiques from the sales team toward the technical department, all act as an "internal peer review mechanism" for the project. The

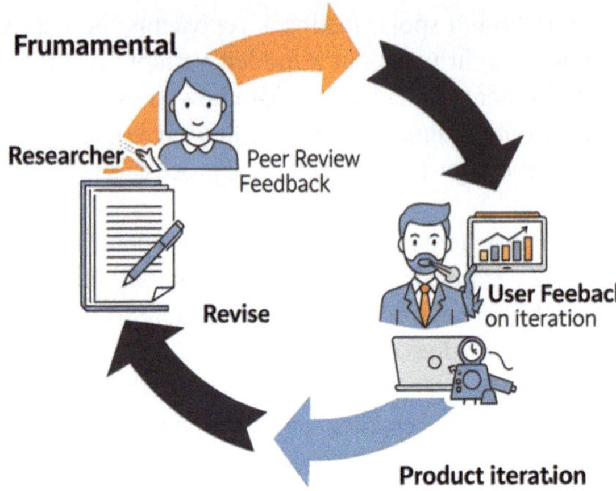


**Fig. 3** In both academic research and entrepreneurship, success is achieved through feedback loops, using insights from feedback to iteratively improve and refine the process

founder must play the role of "editor-in-chief," both adopting useful suggestions and filtering out irrelevant noise, building a feedback-loop system capable of continuous self-optimization. At its core, this skill is about designing organizational structure and communication systems—just as academic research maintains quality through peer review, a business maintains resilience through its internal feedback system.

From this perspective, the entrepreneurial journey is like a multi-year "grand paper." Every product release, market test, and round of investor pitches is a "submission." The market is your final reviewer; users are your anonymous peer reviewers. You must continuously refine your logic, improve your product, and adjust objectives in response to countless "revision suggestions," ultimately producing a sustainable "final version."

Feedback is not punishment but co-creation; it is not denial but an invitation to participate in constructing higher-quality solutions. If paper revision relies on research literacy and writing ability, entrepreneurial revision relies on cognitive flexibility, expressive skill, and organizational learning capacity. These three qualities, passed down from experienced entrepreneurs and mentors, constitute the most valuable growth assets.

## 7 Leveraging Legacy: Standing on Shoulders Beats Closed-Door Reinvention

If the previous sections—creativity, conceptualization, validation, expression, platform selection, and feedback absorption—represent the "operational workflow" of papers and entrepreneurship, then "leveraging legacy and inheritance" is the invisible variable that often determines success or failure. For beginners, this factor is easily overlooked, yet it is an unspoken consensus among successful practitioners.

True, efficient growth is never a solo feat; it is always an evolution built upon prior experience, systematic methodologies, and collaborative networks.

In academic writing, those seemingly "gifted" researchers are often supported by resource-rich, intellectually stimulating research groups. They learn topic selection from advisors, experiment design from peers, revision logic from reviewer comments, and effective expression techniques from prior literature. A high-quality paper is rarely the product of three months of isolated brainstorming in an office; rather, it emerges from the collective dynamics of a "knowledge network." Ignoring this often leads to the illusion of "I must understand everything from scratch," which results in inefficiency, detours, and sometimes abandonment.

Entrepreneurship is no different. Almost every successful entrepreneur, when reflecting on their first company or project, credits a mentor, early investor, experienced partner, professional community, or even a classic book that had a significant impact. These figures provide guidance at critical junctures, emotional support during setbacks, and actionable strategic advice. Without these "shoulders to stand on," entrepreneurship becomes a lonely endeavor, characterized by high self-experimentation and information bottlenecks.

The problem is that many early-stage entrepreneurs—especially those with technical backgrounds—mistakenly equate "originality" with everything, dismissing learning from predecessors as "mere imitation" or even opportunism. They avoid reading classic business books, ignore case studies of past failures, and resist mentor guidance, immersing themselves in self-contained "perfect logic." This is akin to an academic refusing to read literature reviews, ignoring reviewer comments, and insisting on inventing an entirely new writing format—ultimately isolating themselves from mainstream evaluation and risking marginalization or failure.

True "originality" never arises from nothing; it emerges from understanding existing rules and optimizing or surpassing them. Steve Jobs championed "stay hungry, stay foolish," yet he was never a closed-door innovator. He deeply understood industrial design, aesthetics, Japanese Zen philosophy, and strategic histories of Sony and Pepsi, while also valuing networks and talent acquisition. In Apple's rise, every step adhered to the logic of leveraging and collaboration: co-creating product aesthetics with designer Jony Ive, building capital bridges with investors like Wayne, and assembling a dream team of top engineers. Jobs' "genius aura" was in reality a concentrated manifestation of long-term information integration and pattern recognition, not a mystical stroke of insight.

Practically, leveraging legacy comes in multiple forms. First, platform selection. Whether submitting to academic journals or joining incubators, accelerators, or industry conferences, platforms provide rapid access to "collective intelligence." They offer information, resources, and networks, enabling faster learning and reducing detours. Second, mentorship. Whether in a university lab or a startup, finding an experienced, willing-to-share mentor is far more efficient than repeated trial-and-error (Fig. 4). Mentors don't walk every step for you, but they provide guidance when you're stuck, showing that "many have walked this path before—try it this way."

**Fig. 4** Both scientific research and entrepreneurship rely on leveraging legacy and inheritance—drawing strength from mentors, predecessors, and existing knowledge—while looking toward a bright future, achieving a high starting point by standing on the shoulders of giants

Moreover, it involves joining the "peer ecosystem." In academia, there are research groups, peer review systems, and international conferences; in entrepreneurship, there are startup communities, industry salons, product manager conferences, and open-source developer networks. These serve as channels for knowledge flow and experience exchange. Outstanding entrepreneurs regularly interact with peers, learning from others' mistakes and successes, effectively compressing someone else's lifetime of lessons into a week of personal reflection. This ability to systematically absorb others' achievements is, in essence, a true "experience multiplier."

Finally, there is mindset. Those who are willing to leverage others must first admit what they "don't know." This humility is not just a virtue—it is the starting point of growth. The most rapidly ascending entrepreneurs are often not the most intelligent but those who first discard the illusion that they can figure everything out alone. They excel at asking questions, seeking help, and establishing feedback loops, quickly identifying core problems and building their own methodologies. In contrast, those who are arrogant and insist on "reinventing everything" quietly fail during the first round of market testing.

In summary, the logic applies to both academic writing and entrepreneurship: genuine "independent thinking" does not emerge from isolation but from a highly connected world, leveraging collective intelligence, accumulated experience, and integrated invention. If you are fortunate enough to encounter the right platform, mentor, and community at the right time, seize the opportunity to leverage them and learn rapidly. Only by doing so can you truly "stand on the shoulders of giants" and see what others cannot.

# 8 Conclusion

On the surface, academic paper writing and entrepreneurship may seem entirely unrelated, yet in essence, the two are highly aligned—indeed, they can be seen as the "same logic game in different contexts." Whether in research or entrepreneurship, success relies on a rigorous chain of logic: from the spark of inspiration to the construction of theory; from meticulous validation to effective expression; from choosing the right platform to being receptive to feedback and continuous improvement. Each step demands both thorough preparation and flexible adaptation, foresight and a grounded understanding of reality. Missing any link weakens the chain.

More importantly, this mechanism highlights the true nature of "creation": great achievements are never isolated, closed-door endeavors—they emerge from knowledge inheritance, team collaboration, and social interaction. Just as a great paper is rooted in a solid foundation of prior research while pursuing systematic invention, a successful entrepreneurial venture relies on the combined forces of capital, industry ecosystems, and customer demand. Recognizing this helps us move beyond "heroic individualism" toward a more rational and pragmatic view of invention and entrepreneurship.

For researchers, understanding the essence of writing a paper often equates to understanding the essence of entrepreneurship. At their core, both involve constructing a logical system that is internally coherent and externally verifiable. Iterating on theoretical models and experimental data in a paper is akin to validating business models and market feedback for a startup. Paying attention to clarity and accuracy in writing mirrors designing a compelling business plan to attract investors and users. Choosing the right journal aligns with accurately targeting market channels. Responding humbly to reviewers' feedback corresponds to attentively capturing user feedback and iterating products.

This similarity shows that whether one is exploring the academic path or navigating the market, the key capabilities are "systemic thinking and dynamic adjustment." In complex environments, one must identify essentials, key variables, and effective strategies while facing failures and learning from feedback—a continuous evolution. This is not merely methodology but also a mindset and a state of being.

Moreover, success depends on building a "social support system." Whether it's mentorship and academic collaboration, or investor backing and entrepreneurial partnerships, it is always collective wisdom and social capital that drive progress. Fully utilizing and contributing back to these resources allows individuals and teams to grow sustainably and achieve breakthroughs.

Finally, this logical framework not only clarifies the commonalities between entrepreneurship and academic writing but also offers a clear path for action. In the face of uncertainty and challenges, there is no need to struggle alone blindly. Instead, proactively seek and leverage existing knowledge systems, mentor experience, team strength, and market platforms. Standing on the shoulders of giants allows one to see further, move more steadily, and advance faster.

In conclusion, whether you are an aspiring researcher or an entrepreneur stepping into the business arena, understanding and applying this system of logic is an indispensable foundation for success. Through this perspective, we can not only enhance ourselves but also deeply grasp the essence of invention: it does not emerge from nowhere; it arises from inheritance, connection, and collaboration—a spark of collective intelligence, co-written by the individual and the times.

## Further Reading

1. X. Cao, *Modern Business Management*, Palgrave Macmillan, 2025.
2. X. Cao, *Strategic Management and Organizational Development*, Springer, 2025.
3. P. Drucker, *Management: Tasks, Responsibilities, Practices*, Harper & Row, 1973.
4. D. Kolb, *Experiential Learning: Experience as the Source of Learning and Development*, Prentice Hall, 1984.
5. S. Blank, *Four Steps to the Epiphany*, Cafepress, 2006.
6. E. Ries, *The Lean Startup*, Crown Business, 2011.
7. A. Osterwalder and Y. Pigneur, *Business Model Generation*, Wiley, 2010.
8. K. Eisenhardt and J. Martin, "Dynamic capabilities: What are they?" *Strategic Management Journal*, vol. 21, no. 10–11, pp. 1105–1121, 2000.
9. R. Grant, "Toward a knowledge-based theory of the firm," *Strategic Management Journal*, vol. 17, pp. 109–122, 1996.
10. G. Polya, *How to Solve It*, Princeton Univ. Press, 1945.
11. S. Li, *Haircutting Robots*, Switzerland: Springer, 2025.
12. E. G. Carayannis, Ed., *Encyclopedia of Creativity, Invention, Innovation and Entrepreneurship*. New York, NY: Springer, 2013. https://doi.org/10.1007/978-1-4614-6616-1.

# Chapter 5
# Prioritizing R&D or Sales—A Reflection from the British Merchant Mindset vs. The German Rigorous Approach

## 1 Introduction

On the rugged journey of entrepreneurship, founders rooted in research and development often carry an almost stubborn belief: technology reigns supreme, and product excellence comes first. They are convinced that as long as they toil day and night refining code, perfecting algorithms, and polishing every minute detail, the market will inevitably recognize and celebrate their craftsmanship (Fig. 1). Yet, the harsh realities of the market often confound them: why do some companies, whose technology may not be the most advanced, manage to surge ahead triumphantly, while others, endowed with exceptional technological prowess, fade into obscurity in the torrent of the market?

To answer this question, one may need to step beyond the confines of technical details and cast their gaze over the broader sweep of history, examining the grand forces that shaped not only the character of nations and peoples but also the fate of commerce. History does not merely repeat itself, yet it consistently resonates in familiar ways across different times and spaces.

## 2 The Transformation of Britain: From Invention Furnace to Commercial Hub

Imagine Britain in the late eighteenth century. The air was thick with coal smoke and steam, yet it marked one of the most exhilarating chapters in human civilization—the dawn of the Industrial Revolution. At that time, Britain was undeniably the global beacon of invention. Watt's improved steam engine, the Jenny spinning machine, Stephenson's locomotives… these names were not merely cold machines; they were the brightest stars of their era, the most powerful engines driving societal progress (Fig. 2).

 
S. Li, *Bridging the Innovation Gap*, Innovation, Technology, and Knowledge Management, https://doi.org/10.1007/978-3-032-22652-5_5

**Fig. 1** Historical reflection: The interweaving of technology, commerce, and civilization

**Fig. 2** The early technological brilliance of Britain's industrial revolution, when researchers and inventors reaped the greatest rewards

At that time, Britain was like a newborn, emerging track brimming with limitless possibilities. Everything awaited creation, and every technological breakthrough meant explosive growth in productivity and unprecedented economic returns. The meticulous, pragmatic inventors and engineers were the most revered heroes of society. Through their profound understanding of scientific principles and their extraordinary ability to put them into practice, they amassed immense wealth and unparalleled honor. Society as a whole celebrated the exploration of the unknown, the pursuit of rigor, and a fervor for invention. In that era, R&D was the most powerful business model, and invention was the most effective marketing tool. This profoundly shaped the pragmatic, inventive, and perfectionist character of early Industrial Revolution-era Britons, making them truly the "technology pioneers."

However, the tide of history never stops, and every form of advantage experiences diminishing returns. As core industrial technologies such as the steam engine, railways, and steel gradually became widespread, the explosive growth they once brought began to slow. New technological breakthroughs became increasingly difficult; even massive investments might yield only marginal improvements, while market returns lagged far behind. Imagine the first steam engine: its value was revolutionary. Yet when millions of steam engines were already in operation, even slight gains in efficiency could no longer command the same market appeal.

Meanwhile, industrialization on the European continent was just beginning. Countries like Germany and France had a voracious demand for Britain's mature industrial equipment, advanced technologies, and management expertise. For the British of that time, rather than becoming trapped in domestic "involution" and pouring astronomical resources into marginal technological gains, it made more sense to shift focus: exporting mature products and production lines—already low in domestic premium—across the seas to these eager "latecomer markets." In these emerging industrial nations, even Britain's "old technologies" could be sold at higher prices, yielding trade profits far exceeding what further domestic R&D could achieve (Fig. 3).

Thus, a significant shift occurred. The societal scales of reward began to tilt. British merchants who could keenly perceive overseas market demands, establish global sales networks, and manage cross-border financial operations started to replace pure engineers as the new creators of wealth and the focal point of society. University programs in business and finance became highly sought-after, producing successive generations of shrewd and capable commercial talent. This commerce-centered, profit-driven mindset gradually permeated the cultural fabric of Britain, shaping the deeply ingrained "merchant spirit" and acute "trading awareness" we observe today. This does not mean that the British lost their love for scientific research; rather, at that historical juncture, the return on investment in commerce and trade far exceeded that of pure R&D.

## 3 The Rise of Germany: The "Engineer Gene" Forged in Latecomer Advantage

In sharp contrast to Britain was the rise of Germany. As the dividends of the British Industrial Revolution gradually waned and attention shifted toward global trade and finance, Germany was only just beginning its industrialization. This gave Germany

**Fig. 3** During the later stages of the British Industrial Revolution, a commercial wave emerged in Britain, forming a global trade network and achieving a transformation from R&D to trade. Products that had already lost much of their premium value domestically could be sold to late-industrializing countries, where their scarcity commanded substantial markups. At this stage, merchants became the fastest and most lucrative path to wealth in British society

a unique "latecomer advantage": they could directly learn from and adopt technologies and models already proven successful in Britain, thereby avoiding unnecessary detours. Since Germany's industrial revolution progressed later than Britain's, the R&D that had already become "labor-intensive with diminishing returns" in Britain still held significant value in Germany. After all, Germany's technological base was relatively behind at the time, and British industrial products had not yet fully penetrated the German market. Consequently, the R&D returns in Germany were comparable to those enjoyed by early Britain at the dawn of its Industrial Revolution (Fig. 4).

Therefore, in German society, the reverence for technological invention, fundamental scientific research, and engineering excellence reached unprecedented heights. The state invested substantial resources into universities and research institutions, cultivating generation after generation of meticulous, rigorous, and perfection-driven engineers and scientists. In Germany, a product labeled "Made in Germany" signifies quality and reliability—not by chance, but through the collective adherence

**Fig. 4** German industrialization: The forging of Germany's engineering spirit

to an "engineering mindset" passed down over generations. During this phase of technological accumulation and catch-up, every pursuit of precision, every optimization of production processes, and every adherence to quality standards translated directly into tangible competitive advantages and ultimately substantial market returns.

In Germany, a skilled engineer commanded more respect than a successful local businessman. This dedication to logical rigor, process control, and quality excellence became a hallmark of the German national character. They understood that during periods of technological dividend, only through meticulous craftsmanship could one lay a solid foundation, achieve latecomer advantage, and ultimately surpass competitors.

## 4 Lessons for Entrepreneurs: Which "Historical Stage" is Your Company at?

Projecting the evolution of national character and business models during the industrialization of Britain and Germany onto today's entrepreneurial practice—especially for founders with an R&D background—offers profound and highly practical insights. It reveals a core principle: a company's competitive advantage, organizational culture, and talent composition must closely align with the "historical stage" of its industry and product lifecycle.

First, ask yourself: which "historical stage" is your company in? Are you in early-stage Industrial Revolution Britain, late-stage Britain, or modern Germany?

**If you are in an "emerging sector" or "technology boom period": you are early-stage Industrial Revolution Britain.**
**Characteristics:** At this stage, your product is disruptive; industry standards are not yet fully established, and there is enormous space for technological invention. Every breakthrough may represent a transformative market opportunity.
**Core strategy:** Focus intensively on R&D and strive for unparalleled technical leadership. Here, technology itself is your lifeline—it builds barriers and secures premium value. Your product need not be flawless, but it must possess unique inventions that solve core pain points.
**Team composition and culture:** Your team should center on technical experts and R&D personnel, fostering a culture that encourages exploration and tolerates failure. Within the company, technical breakthroughs should be widely revered as the highest achievement.
**If you are in a "mature sector" or "technology stabilization period": you are late-stage Industrial Revolution Britain.**
**Characteristics:** At this stage, product technology is relatively mature, market competition is fierce, products are highly commoditized, and customers care more about price, service, and experience than purely technical performance.
**Core strategy:** Shift from "technology-first" to "business-model invention and efficiency priority." At this point, investing heavily in incremental technological improvements yields low returns. The focus should move to market expansion, sales channel development, brand building, user experience optimization, refined operations, and potentially business model disruption. Consider "technology" as a tradable commodity—how can it be delivered more efficiently and competitively to maximize commercial profit?
**Team composition and culture:** Bring in and prioritize talent in marketing, sales, operations, and branding. Even if the founder comes from an R&D background, they must quickly enhance commercial acumen and learn to balance technical investment against business returns. The company culture should shift from purely "technology-driven" to "business-driven and efficiency-oriented."

Next, entrepreneurs with an R&D background must especially overcome "R&D inertia." It is all too easy to fall into the mindset of "if the product is good enough,

**Fig. 5** The unavoidable strategic choice for modern entrepreneurs—whether to prioritize R&D or sales—must be determined according to the historical stage of the industry in which they operate

the market will follow." When market feedback is poor, we often assume that the product is insufficiently perfect, requiring more features or higher performance, and we continue to pour resources into R&D, falling into a vicious cycle (Fig. 5). However, if your industry track has already matured, user pain points may have shifted from "insufficient functionality" to "too expensive," "inconvenient service," or "lack of brand trust." At this stage, technological upgrades are like deploying troops on the wrong battlefield—they accelerate failure rather than prevent it. Entrepreneurial success is never a victory along a single dimension; it is the result of the complex interplay of technology, market, operations, and management.

Finally, one must understand the iteration of the "profit model." British merchants in the late Industrial Revolution no longer merely sold steam engines—they sold the "industrial productivity" represented by these engines to the world, and further consolidated their commercial empires through financial services and trade networks. As an R&D-driven entrepreneur, your profit model should not be limited to "selling products" or "licensing technology." Which deeper pain points of users can your technology solve? Beyond direct product sales, can you provide technical solutions, SaaS services, data services, or even build an ecosystem based on your core technology? How can your "technology" be "traded" to achieve higher exchange value?

## 5 Conclusion: Business Wisdom Beyond Technology

The sweeping waves of history have not only changed the world but, in their unique ways, shaped national character and provide invaluable guidance for today's entrepreneurs. As founders with a research background, we possess the power to

**Fig. 6** The entrepreneur's Dilemma: The moment of choice between R&D and business

change the world, but to truly unleash this power and translate it into sustainable business success, one must integrate commercial wisdom.

Is your company like Britain in the early Industrial Revolution, where technological invention leads the era? Or is it like Britain in the late Industrial Revolution, where mature technologies must be efficiently commercialized and globalized?

The answer is neither in code nor in the laboratory. It lies in your keen insight into industry trends, your deep understanding of market needs, your clever construction of business models, and—most importantly—the courage to adjust your strategic focus and even transform your mindset at different stages of development. Only by understanding these deeper historical logics and business principles can R&D-driven entrepreneurs navigate farther, more steadily, and ultimately achieve the perfect integration of technology and business (Fig. 6).

# Chapter 6
# Winning Through Strategic Positioning: Insights from the Comparison Between Go and Chess on the Long-Term Value of Corporate Strategy

## 1 Introduction

In the fast-changing world of business, how can a company ensure enduring success rather than fleeting prominence? This chapter draws deeply from the crystallized wisdom of the East—the strategic differences between Go and Chess—to serve as a mirror for analyzing the decisive role of macro-level positioning in corporate strategy, emphasizing its profound value in transcending short-term reactions and shaping a company's long-term destiny.

Go and Chess, both treasures of human intellect, are games of the mind, yet the strategic essence they embody is strikingly different. Chess focuses more on local tactics and direct confrontations, where the gains or losses of each move can immediately affect the battlefield, and victories are often decided in a few critical skirmishes. Go, however, captivates with its complexity and lies in the pursuit of macro-level positioning. At the beginning of a Go match, players place stones across a vast board, where the merit of early moves may not be immediately apparent and can even seem uneventful. As the game progresses, time becomes the ultimate judge, and the hidden risks of an initially flawed layout gradually erode a player's advantage, eventually leading to a comprehensive defeat that may be beyond recovery. This perfectly echoes the Chinese adage: *"He who does not plan for ten thousand years is insufficient to plan for one moment; he who does not plan for the whole is insufficient to plan for a single domain."* It underscores the irreplaceable importance of foresight and holistic planning (Fig. 1).

 
S. Li, *Bridging the Innovation Gap*, Innovation, Technology, and Knowledge Management, https://doi.org/10.1007/978-3-032-22652-5_6

**Fig. 1** As ancient strategy games, Go and Chess exhibit significant differences in their underlying philosophies. Chess emphasizes local tactics within a limited area of the board, using precise coordination and calculation of pieces to execute direct attacks on the king. Go, in contrast, focuses on macro-level positioning and overall board control, leveraging the collaborative interaction of stones to enclose territory and influence the entire board's dynamics, rather than concentrating solely on localized skirmishes between individual pieces

## 2 Strategic Positioning: Building Enterprise Resilience and Sustained Growth Across Cycles

In today's rapidly changing business environment, many managers tend to rely on a "respond as the situation demands" approach. This reactive flexibility can be highly effective in addressing short-term market fluctuations, sudden crises, or localized competitive challenges. It allows a company to quickly adjust its course, avoid immediate losses, and even seize fleeting short-term opportunities.

However, overreliance on short-term reactions may trap a company in a patchwork, symptom-focused mode, constantly busy with day-to-day issues, while neglecting the long-term or even ultra-long-term factors that decisively shape the company's future development.

Much like the opening moves in Go, certain critical strategic decisions may not yield immediate, visible benefits. They often involve substantial upfront investment, long payback cycles, and inherent uncertainty. Examples include:

- Sustained R&D investment in core technologies, such as breakthroughs in AI, biotechnology, or new energy;

- Early positioning and deep cultivation of emerging markets, even when initial market development costs are high;
- Forward-looking development and nurturing of high-quality talent pipelines, rather than scrambling only when talent shortages arise;
- Deliberate cultivation of corporate culture, brand values, and organizational resilience.

These are all long-cycle strategies, whose true value may take years or even decades to fully manifest. Once realized, such macro-level positioning builds formidable competitive barriers, establishes strong first-mover advantages, and allows the company to occupy strategic high ground within its industry—potentially becoming a determinant of the company's future destiny.

For instance, Huawei's long-term investment in 5G technology has cemented its unassailable global leadership in telecommunications, while Amazon's early focus on cloud computing created a sustained, high-margin growth engine. These examples clearly demonstrate that strategic positioning is the cornerstone for navigating economic cycles, resisting external shocks, and achieving enduring growth (Fig. 2).

**Fig. 2** Illustration of long-term strategic investments by enterprises

## 3 Avoiding the "Tactical Busyness" Trap: Returning to Strategic Essence and Top-Level Design

If a company becomes engrossed in short-term tactical busyness, day after day consumed by operational details while lacking a clear macro-level layout and strategic guidance, it is akin to blindly marching without a map. Even if each step is taken quickly, with immense energy and resources invested, the outcome may still veer off course, drifting further from the intended goal—or even losing direction entirely. This "tactical busyness" trap often stems from excessive focus on short-term financial metrics, blind imitation of competitors, and insufficient insight into future trends. In today's VUCA (Volatility, Uncertainty, Complexity, Ambiguity) era, where market conditions change rapidly and competitive landscapes are unprecedentedly complex, enterprises must develop the capability to recognize and seize long-cycle trends.

The fundamental problem with "tactical busyness" is that it limits a company's objectives to "doing what is at hand" rather than "doing what is right." Managers may become mired in the daily operational quagmire—continually optimizing existing product iterations, cutting unnecessary costs, or enhancing marketing efficiency—all of which are undoubtedly important. However, if these efforts are not aligned with a larger strategic vision, they may devolve into inefficient consumption or even strategic misalignment. For example, in Kodak's case, the company's "tactical busyness" in film technology reached its peak, yet it failed to strategically position itself for the long-cycle trend of digital imaging, ultimately leading to its spectacular decline. The root of this trap also lies in an organization's strong preference for short-cycle performance and a natural aversion to uncertainty. Reactions of the stock market to quarterly reports and internal evaluation mechanisms emphasizing short-term profits can subtly guide companies to disproportionately allocate resources and energy toward projects that yield visible short-term results (Fig. 3).

**Fig. 3** A ship adrift—Lost without direction

To escape this trap, enterprises must return to the essence of strategy, re-examining their mission, vision, and core competencies. This requires senior management to possess broad perspectives and forward-looking thinking, enabling them to rise above daily operational minutiae and view the organization from the macro dimensions of the industry chain, ecosystem, and even societal development, thereby engaging in strategic top-level design. This is not merely about drafting an impressive strategy report; it demands that the strategic intent be clearly and repeatedly communicated to every level of the organization, ensuring that from executives to frontline employees, everyone understands and aligns with the company's long-term direction.

Simultaneously, corporate culture must be fundamentally reshaped to cultivate an environment that encourages invention, allows for trial and error, and steadfastly pursues long-term value. This includes patient investment in R&D, nurturing emerging business initiatives, and continuously developing strategic talent—even when these investments may not yield substantial short-term financial returns. A well-executed macro-level strategy helps the enterprise mitigate potential risks, such as technological disruption, policy changes, or market saturation, while also guiding it to seize future growth opportunities, such as emerging technologies, consumption upgrade trends, or global expansion. It ensures that, under limited resources, the company focuses on the most critical and strategically significant areas, optimizing resource allocation, avoiding unnecessary wastage, and preventing scattershot investments. When the market environment changes dramatically, enterprises with a solid strategic layout demonstrate far greater resilience and adaptability than those relying solely on short-term reactive measures; they can swiftly adjust their course, even turning crises into opportunities and uncovering new growth avenues.

## 4 Implementing Long-Term Strategic Layouts: Challenges, Pathways, and the Critical Role of Leadership

However, translating macro-level strategy from paper into reality is no easy task, fraught with complexity and challenges. One of the greatest challenges is overcoming the pervasive short-termism within organizations. In periods of economic downturn or intense competition, management and investors are often driven by short-term financial targets, seeking immediate profit gains rather than focusing on strategic initiatives that require long-term investment to bear fruit. This pressure may lead companies to cut R&D budgets, abandon market cultivation, or even sacrifice brand reputation for short-term performance. Fear of an uncertain future and the lack of effective metrics for evaluating long-term strategic success often constitute additional barriers to implementing long-term plans.

To address these challenges, companies need to establish a performance evaluation system aligned with long-term strategy. This means not relying solely on quarterly or annual financial reports to assess the success of business units, but introducing non-financial indicators that reflect long-term value creation, such as customer loyalty, employee engagement, number of technological patents, market share growth potential, and brand influence. Such a multidimensional evaluation framework helps guide both employees and management to focus on the longer-term horizon. Additionally, the concept of patient capital should be embedded within corporate culture, encouraging sustained investment in strategic initiatives even when early returns are limited. This demands that decision-makers exhibit strategic discipline that transcends immediate gains.

The pathway to implementing long-term strategic layouts is both systematic and iterative. First, enterprises must conduct comprehensive external environment analyses (e.g., PESTEL, Porter's Five Forces) and internal capability assessments (e.g., resource-based view, core competence analysis) to clearly identify strengths, weaknesses, opportunities, and threats. Based on this foundation, companies can formulate a clear and inspiring strategic vision and objectives. These objectives should not be overly broad; they must be specific, measurable, achievable, relevant, and time-bound (SMART principles).

Next, strategy execution requires breaking down the plan into actionable staged tasks and projects, with clearly defined responsibilities and timelines. This involves cross-departmental collaboration, efficient resource allocation, and process optimization. However, strategy is not a rigid, static plan; it is a dynamic process of continuous learning and adjustment. Companies should establish effective strategic review mechanisms, regularly assessing the effectiveness of their layouts and making timely adjustments based on market feedback, technological advances, and changes in internal and external environments. This necessitates cultivating strong organizational learning capabilities and agile decision-making systems that can quickly identify new trends and flexibly adjust strategic directions (Fig. 4).

Finally, and most critically, is the central role of leadership in long-term strategic planning. Strategic leaders are not merely the architects of strategy; they are its steadfast advocates and practitioners. They must possess:

- **Grand Vision and Forward-Thinking:** The ability to anticipate future trends and paint a clear, inspiring blueprint for the enterprise.
- **Strategic Communication and Cohesion:** The capacity to translate complex strategies into messages that employees can easily understand and embrace, fostering a sense of participation and mission across the organization.
- **Decisiveness in Resource Allocation:** The courage to direct resources toward long-term strategic initiatives, even in the face of short-term temptations or internal resistance.
- **Culture Shaping and Resilience:** Cultivating a corporate culture that encourages invention, tolerates failure, and unwaveringly pursues long-term value.
- **Leading by Example:** Leaders' own behaviors and decision-making styles directly influence the organization's belief in and commitment to long-term strategy (Fig. 5).

**Fig. 4** Formulation and execution of strategic planning

## 5 Conclusion

The comparison between Go and Xiangqi offers a profound insight: macro-level strategic layout is the core driver of sustainable corporate development. It transcends short-term tactical considerations, focusing instead on the long-term health and prosperity of the enterprise. In today's highly uncertain business environment, corporate leaders should view their commercial landscape from a higher perspective, dedicating sufficient time and energy to strategic planning, and identifying and investing in areas with long-cycle value. This is not merely an investment in the future—it is a deliberate cultivation of the company's resilience and vitality. Only by doing so can a business remain unshakable amid fierce market competition, ultimately achieve comprehensive victory, and secure enduring success.

**Fig. 5** Only with a far-sighted vision can lasting victory ultimately be achieved

## Further Reading


1. H. Mintzberg, *Strategy Safari: A Guided Tour Through the Wilds of Strategic Management*, Free Press, 1998.
2. X. Cao, *Strategic Management and Organizational Development*, Springer, 2025.
3. R. Grant, *Contemporary Strategy Analysis*, Wiley, 2019.
4. X. Cao, *Modern Business Management*, Palgrave Macmillan, 2025.
5. M. Porter, *Competitive Advantage: Creating and Sustaining Superior Performance*, Free Press, 1985.
6. H. I. Ansoff, *Corporate Strategy: An Analytic Approach to Business Policy for Growth and Expansion*, McGraw-Hill, 1965.
7. G. Hamel and C. K. Prahalad, *Competing for the Future*, Harvard Business School Press, 1994.
8. I. D. Levinthal, "Adaptation on rugged landscapes," *Management Science*, vol. 43, no. 7, pp. 934–950, 1997.
9. J. G. March, "Exploration and exploitation in organizational learning," *Organization Science*, vol. 2, no. 1, pp. 71–87, 1991.
10. B. Henderson, "The Origin of Strategy," *Harvard Business Review*, vol. 67, no. 6, pp. 139–143, 1989.

11. E. G. Carayannis, Ed., *Encyclopedia of Creativity, Invention, Innovation and Entrepreneurship.* New York, NY: Springer, 2013. https://doi.org/10.1007/978-1-4614-6616-1.

# Chapter 7
# Asymmetric Advantage: Transforming Technical Depth into Commercial Moats

## 1 Introduction

Technical professionals are often skilled at "doing the right things" in the laboratory, creating unprecedented technological breakthroughs; however, when these "right things" are brought to the market, they frequently face challenges in "doing things right." In this chapter, we will delve into a core strategy—asymmetric advantage—to help tech entrepreneurs not only bridge this gap but also build formidable barriers in the fiercely competitive commercial landscape.

The legend of Thomas Edison lies not merely in his astonishing number of inventions, but in his ability to transform these inventions into a commercially enduring empire. His success was built on a profound understanding and practice of asymmetric advantage. When he developed a more efficient incandescent lamp, he did not stop at the bulb itself; he focused on building the entire electrical system—from generators, transmission networks, to installation services at the user end. This integrated solution far exceeded what a single technological breakthrough could achieve, creating entry barriers that competitors found nearly impossible to overcome, forming an asymmetric competitive landscape.

The "asymmetric advantage" discussed in this chapter does not simply mean technological leadership. It refers to the ability of tech entrepreneurs, leveraging unique technical depth and systemic thinking, to establish distinctive advantages in key dimensions that are difficult for competitors to imitate or catch up with. This advantage is not merely reflected in superior product specifications, but in the understanding of the essence of problems, the innovative integration of solutions, and the resulting disruptive improvements in cost, efficiency, and user experience. It requires tech entrepreneurs to step beyond a purely technical perspective and view their technological reserves through a broader commercial lens.



S. Li, *Bridging the Innovation Gap*, Innovation, Technology, and Knowledge Management, https://doi.org/10.1007/978-3-032-22652-5_7

## 2 Anticipating the "End-State" in Technology Integration

Building asymmetric advantage first requires entrepreneurs to anticipate the industry's future "end-stage." In this end-state, simply holding a single patent or technology is far from sufficient. True advantage lies in how a series of seemingly independent and complex technologies are organically integrated into a more efficient, disruptive product or service system.

Take artificial intelligence as an example. Many companies possess deep learning algorithms, but only those that can combine algorithmic strength with specific industry data, domain knowledge, and hardware optimization to create end-to-end intelligent solutions can truly establish asymmetric advantage. For instance, a company might have world-leading AI algorithms for medical imaging analysis, but its real asymmetric advantage lies in its deep integration of compliant medical data handling, doctor-centric UI/UX design, and seamless interoperability with existing hospital IT systems. This "technology + data + process + user experience" composite advantage makes it extremely difficult for competitors—even those with similar AI technology—to quickly replicate its market position.

## 3 From "What Others Have, I Have" to "What Others Don't Have, I Have"

Most tech startups initially face a "what others have, I have" competitive situation, where everyone chases similar technology trends. Constructing asymmetric advantage requires entrepreneurs to make strategic early-stage investments in exploring technology paths that currently seem niche but may have exponential potential in the future. These paths may demand longer R&D cycles and larger investments, but once breakthroughs occur, they can create a "what others don't have, I have" scenario.

For example, Elon Musk, in the early stages of the electric vehicle industry, persistently invested in core areas such as battery technology, the Supercharger network, and self-developed autonomous driving chips. At the time, these investments appeared costly and risky, but they ultimately endowed Tesla with unique advantages in energy efficiency, charging experience, and intelligence, enabling it to stand out in a market dominated by traditional giants. This dedication to technical depth and ecosystem integration is key to establishing asymmetric advantage (Fig. 7.1).

Ultimately, technology entrepreneurs, through systematically building asymmetric advantages, converge these efforts into a corporate "moat" that is difficult to breach. This moat is far more than mere legal patent protection; it is a complex ecosystem composed of interrelated and mutually reinforcing elements, making it extremely challenging for newcomers—even those with comparable technical capabilities—to replicate the company's market position in a short period. It is akin to an ancient Roman fortress, whose defense does not rely solely on a high wall but on

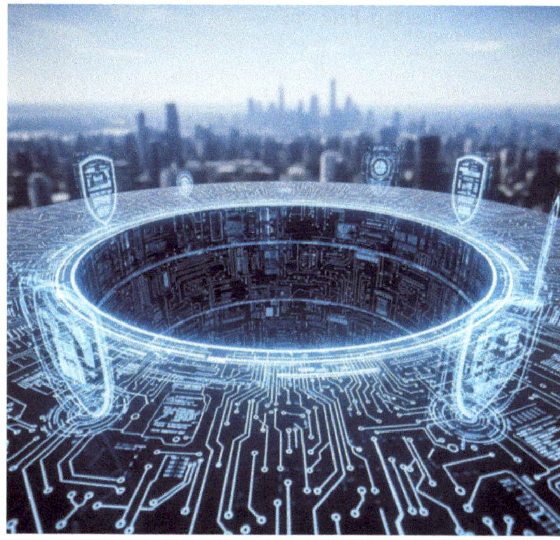

**Fig. 7.1** Technical moat—an impenetrable competitive barrier

a coordinated system of walls, moats, drawbridges, towers, and guards, all working together to form an impregnable defense. We will delve into the four key pillars that constitute this moat and explore how technologists can translate their technical insights into these commercial barriers.

## 4 The Data Flywheel Effect: Symbiotic Evolution of Technology and Data—Building Exclusive "Veins"

In the wave of the digital economy, data has undoubtedly become the most valuable "mineral," while technology is the cutting-edge tool to extract and refine it. However, a true technological barrier is no longer merely about algorithmic sophistication; it lies in the powerful data flywheel effect generated by the combination of algorithms and unique data. This is similar to how Edison did not merely invent the light bulb but established a complete system of power generation, transmission, and distribution. Each expansion of this network allowed him to collect more electricity usage data, improving load prediction and optimizing generation efficiency, thereby making the entire electrical system more efficient and cost-effective.

Imagine an early AI-based diagnostic support system, initially built on limited public datasets and academic models. This is like discovering a small exposed vein of ore. Once the company deploys its technology in real-world settings and convinces several hospitals to adopt it, a transformation begins: every doctor's use, every patient record entered, every diagnostic feedback becomes invaluable, real, professionally annotated clinical data. This data is far from ordinary—it is a "rich vein," meticulously processed, cleaned, and labeled, and extremely difficult for competitors to obtain.

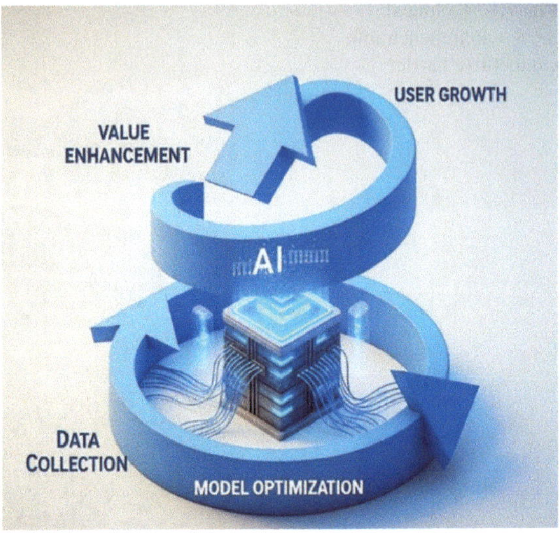


**Fig. 7.2** The data flywheel effect

With this unique, high-quality operational data, the startup can continuously optimize its AI model's accuracy, improve diagnostic efficiency, expand disease coverage, and even uncover new medical insights. As the model's capabilities significantly improve, it naturally attracts more hospitals and physicians, generating larger data flows and creating a self-reinforcing, upward-spiraling loop of data → technology → users → optimized data. Once this loop is activated, its advantages grow exponentially, ultimately forming a profoundly deep "moat" (Fig. 7.2).

For technical professionals, this means that one cannot be satisfied merely with the sophistication of algorithms or the implementation of functionalities. It is essential to approach the problem from a business and strategic perspective: how can products and business models be designed to acquire, accumulate, manage, and effectively leverage unique, large-scale, high-quality datasets in a legal and compliant manner? This includes, but is not limited to:

1. **Innovative data collection mechanisms**: Can new interaction methods, sensor technologies, or collaboration models be used to access data that traditional methods cannot reach?
2. **Data governance and security**: How can the quality, compliance, and security of data be ensured, turning it into a reliable asset rather than a burden?
3. **Extraction of value from unstructured data**: How can innovative technologies be developed to derive deep value from unstructured data such as text, images, video, and audio, turning "noise" into "gold"?

When your AI model is trained on hundreds of millions of real-world clinical data points, while your competitors can only rely on public datasets or small-scale samples, the gap in data depth and breadth creates a formidable barrier. This is not merely a technological advantage but also a business model exclusivity, as data itself is an irreplaceable, non-replicable resource.

## 5 Network Effects: Exponential Value Growth with User Expansion—Weaving an Inescapable "Web of Value"

Certain technology products or services exhibit a core value that grows exponentially with the number of users—a phenomenon known as the classic network effect. For technology entrepreneurs, designing products with strong network effects can weave an inescapable "web of value" in the market, forming an almost insurmountable commercial barrier.

Take the early telephone network as an example: the first telephone had zero value because there was no one to call. The second telephone added some value, as two people could communicate. But as the number of telephone users grew geometrically, the network's value exploded, since each new user increased the potential connections with all existing users. This "the more, the better" dynamic is the essence of network effects.

In today's technology landscape, social media platforms, collaboration tools, online marketplaces, and operating system ecosystems all benefit from strong network effects. For instance, a specialized developer community or code-hosting platform has limited value when only a few programmers use it; yet when millions of developers worldwide share code, exchange experiences, and collaborate, the knowledge base, solution repository, toolchains, and talent connectivity grow geometrically. New entrants, even with similar functionalities, will struggle to convince users to abandon an established platform with strong network effects, as switching entails breaking existing collaborations, losing historical data, sacrificing community support, and incurring significant relearning costs (Fig. 7.3).

At the very start of product design, technical personnel should deeply understand and intentionally build these network effects. This may involve:

**Fig. 7.3** Growth of network effects

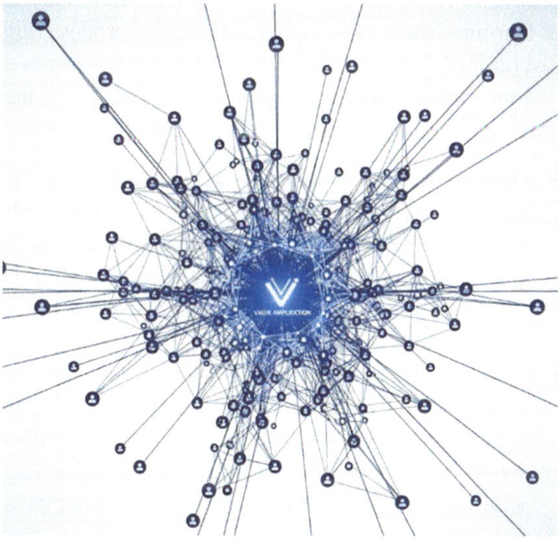

- **Shifting from a single-tool mindset to a platform mindset:** Design open API interfaces to encourage third-party developers to create plugins or applications, enriching platform functionality.
- **Incentivizing user-generated content (UGC):** Provide mechanisms that encourage users to share knowledge, experience, data, or creative works, making them co-creators of value.
- **Building communities and ecosystems:** Actively cultivate user communities, promoting interaction and mutual assistance among users, fostering a sense of belonging and stickiness.
- **Cross-side network effects:** For multi-sided platforms (such as e-commerce platforms connecting merchants and consumers), balance user growth on both sides to ensure mutual reinforcement.

Once network effects take hold, they can generate powerful "winner-takes-all" or "winner-takes-most" dynamics, concentrating market share in the hands of a few leading players and making it extremely difficult for new competitors to establish a foothold. This occurs because, under the influence of network effects, leaders can pull ahead of followers at an accelerating pace, creating a self-reinforcing growth pattern that makes market competition highly asymmetrical.

## 6 High Switching Costs: The Invisible Chain of User Stickiness—Making Users "Willing to Stay"

The cost that users must bear when attempting to switch to a competitor's product or service is known as the switching cost. The higher this cost, the stronger the user stickiness, thereby forming a powerful technical barrier for the enterprise. These costs are not limited to monetary expenditures; they also include time, effort, cognitive load of learning a new system, risks of data or process migration, and even psychological discomfort.

For complex technical products, especially enterprise software, data analytics platforms, or design tools, high switching costs typically arise from several factors:

- **Deep data accumulation and lock-in:** Users have accumulated significant, sensitive data within the system (e.g., financial records in an ERP system, client data in a CRM, core design files in CAD software). This data is often highly structured and tightly linked to business processes; migrating it to a new system entails massive data export, cleaning, and import work, along with the risk of data loss or corruption.
- **Specialized skills and habits:** Users have invested significant time learning and mastering the complex operations, shortcuts, and workflows of a specific software or tool. These skills are essential to daily work efficiency. Switching to a new system requires relearning and adaptation, which temporarily reduces productivity—this learning cost and efficiency loss are invisible but substantial.

- **Deeply embedded processes and business dependencies:** The product is deeply integrated into every aspect of the enterprise's or individual's daily workflow, becoming indispensable "blood flow." For example, if a project management tool has been used long-term by a team, its internal communications, task allocation, file storage, progress tracking, and approval workflows are all highly dependent on it. Replacing it could disrupt the entire team's workflow, causing confusion and stagnation.
- **Ecosystem and integration lock-in:** Users not only rely on the core product but also on a suite of surrounding APIs, plugins, third-party applications, and even compatible hardware. This forms a complete solution. Changing the core product could invalidate the entire ecosystem, requiring a full rebuild.

This high switching cost, when deliberately designed and reinforced, ensures that users remain "willing participants" in the ecosystem, creating a robust and defensible commercial moat (Fig. 7.4).

When designing products, technical personnel should consciously enhance user "engagement," enabling users to continually accumulate "assets" through product usage—whether in the form of data, skills, content, or business processes built upon the product. This accumulation of assets eventually evolves into intangible switching costs, making users more inclined to continue using the existing product rather than switching to a competitor. Importantly, this should not be achieved through coercive "lock-in" tactics, but by delivering continuous, meaningful value, so that the more users invest, the greater the convenience and benefits they receive, naturally encouraging them to stay. High-quality products, excellent user experience, and deep resolution of core pain points are prerequisites for cultivating this kind of "willing" loyalty.

**Fig. 7.4** High switching costs—barriers to user migration

# 7 Brand and Trust: The Intangible Asset of Technical Strength—Forging an Impregnable "Mental High Ground"

In today's era of information overload and abundant choices, the quality and sophistication of a technology product ultimately crystallize into an intangible yet extraordinarily valuable asset—brand and trust. For technology startups, establishing professional authority and user trust in a specific domain is itself a formidable barrier, sometimes even more penetrating than patents.

The establishment of such brand and trust stems from cumulative, meticulous effort, including:

- **Sustained investment and excellence in R&D:** Constantly staying at the technological forefront, launching breakthrough products and features, allowing the market to perceive the company's leadership and invention in technology.
- **Exquisite product quality:** Whether software stability, superior performance, or hardware reliability and craftsmanship, products should embody perfection, integrating a "craftsmanship spirit."
- **Rapid response and deep listening to user feedback:** Actively interacting with users, converting their pain points and needs into product iteration drivers, making users feel valued and understood.
- **Setting industry standards or solutions:** Leveraging invention and influence to drive or participate in industry standards, establishing the company's technology as the de facto benchmark.
- **Transparent and responsible corporate culture:** Upholding high standards in data privacy, ethical AI, and related areas, earning users' respect and long-term trust.

Edison was able to build a vast commercial empire not merely because of his inventions, but because the name "Edison" itself came to represent invention, reliability, and light, even becoming a symbol of quality. This powerful brand image made his products more easily accepted by the market and attracted top-tier talent, forming a "talent moat." For modern technology entrepreneurs, this means that while pursuing technological breakthroughs, we must also focus on outwardly communicating our technological vision, participating in industry conferences, actively sharing knowledge within professional communities, writing white papers, and always placing user interests first. Through consistent successful deliveries, reliable service, and responsible corporate behavior, this invaluable "trust asset" is gradually accumulated. Once established, this trust occupies a "high ground" in users' minds, creating deeply rooted preference and loyalty, becoming the enterprise's most powerful intangible asset and its most formidable business barrier (Fig. 7.5).

**Fig. 7.5** The radiating effect of brand and trust

## 8 Conclusion

The entrepreneurial journey for technologists is far more than simply bringing laboratory inventions to the market. It is a systematic game that requires transforming technological "points" into commercial "planes," thereby constructing a series of robust "asymmetric advantage" fortresses. Only when technological depth truly permeates every aspect of business operations, forming a composite strength that is difficult to replicate, can the flower of technological entrepreneurship bloom brilliantly on the fertile soil of commerce, enduring and ever-renewing.

## Further Reading

[1]. P. Ghemawat, *Commitment: The Dynamic of Strategy*, Free Press, 1991.
[2]. X. Cao, *Modern Business Management*, Palgrave Macmillan, 2025.
[3]. B. Wernerfelt, "A resource-based view of the firm," *Strategic Management Journal*, vol. 5, no. 2, pp. 171–180, 1984.
[4]. X. Cao, *Strategic Management and Organizational Development*, Springer, 2025.
[5]. J. Barney, "Firm resources and sustained competitive advantage," *Journal of Management*, vol. 17, no. 1, pp. 99–120, 1991.
[6]. M. E. Porter, *Competitive Strategy: Techniques for Analyzing Industries and Competitors*, Free Press, 1980.
[7]. R. Rumelt, *Good Strategy Bad Strategy*, Crown Business, 2011.
[8]. C. Shapiro and H. Varian, *Information Rules: A Strategic Guide to the Network Economy*, Harvard Business School Press, 1999.
[9]. K. Eisenhardt and J. Martin, "Dynamic capabilities: What are they?" *Strategic Management Journal*, vol. 21, no. 10–11, pp. 1105–1121, 2000.
[10]. A. Brandenburger and B. Nalebuff, *Co-opetition*, Doubleday, 1996.

# Chapter 8
# Differentiation and Homogenization in Team Building

## 1 Introduction

In today's highly competitive and complex business environment, teams serve as the core units for invention and value creation, and the way they are built directly impacts organizational performance and long-term sustainability. The tension between differentiation and homogenization among team members is a common and challenging issue in management practice. On the one hand, differences in skills and backgrounds can bring rich resource complementarity and innovative energy, achieving a "$1 + 1 > 2$" synergy effect. On the other hand, cognitive differences may lead to communication barriers, conflicts of interest, and collaborative friction, undermining team stability and efficiency. Conversely, members with highly aligned cognition may find it easier to reach consensus, but they often lack the drive for breakthrough collaboration, making it difficult to meet the demands of rapid organizational change. This chapter systematically analyzes the advantages and disadvantages of differentiated versus homogeneous team members, and explores how corporate culture, rules and regulations, and incentive mechanisms can be leveraged to resolve conflicts and enhance cohesion, aiming to provide theoretical guidance and practical insights for managers to achieve a dynamic balance between differentiation and homogenization in team building.

## 2 What Truly Holds a Team Together Is Not Shared Beliefs

In the business world, what often surprises people is not why teams fail, but how they initially came together. Many startup teams resemble the "brotherhoods" of college dormitories—similar majors, comparable backgrounds, shared interests, and even strikingly similar working styles. Founders often proudly recount in interviews: "The three of us were college buddies; our way of thinking was almost identical."

 
S. Li, *Bridging the Innovation Gap*, Innovation, Technology, and Knowledge Management, https://doi.org/10.1007/978-3-032-22652-5_8

Yet reality rarely indulges sentiment. Once a project enters phases of financing, expansion, equity allocation, or role adjustment, that so-called alignment quickly becomes the root of the hardest-to-reconcile conflicts. When cognition is identical, everyone wants the same thing; no one is willing to step back or fill gaps, and clashes erupt over "who leads, who follows." Ultimately, it is not shared beliefs that fracture, but interests.

We often assume that shared beliefs are the foundation for long-term teamwork. But alignment only solves the "easy communication" problem—it cannot address the reality of "who does the dirty work, who takes responsibility." Two people may both excel at strategy, yet no one wants to handle client relations; two may be product-oriented, yet none understands sales. Teams with highly aligned cognition may initially enjoy collaborative ease, but they frequently stumble in complex situations.

Conversely, many of the most successful teams begin with "misunderstanding." One member excels at operations, another at product, and another drives decisions through sales—though their discussions may get heated, together they ultimately guide the company on track. These team members possess highly complementary abilities, with clearly delineated responsibilities: you handle what you excel at, I manage what I know best. Appearing discordant on the surface, the team is actually stable. The key is not whether cognition aligns, but whether a "win-win yet divided" system can be established.

Why is this the case? Even the most aligned beliefs can crack under the pressure of real money. What truly sustains a team is not shared ideology, but institutional arrangements. Only when a system makes each member understand—"I gain more by staying in this team than by leaving"—does long-term cooperation become possible. Mechanisms shape behavior; interests stabilize relationships.

This is even more evident in marital relationships. Couples who are well-matched in social status or education often communicate more smoothly. They naturally agree on issues such as child-rearing, finances, and household management. Yet such marriages are also prone to a "consensus bubble." A husband and wife both engaged in research may have deep academic discussions but may struggle with mundane, diverse aspects of daily life, such as family finances, elder care, or home maintenance. The ideal marital pairing is often one of complementary personalities and abilities: one excels at long-term planning, another at immediate adaptation; one is rational and precise, the other emotionally perceptive. At minimum, one should be able to support the other in their "weak spots." We always emphasize avoiding close-relative marriage because it increases the risk of expressing disadvantageous shared genes. In fact, individuals who are completely aligned in beliefs and background may also be engaging in a form of "inbreeding" that sacrifices diversity (Fig. 1).

A company operates in much the same way. A truly effective team is not about replicating another version of yourself, but about filling in the gaps you lack. A great CEO does not need three vice presidents who think exactly like him; rather, they need a CFO with financial expertise, a CMO with marketing acumen, and a COO skilled in operations. These individuals may hold different values, have contrasting styles, and even clash on certain issues. Yet as long as organizational systems are

**Fig. 1** Diverse individuals collaboratively build a strong organization through cooperation and shared benefits, realizing the company's core values under the guidance of corporate culture

clear and the structure of incentives is well designed, they will reach a stable balance because "cooperation yields greater benefits than conflict." This balance is the real adhesive that holds the organization together.

One might ask, what about disagreements within the team? Don't conflicts slow down efficiency? Indeed, complementary teams often incur higher communication costs initially compared to homogeneous ones. One person might insist "the customer comes first," while another prioritizes "product above all"—to outsiders, it might sound like speaking different languages. But the solution is not to enforce cognitive alignment; it is to establish systems that clarify boundaries and responsibilities: you handle external affairs, I manage internal operations; you set strategy, I execute; you make decisions, but you are accountable if things go wrong. Supplement this with effective culture-building, regular team activities, and cross-functional collaboration, and what was once "not understanding each other" gradually evolves into "understanding and trust."

This is precisely the core significance of corporate culture. It is not about making everyone the same; it is about ensuring that even when we are different, we can still win together. Company culture is not a slogan—it is a buffer that prevents diversity from collapsing. Coupled with rational economic incentives, such as equity binding, phased incentives, and exit penalties, individual interests are tied to organizational value, creating an organizational logic of "we cooperate not because we agree, but because cooperation is more advantageous."

In summary, the key logic in team building is this: cognitive differences are not to be feared; what is dangerous is lacking systems and mechanisms to reconcile them. Only complementary teams possess structural integrity, and the greatest threat to structural integrity is not disagreement itself but the absence of rules to manage it.

Teams that endure are not those who share mutual understanding, but those who are mutually dependent, operate within clear systems, and maintain stable cooperation.

Therefore, when building a team, don't just look for people you "get along with." Look for those you can "work with"—people who can combine responsibilities, create value together, and thrive within a well-designed system.

## 3 The Challenge of Complementarity—The Necessity of Management, Division of Labor, and System Design

If team member complementarity is a strategic resource, activating it does not happen naturally. It is more like an uncut gemstone—full of potential, yet containing hidden flaws. In practice, teams composed of members with highly divergent backgrounds and strong knowledge complementarity, while theoretically capable of "$1 + 1 > 2$" synergy, can easily slip into a "$1 + 1 < 1$" internal conflict trap without proper system design and clear division of responsibilities.

I once observed a startup team where the founder was a product expert, the co-founder a seasoned marketer, and an early-joining partner handled technology. Their backgrounds were completely different. Initially, collaboration was smooth, and division of labor was clear. However, as the business progressed, tensions emerged between product roadmaps and market timing: the founder and marketing co-founder disagreed on priorities, while the technical partner pursued cutting-edge, complex solutions that increased project uncertainty. Each had valid points, yet the "everyone for themselves" dynamic began to appear, meetings became long and contentious, execution efficiency dropped, and eventually a third party had to step in to help restructure the decision-making process. This case clearly illustrates that complementarity alone is insufficient; what truly enables organizational synergy is clear division of labor and accountability built on top of complementarity.

Division of labor may seem basic, but in teams with diverse backgrounds, it often becomes complex. On the one hand, members may not understand each other's professional boundaries, leading to misjudgments about task ownership. On the other hand, even with clearly defined roles, interference can occur in execution because everyone thinks they see a "better solution." Underlying this is a deeper insecurity: trust among members has not been fully established, and understanding of team goals has not been aligned, resulting in divergent paths despite shared objectives.

The key to resolving this issue is not simply "getting along," but systematic organizational design. First, a clear responsibility matrix is essential. Each core member's "domain" must be defined: who is accountable for which outcomes, who holds final decision authority—no ambiguities. Second, communication mechanisms must be institutionalized. Many conflicts do not stem from value differences but from misunderstandings caused by information asymmetry. Regular strategic alignment meetings and cross-functional sharing sessions are effective ways to reduce miscommunication and enhance transparency (Fig. 2).

**Fig. 2** Systems play a crucial role in activating collaboration, ensuring the team transitions from chaos to harmony

Furthermore, effective system arrangements require building consensus both culturally and economically. Culturally, the emphasis is on the principle of "focus on the matter, not the person," guiding everyone to understand that differences are organizational assets, not fissures; economically, incentive mechanisms should be designed with long-term alignment in mind. For example, in equity allocation, a "time-for-rights" vesting mechanism ensures that team members can only realize value through sustained collaborative work. On the surface, this mechanism appears to "lock people in," but in essence, it "locks in unity," as it forces everyone to recognize that only through mutual success can individual maximum benefit be achieved.

We can perhaps use another analogy to understand the necessity of such systems—a symphony orchestra. Violins, cellos, pianos, percussion, each with different timbres and styles, if left to play freely, could easily become a disaster. Yet, under the coordination of a conductor and a musical score, each difference becomes a supporting element of the overall harmony, creating a breathtaking performance. Teams are similar: complementary individuals must rely on the "baton" of rules and the "score" of division of responsibilities to collaborate and produce an outstanding business "symphony."

Therefore, we can draw a clear conclusion: in highly complementary teams, systems are not shackles that constrain creativity; rather, they are the prerequisite for activating collaboration. If managers only see the potential brought by complementarity but neglect the foundational work of system construction, the battle of team building is likely to be doomed from the start.

## 4 Culture as the Adhesive—Building a Hidden Mechanism for Sustainable Collaboration

If division of labor and systems are the skeleton of team collaboration, then culture is the ligament woven throughout the bones, determining whether the organization is truly flexible and vibrant. Especially in complementary teams, no matter how clear the division of labor or how meticulous the systems, without an internalized cultural mechanism as lubrication, sustained, efficient, and enjoyable collaboration is difficult to achieve.

The role of culture is not to constrain, but to guide. Unlike the "explicit constraints" of systems, it functions as an "implicit norm," creating an atmosphere that encourages voluntary collaboration. In a team with strong culture, even when facing disputes, misunderstandings, or disagreements, members can address issues constructively rather than harbor suspicion, shirk responsibility, or lose emotional control.

This is particularly critical in teams with high diversity. Members with different experiences, educational paths, and cognitive styles are prone to communication biases and misalignment in understanding, and culture serves as the buffer that balances these tensions. A culture that emphasizes "open discussion, mutual respect, and focus on issues rather than individuals" can effectively reduce friction caused by complementary differences, allowing members to express differing viewpoints without feeling attacked or attacking others.

However, culture is not a slogan or a poster on the wall. Its establishment comes from repeated behavioral guidance and reinforcement through organizational rituals. A team emphasizing collaboration must reward cooperative behavior, tolerate failure in the team atmosphere, and actively guide listening in management practices. For instance, organizing regular team-building activities is not just about "food, drinks, and fun," but about getting team members out of their role identities to understand each other's life trajectories and values, thereby building deeper emotional trust. This trust forms the foundation for members to remain calm during conflicts and continue to collaborate.

A frequently overlooked detail: many early-stage startup teams do not value "culture building," seeing it as something only large companies need. Yet, precisely because small teams have limited resources, high pressure, and more frequent differences of opinion, cultural mechanisms are essential to buffer conflicts and maintain cooperative enthusiasm. Some companies resolve issues through systems but lose the hearts of their people when culture is absent; others may have imperfect systems, but strong culture makes them highly resilient, allowing rapid self-healing in crises.

Cultural mechanisms can also provide "humanized coverage" in gray areas that systems cannot fully govern. For example, if a technical partner temporarily takes a three-week leave for family reasons and the system provides no formal leave basis, tasks may be delayed. In a team with a culture of "empathy" and "mutual support first," however, members are willing to temporarily cover for each other and tolerate

**Fig. 3** In a diverse team, corporate culture plays a crucial role; it serves both as a buffering mechanism and as a driver of collaborative synergy

delays without worrying about performance evaluation. This "automatic collaboration" behavior cannot be fully dictated by systems but is a direct manifestation of cultural strength (Fig. 3).

Furthermore, culture also carries a strategic "path dependency" effect—it determines the quality of team member turnover. When a team's cultural core is clear and resilient, new members are not forced to assimilate but are naturally attracted; those who do not align with the culture will leave on their own; and truly like-minded individuals will demonstrate greater loyalty due to cultural alignment. In the long term, this mechanism significantly reduces personnel issues such as "internal friction hiring" and "misaligned values."

From a strategic perspective, we must recognize that in a diverse team, culture is not an optional "soft asset" but a key strategic resource for ensuring collaboration efficiency and team longevity. Only when culture becomes a shared consensus among team members can an organization evolve from a "temporary collaborative entity" into a "community of shared destiny."

## 5 Designing a Win-Win Structure—Binding the Team's Fate through Incentive Mechanisms

If culture is the subtle lubricant of collaboration, then incentive mechanisms are the driving system that sustains long-term team operation. A truly stable and effective team relies not only on shared ideals, personality compatibility, or clear division of labor, but also on an institutionalized "win-win mechanism"—explicitly signaling to each member: the team succeeds, and you succeed; disrupt the collaboration, and your own interests suffer.

This is not merely an incentive tool but a strategically significant institutional arrangement. In highly complementary teams, members often possess different core resources or capabilities, are interdependent, yet lack interchangeability. Without precise design of benefit allocation and exit mechanisms, any imbalance of interests or breach of trust can easily lead to "key member exits" or "internal hijacking," directly undermining the team's collaborative structure.

From a management perspective, there are two mechanisms that can stabilize such highly complementary teams: one is a delayed benefit realization mechanism, and the other is an asymmetric exit penalty mechanism (Fig. 4).

The first mechanism involves linking individual rewards to the team's collective milestones through approaches such as "delayed outcomes" and equity vesting periods. In simple terms, an individual can only realize their equity or dividends once

**Fig. 4** Binding the Team's Fate Through Incentive Mechanisms

the company reaches a certain stage or milestone. For example, early-stage startups often set a four-year vesting schedule for founders' shares, with 25% released each year, and include a one-year cliff, meaning no shares are allocated if the individual leaves within the first year. This approach is fundamentally designed to prevent "free-riding" and reinforce incentives for long-term, collaborative effort.

The second mechanism imposes proportionate penalties on members who exit uncooperatively or prematurely, safeguarding the interests and motivation of those who remain. For instance, if a key partner leaves suddenly during an early financing stage, they may only be able to repurchase shares at a very low valuation or lose unvested equity entirely. While this may seem harsh, it is crucial for maintaining overall team stability and preventing morale and fairness from being undermined by opportunistic exits.

Such mechanisms also have parallels in marital relationships. Community property laws and spousal support obligations are, in essence, structural arrangements that ensure "cooperation leads to mutual gain, while separation leads to loss for both." Though business teams are not emotional contracts, their collaborative relationships similarly require structural institutional binding.

It is important to note that designing incentive mechanisms does not mean enforcing egalitarianism or strict symmetry; rather, it should be tailored to the individual and their role. True design artistry lies in balancing contribution, scarcity, and risk. A partner who controls critical technology should receive far greater incentives than a more easily replaceable functional manager; a CEO responsible for financing must have a compensation structure reflecting their excess risk in resource integration and strategic maneuvering. If incentives fail to reflect such "value differences," psychological imbalance can emerge, ultimately undermining team collaboration.

An elevated level of incentive design allows members not only to receive immediate rewards but also to participate in the future growth dividends. This embodies the so-called long-term partnership culture—members are not mere employees, but co-builders. For example, some platform companies use virtual equity, performance options, or growth incentive pools to tie the organization's overall growth to individuals' future gains, ensuring that each core member thinks, acts, and bears responsibility like a founder.

Ultimately, any incentive mechanism answers a fundamental question: do we have the courage to discuss "exit" from the very beginning? Many teams avoid conversations about rewards, failure, or exit at the startup stage, attempting to preserve superficial harmony through idealism. Yet, teams that shy away from confronting differences are likely to fracture over them. Truly mature teams design for the "worst-case scenario" from the outset—only then can they advance farther, more stably, and with greater trust.

## 6 Corporate Culture and Regulations—The Lubricant for Cohesion in Differentiated Teams

The previous sections analyzed the tension between differentiation and homogeneity among team members and highlighted the necessity of constructing win-win cooperation through incentive mechanisms. While members' diverse backgrounds and complementary cognition bring invention and maximize value, they inevitably generate disagreements and conflicts. So how can team stability and harmony be maintained amid such differentiation? The role of corporate culture and regulations is especially critical (Fig. 5).

First, clear corporate rules and regulations delineate the behavioral boundaries for team collaboration. Ensuring that each team member focuses on their assigned responsibilities is a core aspect of these regulations. This not only prevents friction caused by "overstepping" but also avoids shirking due to unclear responsibilities. When everyone understands their role and duties, internal conflicts and misunderstandings stemming from ambiguous responsibilities are minimized.

Second, corporate culture serves as the spiritual bond that fosters team identity and a sense of belonging. Emphasizing a harmonious culture and a spirit of mutual support is not merely a slogan but a management strategy manifested through tangible actions. For instance, regularly organizing team-building activities strengthens mutual understanding and trust among members, alleviating the barriers created by cognitive differences. A culture of tolerance and understanding helps team members better accept each other's differences, turning disagreements into advantages derived from diversity.

**Fig. 5** Corporate culture and regulations serve as the lubricant for team cohesion

It is important to note that corporate culture and regulations are not static; they require continuous adaptation and refinement to accommodate changes in team composition and business development. Only in an environment where "rules are clear and widely accepted, and culture is inclusive and positive" can members of a diverse team find a balance for collaboration and achieve genuine synergy.

Returning to the analogy of marriage, even when two people have similar cognitive frameworks, the absence of effective communication and shared life rules can still lead to conflicts. Similarly, in corporate teams, building culture and regulations is crucial—they act as the lubricant that resolves cognitive differences and enables efficient collaboration.

In summary, corporate culture and regulations are both tools for managing differences and guarantees for team stability. They enable differentiated members to collaborate respectfully, creating a productive environment, maximizing overall team value, and advancing organizational strategic goals.

## 7 Conclusion: Strategic Balance between Differentiation and Homogeneity—Building an Efficient and Stable Team System

This chapter has delved into the core tension in team building—the balance between differentiated and homogeneous team members. In today's business environment, teams require complementary skills and cognition to maximize invention and value creation, yet they simultaneously face the challenges of cognitive discrepancies and potential conflicts of interest.

First, we clarified that while differentiated team members can produce a "1 + 1 > 2" synergistic effect, they inevitably bring cognitive and background inconsistencies that may cause friction and conflicts. In contrast, homogeneous members may achieve high tacit understanding but lack complementary advantages, struggle to break through invention bottlenecks, and are not guaranteed harmony in conflicts of interest.

Second, this chapter emphasizes the critical role of corporate culture, regulations, and incentive mechanisms in resolving these tensions. Properly designed incentive structures can tightly bind team members into a shared-interest entity, preventing zero-sum games from undermining collaboration. Clear division of labor rules, along with an inclusive and harmonious corporate culture, provide the foundation and lubricant for collaboration among differentiated members, enhancing cohesion and stability.

Finally, drawing analogies from family and particularly marital relationships further validates the strengths and limitations of cognitive similarity and complementary differences. It also illustrates that whether in teams or families, the design of interests and rules is fundamental to sustaining long-term cooperation.

In conclusion, building an efficient and stable team does not mean pursuing homogeneity or differentiation alone; it is about finding a dynamic balance between the two. By scientifically designing incentive mechanisms and fostering corporate culture and regulations, organizations can leverage the advantages of differentiation while mitigating its risks, thereby truly achieving synergistic performance and long-term development. This strategic balance is key for modern enterprises to maintain competitiveness and invention in a complex and ever-changing environment, and it is a critical concept that managers must deeply understand and implement.

## Further Reading

[1] R. M. Grant, "Toward a knowledge-based theory of the firm," *Strategic Management Journal*, vol. 17, pp. 109–122, 1996.
[2] X. Cao, *Strategic Management and Organizational Development*, Springer, 2025.
[3] R. S. Burt, *Structural Holes: The Social Structure of Competition*, Harvard Univ. Press, 1992.
[4] X. Cao, *Modern Business Management*, Palgrave Macmillan, 2025.
[5] J. Katzenbach and D. Smith, *The Wisdom of Teams: Creating the High-Performance Organization*, Harvard Business School Press, 1993.
[6] E. Lawler, *High-Involvement Management*, Jossey-Bass, 1986.
[7] A. Edmondson, "Psychological safety and learning behavior in work teams," *Administrative Science Quarterly*, vol. 44, no. 2, pp. 350–383, 1999.
[8] J. Pfeffer, *Competitive Advantage Through People*, Harvard Business School Press, 1994.
[9] F. J. Yammarino and F. Dansereau, "Individualized leadership," *Journal of Leadership Studies*, vol. 1, no. 2, pp. 133–139, 2007.
[10] R. Hackman, *Leading Teams: Setting the Stage for Great Performances*, Harvard Business School Press, 2002.
[11] E. G. Carayannis, Ed., *Encyclopedia of Creativity, Invention, Innovation and Entrepreneurship*. New York, NY: Springer, 2013. doi:https://doi.org/10.1007/978-1-4614-6616-1.

# Chapter 9
# Automation Vs. Centralization: The Hidden "Marginal Cost" of Centralization

## 1 Introduction

On the vast currents of modern business, the banner of efficiency flies high. From the roar of steam engines to the glimmer of microchips, humanity's pursuit of "less input, more output" has never ceased. For years, we have regarded automation as the holy grail of efficiency—the "lights-out factory," where machines run themselves and processes require no human intervention, has been the ultimate dream of countless entrepreneurs. Yet, when dreams meet reality, we find that the path to full automation is fraught with thorns; its high costs and fragile reliability often dash ambitious plans against the rocks.

This chapter will present a disruptive core argument: in the journey of chasing efficiency and value maximization, we may have overestimated the magic of pure automation while greatly underestimating the enormous marginal cost dividends that centralization can bring. A deeper insight is that the core mission of automation is to break through potential human efficiency bottlenecks within a centralized model, while centralization itself generates value through economies of scale, resource sharing, and optimized management. These two are not substitutes but complementary forces, jointly driving a revolution in efficiency. For aspiring entrepreneurs, understanding and mastering this dual-engine system is key to navigating toward success.

## 2 Automation: The Allure of the Stars and the Reality of Reefs

When automation is mentioned, people often envision scenes straight out of a sci-fi film: robots operating flawlessly on production lines, documents flowing automatically through offices, robotic chefs cooking meals in kitchens—the whole world

 
S. Li, *Bridging the Innovation Gap*, Innovation, Technology, and Knowledge Management, https://doi.org/10.1007/978-3-032-22652-5_9

**Fig. 9.1** The complexity and challenges of full automation

seemingly running in a "worry-free" mode. This vision of full automation (Fully Autonomous) is undeniably enticing; it promises to completely liberate humans from heavy, repetitive labor and deliver exponential leaps in productivity (Fig. 9.1).

However, reality is often far more complex than the ideal. Automation is not monolithic; it exists in layers. At the most basic level, there is teleoperated autonomy, where machines function more like an "extension of human limbs." Think of remotely piloting a drone for aerial photography, or a surgeon using the Da Vinci surgical system for precise operations. While the machine executes the physical actions, every decision and command originates from the human brain. The primary value of this mode lies in extending human capabilities—such as entering hazardous environments or performing ultra-precise tasks—but the efficiency gains are essentially a physical extension of human efficiency, not a fundamental transformation of system efficiency.

A more intelligent and flexible approach is what we commonly call supervised autonomy, or semi-automation. In this mode, machines handle the bulk of routine, repetitive tasks, while humans step back to act as "supervisors" and "exception handlers." This is akin to using Level 2 or Level 3 driver-assist systems in daily driving: the system can keep the vehicle centered and follow the car ahead on the highway, but the driver must remain alert, ready to take over in complex or unexpected situations. Similarly, intelligent customer service robots can resolve most common inquiries, while complex issues are seamlessly transferred to human agents. Supervised automation has found widespread real-world applications, striking an optimal balance between improving efficiency and ensuring reliability.

So why is truly full automation—the kind of utopia requiring no human intervention—so difficult to achieve? The core reason lies in a seemingly simple mathematical principle, grimly known as the "multiplication of reliability." Imagine a complex task

**Fig. 9.2** The automation process typically involves numerous interconnected steps, and the overall system reliability follows the multiplication-of-reliability principle. Even a small flaw or issue in any single step can accumulate, sharply reducing the overall success rate and potentially causing total system failure

composed of ten interdependent steps, like a line of dominoes: one misstep, and the whole system fails. Even if each step has a 99% automation success rate—which is already extremely high in engineering terms—the overall system success rate would only be $0.99^{10} \approx 90.4\%$. If the number of steps rises to 100, the success rate plummets to $0.99^{100} \approx 36.6\%$. This illustrates the harsh reality that in complex, multi-step tasks, system reliability declines exponentially. To reach the extremely high-reliability standards often required in business operations—such as the "five nines" (99.999%) or higher—each step must operate near perfection. Achieving this is not only technically daunting but also exponentially expensive in terms of development and testing, often discouraging startups from attempting full automation (Fig. 9.2).

This is the stark reality of the famous "Moravec's Paradox"—machines excel at precise calculations and repetitive tasks, yet struggle with perception, judgment, and common-sense reasoning that humans perform seemingly effortlessly. Entrepreneurs who attempt to build a fully automated empire from the outset may deplete their resources, only to end up with a "castle in the air" of theoretical achievements.

## 3 Centralization: The Infinite Magic of Marginal Cost Dividends

If full automation is a distant star, then centralization is the fertile ground beneath our feet. It may lack the dazzling technological aura of automation, yet the marginal cost dividends it contains are tangible, accessible wealth—often underestimated (Fig. 9.3).

Imagine a city with millions of residents, where all dining needs are served through a single unified platform. Even if the backend still relies heavily on human labor,

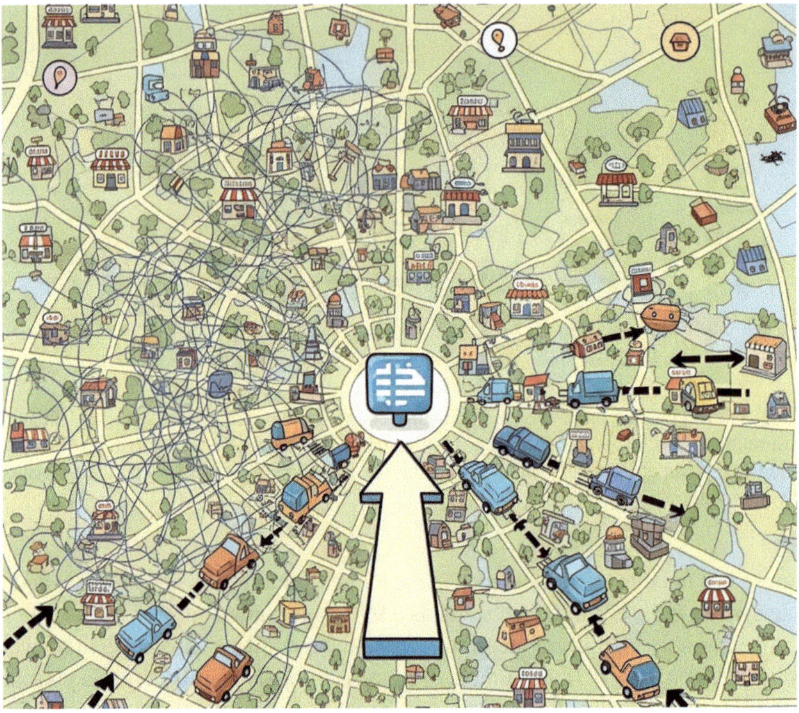

**Fig. 9.3** The order and efficiency brought by centralization

the efficiency gains and cost savings are remarkable. This efficiency stems from centralized management: restaurant onboarding standards, food safety regulations, and staff training can all be standardized, reducing chaos and improving overall service quality. Even more striking is the marginal cost miracle brought by centralized logistics. If a delivery person delivers one meal, the cost is X; if they can deliver two meals along the same route, the additional cost is negligible, yet revenue doubles. This is the power of shared resources and sharply reduced marginal costs. Platforms like Meituan or Ele.me, as well as urban bike-sharing systems, achieve this by centrally coordinating resources, maximizing utilization, and minimizing unit costs.

Moreover, the platform can implement a unified supply chain, purchasing ingredients in bulk to gain stronger bargaining power, ensuring quality and stable supply while lowering procurement costs for individual merchants. Finally, a unified channel allows consumers to browse countless restaurants through a single app, saving the time of visiting each individually. The platform also lowers customer acquisition costs for each restaurant through centralized marketing and brand promotion.

The magic of this model is not limited to dining. Take e-commerce giants like Amazon and JD.com: their core competitiveness lies in establishing vast and efficient centralized warehouses, logistics, and supply chain networks. While they continually advance automation, their initial value creation came largely from centralizing dispersed products, suppliers, and consumers—using scale and unified management to dilute the per-order costs of storage, packaging, and shipping to the extreme (Fig. 9.4).

Consider cloud computing. Providers like Amazon AWS and Alibaba Cloud build massive centralized data centers, offering computing, storage, and other IT resources as on-demand services. Users no longer need to invest in costly, complex-to-maintain servers; they simply pay for what they use, dramatically reducing the marginal cost of IT for businesses.

Clearly, centralization sets up a vast stage where resources, information, and demand can efficiently converge and flow, generating substantial marginal cost benefits. These benefits do not necessarily rely on cutting-edge automation technology; rather, they stem more from inventions in business models and thinking, and from optimized resource allocation. Centralization is relatively easier to implement, yet it can deliver immediate and tangible results. For entrepreneurs with limited resources, identifying and fully leveraging the marginal cost advantages of centralization early

**Fig. 9.4** Inside a massive warehouse, towering shelves are stacked with goods, yet few robots are present—only a handful of workers in uniforms move about in an orderly fashion. This illustrates that even without extensive automation, significant efficiency gains can still be achieved purely through the marginal cost reductions brought by centralization

on is often a more practical path to survival and establishing a foothold than chasing the elusive ideal of full automation from the outset.

## 4 Dual-Engine Drive: How Automation Empowers Centralization

We can now better understand the relationship between automation and centralization. They are not opposites; rather, they complement each other, jointly enhancing overall efficiency and value. If centralization is like laying down a highway, automation is the engine that allows vehicles on that highway to run faster and more smoothly (Fig. 9.5).

The core function of automation within a centralized system is to address potential efficiency bottlenecks caused by human operations. In a highly centralized system, a large number of transactions and interactions may still require human involvement. Any inefficiency at a single step can be magnified into a bottleneck for the entire system. Automation can intervene precisely, much like a surgeon removing these efficiency "tumors."

First, automation can significantly enhance human efficiency within the system. In large call centers, intelligent customer service bots can handle 80% of common inquiries, freeing human agents to focus on more complex and challenging issues. Automated banking approval systems can quickly process most standardized loan applications, with humans only reviewing exceptions or high-risk cases. This does not entirely replace humans; rather, it allows them to focus on higher-value tasks that truly require human intelligence.

**Fig. 9.5** The synergy between centralization and automation generates both value and growth

Second, automation can compensate for human limitations. In high-concurrency, high-intensity, high-precision, or hazardous environments, humans often struggle to keep up. Sorting robots in automated warehouses can operate 24/7 with minimal error rates, far exceeding human capability. Similarly, high-frequency trading algorithms in financial markets process data and execute trades at speeds and complexities beyond human reach.

Third, automation enables data-driven decision optimization. Automated systems can collect and analyze massive amounts of data in real time, providing centralized operations with precise insights. Ride-sharing platforms, for example, use automated algorithms to match supply and demand in real time, optimizing dispatch routes and minimizing idle mileage—tasks nearly impossible for humans to perform efficiently.

Finally, automation can enhance the reliability of centralized systems. For repetitive and standardized tasks, automated systems generally offer greater consistency and stability than humans, improving overall system reliability and product quality while reducing losses from human error.

Supervised automation (Supervised Autonomy), when integrated with centralization, demonstrates unparalleled advantages. It avoids the high costs and low-reliability risks of full automation while providing flexibility and resilience through human oversight and intervention, allowing the system to handle unexpected situations with ease. In this model, human-machine collaboration becomes critical: human judgment, creativity, and problem-solving combine seamlessly with the precision, speed, and data-processing capabilities of machines, achieving a synergy greater than the sum of its parts ("$1 + 1 > 2$").

For entrepreneurs, this means that when designing products or services, one cannot neglect human-machine interaction. The interface must be intuitive and efficient, allowing operators to quickly understand system status, detect issues, and intervene effectively—ensuring that human contribution flows seamlessly through automated processes, neither dragging down efficiency nor leaving gaps in machine capability. This is an essential skill for any "smart" entrepreneur.

## 5 Navigating for Entrepreneurs: Centralize First, Automate Later

So, what does this "automation, semi-automation, and centralization" efficiency revolution mean for entrepreneurs aiming to carve out new markets? It provides clear guidance, pointing the way toward successful outcomes.

In the early stages of a startup, the wisest choice is often to prioritize centralization. Entrepreneurs may be dazzled by flashy technological concepts, dreaming of immediately building a fully automated, high-tech product. However, startup resources are limited. Instead of pouring capital into a high-risk, low-reliability full automation system, it is wiser to focus on constructing a core centralized platform or model, capturing the largest "marginal cost dividend" first.

**Fig. 9.6** Centralization as a key driver of industry advancement

Carefully examine your industry: are there abundant scattered resources and inefficient processes? Can you consolidate these disparate elements through a unified platform or standardized processes to generate scale effects and shared benefits? For example, a local life-service platform in its early stages may not need sophisticated AI scheduling algorithms. As long as it can efficiently connect local merchants and consumers for fast service delivery, it can quickly capture market share. Prioritizing network effects and establishing user/merchant barriers will create the strongest early-stage moat for your venture (Fig. 9.6).

When your centralized platform reaches a certain scale and business volume grows rapidly, new bottlenecks often emerge—typically, human efficiency can no longer keep up. This is precisely when automation can shine, empowering your centralized system. Examine your daily operations: which processes are highly repetitive, time-consuming, error-prone, and standardized? These are the prime candidates for introducing supervised automation. For example, if a surge in customer inquiries slows down human response, deploy intelligent customer service bots while retaining human agents for complex issues. If order processing is complicated and prone to mistakes, develop an automated order management system but provide interfaces for human review and exception handling. This "small steps, rapid iteration" strategy allows you to gradually improve efficiency without compromising reliability (Fig. 9.7).

Entrepreneurs must also embrace the concept of "semi-automation" and recognize it as the future mainstream. Do not view machines as "replacements," but rather as "collaborators." In the vast majority of real-world scenarios, human judgment,

**Fig. 9.7** Centralization boosts efficiency by lowering marginal costs, while automation enhances efficiency by replacing human labor with machines

creativity, and emotional intelligence remain irreplaceable by machines. Consequently, you need to cultivate your team to evolve from traditional "executors" into "supervisors," "optimizers," and "problem solvers." This means that when designing products or services, resources must be invested in user experience (UX) and human-machine interface (HMI) design, ensuring that when machines require assistance, humans can intervene quickly and intuitively, providing effective feedback. For example, designing a clear dashboard allows operators to monitor the health of automated systems in real time and receive unambiguous alerts in case of anomalies.

Furthermore, data is the fuel driving everything. Both centralization and automation rely heavily on data support. Data is the "fuel" for optimizing processes, identifying bottlenecks, and improving efficiency. Therefore, it is crucial to establish data collection and analysis systems from the very beginning of your venture. Your centralized platform will generate massive amounts of data, while automated systems will produce even more operational data. Leveraging this information allows you to pinpoint efficiency pain points, optimize resource allocation, and even uncover new business opportunities.

Finally, entrepreneurs must understand that resilience outweighs everything else—survival is the ultimate priority. The fragility of full automation lies in the "weakest link" effect: a single failure can paralyze the entire system. In the early stages of a startup, system resilience and adaptability are more critical than extreme automation. Supervised automation adds a layer of "insurance" by incorporating human intervention, allowing the system to adjust flexibly in the face of uncertainty and unexpected events, preventing total failure. Only organizations and systems capable of rapid adaptation and adjustment can survive and thrive amid fierce competition and accelerated technological iteration.

## 6 Conclusion: Humans and Machines in Harmony, Navigating toward Shared Prosperity

Efficiency gains are never the solo performance of a single technology; they are a grand symphony orchestrated through systemic thinking and composite strategies. Centralization is akin to a massive ship, carrying immense value potential, where scale effects and resource sharing reduce marginal costs to the utmost. Automation—particularly in the form of supervised automation—acts as the ship's most advanced engine, precisely eliminating resistance along the voyage while granting higher speed and enhanced resilience against risks (Fig. 9.8).

For every aspiring entrepreneur, do not be trapped by the illusion of "full automation." First, take a step back and consider how your business can create unique marginal cost advantages and network effects through centralization. Once this foundation is firmly in place, strategically and selectively introduce supervised automation, making machines your most capable assistants rather than distant, untouchable substitutes.

The future business world belongs to those enterprises that understand and can harness this "dual-engine" system. This is not merely about commercial success—it is about navigating a new paradigm of human-machine collaboration, collectively moving toward a future that is more efficient, resilient, and ultimately capable of

**Fig. 9.8** With the development of efficient transportation and communication systems, the world increasingly resembles a "global village," becoming highly centralized and interconnected. Combined with automation and robotics, this connectivity further enhances overall efficiency

shared prosperity. This pathway is rich with opportunities, awaiting entrepreneurs who are both grounded and daringly innovative to explore and conquer.

## Further Reading


1. J. Galbraith, *Designing Complex Organizations*, Addison-Wesley, 1973.
2. H. Simon, *The Sciences of the Artificial*, MIT Press, 1969.
3. X. Cao, *Modern Business Management*, Palgrave Macmillan, 2025.
4. J. March and H. Simon, *Organizations*, Wiley, 1958.
5. C. Perrow, *Complex Organizations: A Critical Essay*, McGraw-Hill, 1986.
6. X. Cao, *Strategic Management and Organizational Development*, Springer, 2025.
7. E. Brynjolfsson and A. McAfee, *The Second Machine Age*, W. W. Norton, 2014.
8. C. Christensen, *The Innovator's Solution*, Harvard Business School Press, 2003.
9. D. Tapscott, *Blockchain Revolution*, Penguin, 2016.
10. J. Bessen, "AI and jobs: The role of demand," *NBER Working Paper*, No. 24235, 2018.

# Chapter 10
# Supply Chains: The Cornerstone of Corporate Strategy—with a Discussion on the Boundaries of Independent R&D

## 1 Introduction

In today's business environment, where globalization and digitalization are deeply intertwined, enterprises face unprecedented opportunities and challenges. Market demands shift rapidly, technological iterations accelerate, and competitive landscapes grow increasingly complex. Against this backdrop, the effective allocation of resources, risk mitigation, and achievement of sustainable growth have become central concerns of corporate strategic management.

This chapter delves into the pivotal role of supply chains in corporate strategy and the unique value they provide. On this foundation, it carefully analyzes the inherent risks and boundaries of independent research and development (R&D), aiming to elucidate the profound significance of the strategic principle: *"If a supply chain can be leveraged, do not engage in independent R&D."* Furthermore, it reveals the quantitative relationship between project complexity and the probability of failure, offering deep insights for enterprises seeking to build a strategic system that is both resilient and efficient (Fig. 1).

## 2 The Strategic Anchor of Supply Chains: Near-100% Reliability

As a complex network connecting internal and external resources to realize value creation, the most notable characteristic of a supply chain is its ability to provide near-100% reliability or success rate. This high level of certainty is not accidental; it stems from the long-term development of specialized division of labor, economies of scale, standardized processes, and risk diversification mechanisms. At the strategic level, this high reliability renders the supply chain an irreplaceable cornerstone for the enterprise (Fig. 2).



S. Li, *Bridging the Innovation Gap*, Innovation, Technology, and Knowledge Management, https://doi.org/10.1007/978-3-032-22652-5_10

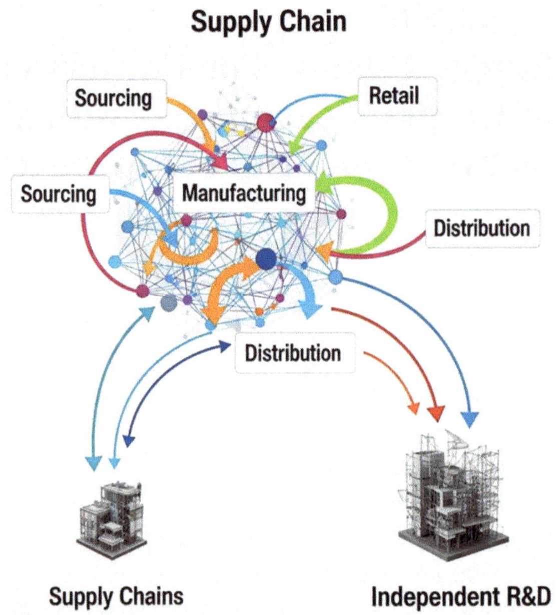


**Fig. 1** The strategic importance of supply chains in today's business environment and the potential risks of independent R&D

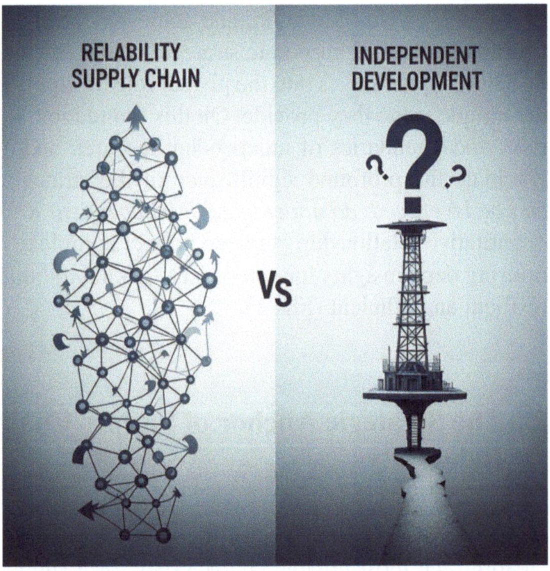


**Fig. 2** The supply chain is a network connecting various suppliers. Although complex, it offers near-100% reliability and certainty, whereas R&D, in contrast, is exploratory and inherently risky

First, the reliability of the supply chain provides enterprises with a stable and predictable operational foundation. In any manufacturing enterprise, a consistent supply of raw materials and components is the prerequisite for maintaining uninterrupted production. A mature and efficient supply chain system, through establishing long-term stable partnerships with upstream suppliers, implementing rigorous supplier selection and performance evaluation mechanisms, and leveraging advanced inventory management (such as Just-In-Time, JIT) and logistics systems, can minimize the risks of supply disruptions, quality defects, or delivery delays. For instance, in precision manufacturing industries such as semiconductors or aerospace, the delay of even a single critical component can halt an entire production line, causing enormous economic losses and damage to market reputation. By relying on a highly reliable global supply chain, these companies can ensure that tens of thousands of complex components arrive at the assembly line precisely on time, guaranteeing the smooth execution of production schedules and on-time product delivery. This stability and predictability allow enterprises to make more accurate production plans, sales forecasts, and financial budgets, providing a solid foundation for long-term development.

Second, the reliability of the supply chain is a key pathway for optimizing cost structures. By leveraging the economies of scale within the supply chain, enterprises can achieve lower procurement costs. Large suppliers typically possess stronger bargaining power and more efficient production processes, enabling them to offer high-quality products or services at more competitive prices. At the same time, efficient logistics management and inventory optimization can significantly reduce warehousing costs, transportation costs, and the capital tied up in excess inventory. For example, the success of global retail giant Walmart is largely attributed to its unparalleled supply chain management capabilities. Through close collaboration with suppliers, advanced logistics networks, and data-driven inventory management, Walmart compresses the entire flow cost from producer to consumer to the extreme, realizing its "Everyday Low Price" strategy. This provides consumers with highly attractive prices while maintaining high profit margins. Such cost advantages are not achieved by compromising quality or service but are a direct reflection of supply chain efficiency and reliability.

Furthermore, supply chain reliability significantly enhances a company's market responsiveness and flexibility. In the context of rapidly changing consumer demand and increasingly shortened product life cycles, enterprises need the ability to quickly respond to market changes and flexibly adjust product strategies. A flexible and reliable supply chain ensures that companies can rapidly allocate resources to meet sudden spikes in orders, seasonal fluctuations, or market trend shifts. For example, fast-fashion brand ZARA stands out in the global fashion industry, with one of its core competitive advantages being its "small batch, multiple batch, rapid replenishment" supply chain model. ZARA can transform the latest design concepts into store products within one to two weeks, thanks to the vertical integration and high-efficiency coordination across its entire supply chain, including design, production, logistics, and retail. This rapid response capability allows ZARA to closely follow fashion trends, reduce overstocked inventory, and continuously attract consumers, thereby maintaining a leading position in the highly competitive fashion market.

Finally, the reliability of the supply chain is also reflected in risk diversification and specialization advantages. By establishing partnerships with multiple suppliers, companies can spread the risk associated with relying on a single supplier. Additionally, by outsourcing non-core business to specialized supply chain partners, enterprises can leverage external expertise, technology, and experience to enhance overall operational efficiency and product quality. For instance, many technology companies choose to outsource chip manufacturing and assembly to specialized contract manufacturers like TSMC or Foxconn. These firms possess world-leading capabilities in their respective fields and can provide high-quality, efficient services. This specialized division of labor not only reduces operational costs and risks for the enterprise but also allows the company to focus more on its core competencies, such as product design, brand building, and marketing.

## 3 The Risk Boundaries of Independent R&D: Natural Constraints on Success Probability

In stark contrast to the near-100% certainty offered by supply chains, independent R&D (Research & Development) is often accompanied by significant risks, with success probabilities far lower than the certainty of supply chains. The essence of technology R&D is exploration into unknown territories, filled with uncertainties, repeated trials, and potential failures. When considering independent R&D, enterprises must clearly recognize its inherent risk boundaries.

First, technological R&D carries inherent technical risks. From the conception of a new technology to its eventual mature application, a series of technical challenges must be overcome. Even with massive financial investment, top-tier talent, and extended development cycles, success is not guaranteed. For example, in pharmaceutical development, a new drug often requires years or even decades and billions of dollars in investment, yet only a small fraction successfully reaches the market (with success rates typically below 10%), with the vast majority failing during clinical trials due to insufficient efficacy or safety concerns. Similarly, in artificial intelligence, many cutting-edge algorithms and models perform well in laboratory settings but may fail to meet expectations in real-world applications due to data bias, computational limitations, or poor generalization. These examples clearly illustrate the natural technical uncertainties associated with independent R&D.

Second, independent R&D faces substantial market risks. Even if a company achieves a breakthrough in technology, there is no guarantee that the market will accept the new technology or product. Market demand is dynamic; consumer preferences, competitors' strategies, and macroeconomic fluctuations can all result in new products failing after launch. For example, some high-tech products developed with substantial investment may fail in the market due to excessive pricing, redundant functions, poor user experience, or failure to address consumer pain points, becoming "praised but unsold" cases. Google Glass, for instance, was technologically innovative but failed to achieve mass adoption due to privacy concerns, high costs, and limited practical use scenarios. This demonstrates that technical success does not equate to commercial success, and market uncertainty represents another significant risk that independent R&D must confront (Fig. 3).

Moreover, independent R&D entails high sunk costs. R&D investments are typically substantial, encompassing salaries for research personnel, laboratory equipment purchases, consumption of experimental materials, patent application fees, and the time cost associated with lengthy development cycles. Once an R&D project fails, these investments become unrecoverable sunk costs, placing significant financial pressure on the enterprise. This is particularly acute in high-tech sectors, where R&D expenditures can reach hundreds of millions or even billions of dollars. A failed project can be a severe blow to any company and potentially fatal for small

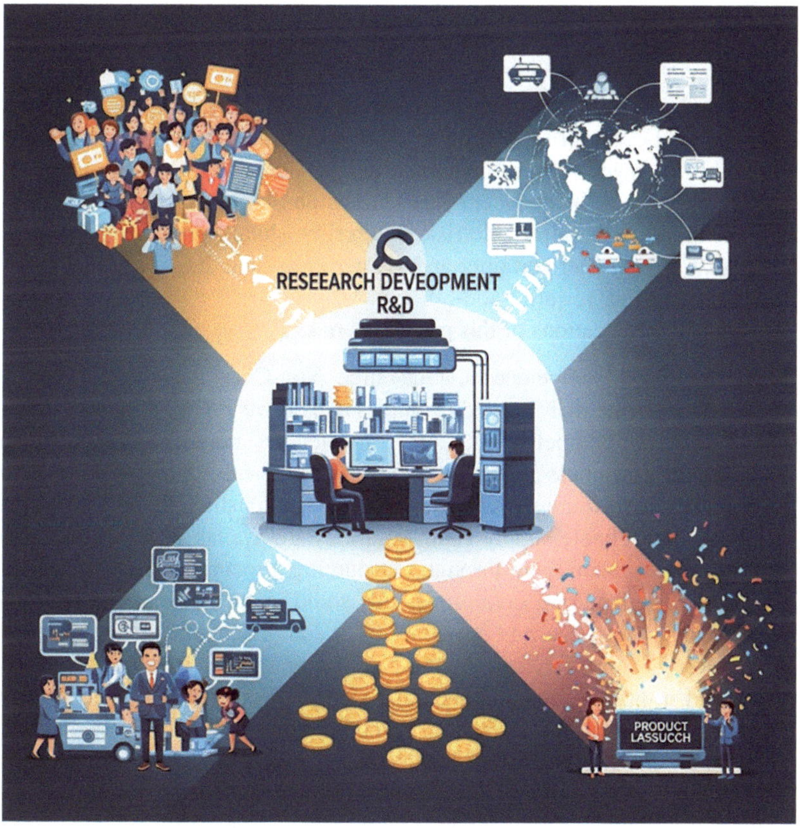


**Fig. 3** Independent R&D can lead to resource dispersion and opportunity cost issues

and medium-sized enterprises. For example, during the early stages of its smartphone transition, the former mobile giant Nokia invested heavily in R&D. However, due to its failure to timely adapt to market shifts and technological trends, its smartphone business eventually declined, rendering the substantial prior R&D investments effectively wasted.

Finally, independent R&D also involves issues of resource dispersion and opportunity cost. Choosing to pursue independent R&D means dedicating valuable financial, human, and temporal resources to a specific domain. This can result in insufficient investment in other areas that may hold greater strategic significance or higher potential returns, causing missed development opportunities. For resource-constrained enterprises, overly dispersed R&D efforts can prevent any single project from receiving adequate support, ultimately slowing or jeopardizing the progress of all initiatives.

## 4 Strategic Choice: If You Can Leverage the Supply Chain, Don't Pursue Independent R&D

Given the high reliability offered by supply chains and the high risks inherent in independent R&D, enterprises should adhere to a core strategic principle: if a supply chain can be leveraged, do not undertake independent R&D. This principle does not negate the value of independent R&D but emphasizes that, under conditions of limited resources and controllable risk, enterprises should prioritize supply chain solutions that offer higher certainty and greater efficiency. It is a rational strategic choice based on a risk-reward trade-off (Fig. 4).

The strategic implications of this principle are as follows:

1. Focus on Core Competencies, Outsource Non-Core Activities: Enterprises should concentrate their limited resources and efforts on building and strengthening their core competencies. Core competencies are the unique advantages upon which a business relies for survival and growth, distinguishing it from competitors in the market. For aspects that do not constitute core competencies, if mature and reliable supply chain solutions are available, companies should not hesitate to obtain them through outsourcing, procurement, or partnerships. For most manufacturing enterprises, this could include automated production equipment, enterprise-level IT systems, basic component manufacturing, or even certain R&D testing services, all of which can be sourced externally rather than developed in-house. This approach allows firms to focus their energy, capital, and top talent on product invention, brand building, breakthrough technologies, marketing, and customer relationship management—areas that truly generate differentiated value and high added value. Such strategic focus enables a company to develop a competitive advantage that is difficult to replicate.
2. Mitigate Unnecessary Risks and Reduce Operating Costs: Leveraging mature supply chains allows enterprises to effectively avoid the technical, market, and

**Fig. 4** By outsourcing non-core activities, enterprises can concentrate and focus on their core competencies

financial risks associated with independent R&D. External suppliers have typically been market-validated, and their products or services exhibit high maturity and reliability. Moreover, suppliers often benefit from economies of scale and specialized services, allowing enterprises to enjoy lower procurement costs and higher operational efficiency. For example, a clothing brand attempting to build an in-house fabric R&D team would face substantial investment and uncertain success, including long development cycles, high costs, and uncertain market acceptance. Collaborating with leading global fabric suppliers, however, provides high-quality and diverse materials while avoiding high R&D costs and risks, enabling faster product-to-market cycles. This "leveraging external strengths" strategy allows firms to achieve high-quality outcomes at lower cost and risk, enhancing overall competitiveness.

3. Accelerate Market Response and Enhance Agility: Relying on established supply chains can significantly shorten time-to-market. External suppliers often have streamlined production processes, efficient logistics networks, and rapid response mechanisms, enabling enterprises to quickly bring products to market and seize fleeting business opportunities. This is particularly crucial in fast-iteration, highly competitive industries. For instance, in consumer electronics, product lifecycles are increasingly short, requiring rapid product launches to maintain market share. Utilizing global component supply chains and contract manufacturing allows enterprises to quickly integrate resources for rapid design, production, and launch. Supply chain flexibility also enables easier adjustment of production scale and product variety to meet changing market demand, enhancing enterprise agility.

4. Optimize Resource Allocation and Improve Capital Efficiency: Corporate resources—including capital, talent, technology, and time—are limited. Investing these scarce resources in high-risk, low-certainty independent R&D may lead to waste and low capital efficiency. By leveraging supply chains, companies can allocate resources to higher-return, lower-risk areas, thereby improving overall capital efficiency. For example, outsourcing non-core manufacturing allows companies to redirect saved funds toward market expansion, brand development, or breakthrough core technology R&D, optimizing resource allocation.
5. Quantifying Complexity and Failure Probability: More Elements, Greater Risk: To further deepen the principle of "if you can leverage the supply chain, don't do independent R&D," we can introduce a probabilistic perspective: the more elements of a project require independent R&D, the higher the likelihood of failure. From a probabilistic standpoint, there is a clear negative correlation between project complexity and overall success probability.

Assume a project contains N key elements, each requiring independent, from-scratch R&D. Let the success probability of element i be Pi ($0 < Pi < 1$), and assume the success of each element is independent. Then the total success probability P of the project is the product of the success probabilities of all R&D elements:

P = P1* P_2*… * P_N

This formula clearly shows that as N increases, even if each Pi is relatively high, the overall P decreases significantly. For example:

- A project requiring only one key R&D element with an 80% success rate (P1 = 0.8) has a project success probability of 80%.
- With two key R&D elements, each at 80% success (P1 = P2 = 0.8), overall success drops to $0.8 \times 0.8 = 0.64$, or 64%.
- With three key R&D elements at 80% each, overall success is $0.8^3 = 0.512$, or ~ 51.2%.
- For five key elements, overall success falls to $0.8^5 \approx 0.32768$, or ~ 32.77%.

This mathematical relationship illustrates the exponential negative correlation between project complexity (number of elements requiring independent R&D) and final success probability. Even if individual R&D success rates seem reasonable, bundling multiple elements under a single project dramatically lowers overall success chances.

For enterprises, this means that decisions about independent R&D must include a detailed analysis of project components, assessing which elements can be sourced via mature supply chains. A project requiring independent breakthroughs across multiple elements entails exponentially higher strategic risk, potentially reaching levels beyond what the company can tolerate.

For example, a startup attempting to independently develop new battery materials, a battery management system (BMS), and a full vehicle platform may have independent R&D success rates of 70%, 80%, and 60%, respectively. The probability of successfully completing all three elements is $0.7 \times 0.8 \times 0.6 = 0.336$, or only 33.6%.

If, instead, the company focuses solely on battery materials and outsources the BMS and vehicle manufacturing to mature supply chain partners, its success probability significantly increases, as it only needs to ensure success in its core R&D. This approach concentrates resources on critical invention points, whereas attempting all elements independently risks failure at any one stage, potentially collapsing the entire project.

Hence, when planning strategic projects, companies should aim to **"decouple"** initiatives, stripping out elements obtainable through the supply chain and retaining only truly core, differentiated elements for independent R&D. This reduces overall project risk and allows companies to concentrate precious resources on areas with the highest value creation and competitive advantage potential.

## 5 Conclusion and Outlook: Building a Strategic System of Resilience and Efficiency

In today's uncertain business environment, strategy formulation and execution are critical. This chapter examined the fundamental difference between the near-100% reliability of supply chains and the high-risk nature of independent R&D, emphasizing the necessity and rationality of the principle: "If you can leverage the supply chain, don't do independent R&D." Quantitative analysis further demonstrated the strong link between project complexity and failure probability—more elements requiring independent R&D mean higher failure risk.

Supply chains, with near-perfect reliability, provide enterprises with a stable operational foundation, optimized cost structure, enhanced market responsiveness, and specialized risk diversification—serving as the strategic cornerstone for efficient operations and sustainable growth. Independent R&D, while a source of technological breakthroughs and differentiation, carries inherent technical, market, and sunk cost risks, necessitating extremely cautious investment.

Looking ahead, enterprises should strive to build a strategic system that combines resilience and efficiency, which entails:

1. Deepening Core Supply Chain Partnerships: Elevate supply chain management from procurement to strategic collaboration. Establish long-term, deep partnerships with core suppliers, jointly invest in R&D, share risks and rewards, and form an interdependent ecosystem. Through information sharing, joint planning, and continuous improvement, create a highly efficient, risk-sharing supply chain ecosystem.
2. Careful Evaluation and Precise Targeting of Independent R&D: Before launching any independent R&D project, conduct strict cost–benefit and risk assessments. Define the boundaries of R&D, identify which technologies require independent breakthroughs, and which can be sourced externally. Focus investments on areas that build unique competitive advantages with promising market potential, avoiding blind investment and resource dispersion. For non-core,

non-differentiated technologies, prioritize external procurement, licensing, or collaborative development.

3. Building an Open Invention Ecosystem: Invention should not be confined internally. Embrace open invention through partnerships with universities, research institutes, startups, and even competitors to jointly solve technical challenges and share results, reducing in-house R&D risks and costs. For example, invest in or incubate startups to access frontier technologies, or join industry alliances to develop standards and advance the sector.
4. Continuous Supply Chain Optimization and Digital Transformation: Utilize big data, AI, IoT, and other advanced technologies to enhance supply chain transparency, traceability, and predictive capabilities. Real-time data analysis enables accurate market demand forecasting, inventory optimization, logistics efficiency, and proactive risk management. Digital transformation improves both efficiency and resilience, strengthening resistance to unexpected events such as natural disasters or geopolitical conflicts.
5. Establish a Dynamic "Make-or-Buy" Decision Mechanism: Regularly review product and service components, dynamically assessing whether to manufacture internally or source externally. As technologies and markets evolve, previously in-house R&D elements may become mature supply chain products, while new core competencies may require fresh independent R&D. A dynamic decision mechanism ensures optimal resource allocation at all times.

In an uncertain business world, enterprises that wisely leverage supply chain reliability and carefully manage independent R&D risk are more likely to thrive and achieve sustainable growth. This is not only the art of strategic management but also the wisdom of corporate survival and development. By making supply chain reliability the strategic foundation and conducting precise, bounded independent R&D, companies can build a strategic system that is both highly efficient and resilient, securing an unbeatable position in future market competition.

## Further Reading

[1] M. Christopher, *Logistics and Supply Chain Management*, Pearson, 2016.
[2] X. Cao, *Strategic Management and Organizational Development*, Springer, 2025.
[3] J. H. Dyer and H. Singh, "The relational view: Cooperative strategy and sources of interorganizational competitive advantage," *Academy of Management Review*, vol. 23, no. 4, pp. 660–679, 1998.
[4] X. Cao, *Modern Business Management*, Palgrave Macmillan, 2025.
[5] M. Porter, *The Competitive Advantage of Nations*, Free Press, 1990.
[6] H. L. Lee, "The triple-A supply chain," *Harvard Business Review*, vol. 82, no. 10, pp. 102–112, 2004.
[7] Y. Sheffi, *The Resilient Enterprise: Overcoming Vulnerability for Competitive Advantage*, MIT Press, 2005.
[8] C. Fine, *Clockspeed: Winning Industry Control in the Age of Temporary Advantage*, Perseus Books, 1998.
[9] J. L. Gattorna, *Dynamic Supply Chains: Delivering Value Through People*, Pearson, 2015.

[10] S. Chopra and P. Meindl, *Supply Chain Management: Strategy, Planning, and Operation*, Pearson, 2023.

# Chapter 11
# Paradigm Shift in Business Logic: From Products to Scenarios, from Industries to Ecosystems

## 1 Introduction

The history of human commercial civilization is, from ancient times to the present, a chronicle of continuous evolution and iteration. From primitive barter to the advent of currency, from the rise of artisanal workshops to large-scale industrial production, each era has its unique business logic and core driving forces. However, with the extraordinary development of social productivity, the continual perfection of supply chains, and the awakening of consumer demands, we are now at an unprecedented turning point in a commercial paradigm revolution. As Zhang Ruimin, the founder of Haier Group, insightfully stated: "Products are replaced by scenarios; industries are encompassed by ecosystems." This observation not only reveals the trajectory of future business evolution but also heralds the arrival of a new consumer-centric era in commerce.

The profundity of this assertion lies in its direct focus on the essence of commercial competition: the shift from pursuing individual product features and price to constructing complete user experiences and value networks. If efficiency was the core of the industrial era, then experience is the core of the information and intelligent era. The future vitality of enterprises will no longer depend on how many products they produce, but on how many emotionally compelling scenarios they create and how many ecosystems they integrate to support these scenarios.

This chapter will analyze this thesis from three perspectives: macro historical evolution, micro business practice, and future trends. We will first review the development history of computer programming languages as a vivid metaphor for understanding the evolution of business logic. Then, we will explore how business models have shifted from "producer-centric" to "consumer-centric" under varying levels of productivity. Finally, we will examine how "scenarios" and "ecosystems" will become the core of sustainable enterprise vitality and the disruptive impact this shift brings across industries.

 
S. Li, *Bridging the Innovation Gap*, Innovation, Technology, and Knowledge Management, https://doi.org/10.1007/978-3-032-22652-5_11

## 2 Lessons from the History of Computer Programming: From "Adapting to Machines" to "Adapting to Humans"

To grasp the essence of consumer-centric business, it is instructive to look at the evolution of computer science. As one of humanity's greatest inventions, the evolution of programming languages mirrors the changing relationship between humans and machines—a transformation remarkably analogous to that in the business world.

At the dawn of computing, programming was an extraordinarily arduous task. Programmers had to master machine code, inputting binary instructions of 0 s and 1 s via switches or punched cards. At this stage, programmers were entirely "adapting to the machine," as computers had extremely limited capabilities, and humans had to communicate using the primitive "language" that machines could understand. Programming at this time resembled advanced electronic engineering more than a discipline accessible to the general populace. Programmers needed an in-depth understanding of the internal logic and hardware structure of computers; every operation involved compromises to accommodate the machine, making the process highly inefficient. Even a simple addition operation could require dozens or even hundreds of machine instructions, testing the programmer's patience and limiting the technology's diffusion and application. Programming thresholds were like high mountains, keeping the vast majority of people outside the gate.

The advent of assembly language marked a critical step forward. Using mnemonic codes (e.g., ADD, SUB) to replace complex binary instructions, assembly language greatly lowered the entry barrier. Yet it remained a "machine-adaptive" language, with each instruction corresponding directly to a specific hardware operation. Despite the progress, programmers still needed deep understanding of hardware architecture; the essence of programming remained dictated by the physical constraints and logical rules of the machine. For instance, to implement a simple loop, a programmer had to manually manage memory addresses and registers, keeping programming within the domain of specialized professionals.

The real turning point came with the emergence of high-level programming languages, such as C, Fortran, Java, and Python. These languages no longer corresponded directly to hardware instructions but aligned more closely with human cognitive logic. This was a "paradigm revolution" in the programming world. They introduced the concept of "abstraction," encapsulating complex machine operations into simple and comprehensible functions and commands. For example, in Python, a programmer can effortlessly output print("Hello, World!") without worrying about how the operating system is called or how hardware is accessed. These languages shortened learning cycles, improved usability, and clarified logic. Their core idea was to make the computer adapt to humans, allowing programmers to "speak" to machines in human terms. From the procedural C language to object-oriented Java, and eventually to user-oriented Python, the evolution of programming languages shows a clear trend: shifting focus from how machines operate to how humans think (Fig. 1).

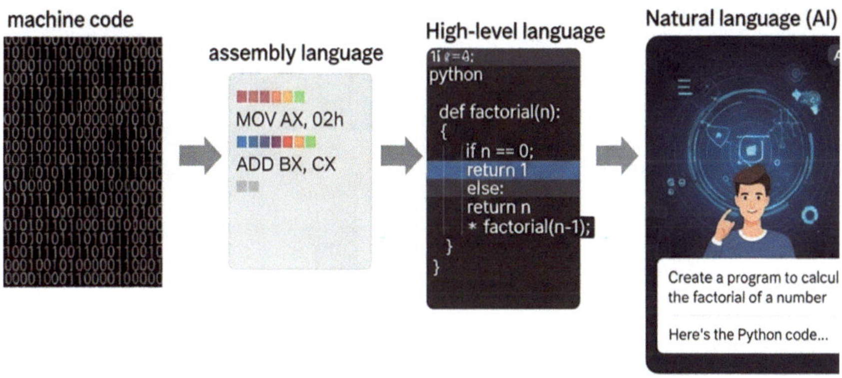


**Fig. 1** The evolution of programming languages—from machine code (binary) to assembly language (mnemonics), then to high-level languages (e.g., Python), and ultimately to natural language (AI). Each stage reduces complexity, gradually transitioning from a "computer-centric" approach to a "human-centric" approach

In the past two years, the rise of large language models has pushed this trend to its extreme. Today, people can simply use natural language to tell an AI, "I need a program that performs a specific function," and the model can automatically generate executable code. This suggests that, in the future, humans may no longer need to learn any specific programming language to collaborate efficiently with computers.

Tracing the trajectory from machine code to natural language, the history of computer programming clearly demonstrates that technological progress ultimately serves to liberate humans and lower the barriers to use. When technology becomes sufficiently advanced, it transforms from a "distant, high-perched" entity that humans must adapt to, into a capable assistant that adapts to humans instead. Each technological leap reduces cognitive load and enhances creative efficiency, providing an excellent reference for understanding the evolution of the business world.

## 3 Mapping to the Business World: The Paradigm Shift from "Producer-Centric" to "Consumer-Centric"

Projecting the lens of computer programming history onto the business world reveals a striking similarity. In the early era of low productivity and scarce products, business models were typically "producer-centric." Take home renovation as an example: if a family wanted to renovate, they had to individually seek out flooring suppliers, bathroom fixture vendors, appliance manufacturers, and then separately communicate, purchase, and coordinate installation. In this process, the consumer played a passive, running-around role—they had to "adapt to the producer," because each company focused only on its own product, leaving the consumer to piece together the final scenario.

**Fig. 2** In traditional business models, producers manufacture products, and consumers must piece together their desired outcomes by going to multiple, different producers

This pattern extends beyond renovation—it was pervasive across nearly all sectors. Consumers were the disadvantaged party facing opaque information; they had to invest extra time and learning costs to understand different products, suppliers, and pricing systems, and personally assume the burden of integrating all these elements (Fig. 2).

Another classic example of this model can be seen in the early automotive industry. During Henry Ford's assembly line era, the Model T became a global sensation due to its low price and standardized specifications—but consumers had no choice, as Ford famously quipped: "Any color you like, as long as it's black." This approach maximized production efficiency while completely ignoring consumers' desire for personalization. At that time, what consumers purchased was merely a means of transportation, not a lifestyle or a form of self-expression. Similarly, in the early electronics market, consumers could only buy single-function radios, TVs, or record players, with all design and functionality dictated by manufacturers, leaving consumers virtually no voice.

However, as social productivity soared, supply chains matured, and product homogenization intensified, consumers no longer paid for "scarcity"; they began to pay for "experience." This marked a fundamental shift in business models, transitioning toward a "consumer-centered" approach.

A prime example of this shift is companies that "sell scenarios." Businesses in full-home customization, smart home integration, one-stop wedding services, and even Mobility as a Service (MaaS) emerged. These companies no longer merely sell a floorboard, a toilet, or a TV; they offer a complete lifestyle solution. They handle design, procurement, construction, installation, and after-sales service, liberating consumers from the tedious coordination work. Consumers simply state their needs and can enjoy a turnkey experience. Here, the product is no longer the ultimate goal—it is merely a necessary element for constructing a specific scenario. What consumers are truly buying is a more comfortable, convenient, and lifestyle-aligned "scenario experience."

The fundamental shift in this business model also redefines value distribution along the commercial chain. In the past, product manufacturers—directly serving end customers—typically captured the highest profits. In the post- "scenario revolution" era, the entities directly engaging with consumers are no longer the product manufacturers themselves, but the "scenario solution providers" who integrate diverse products and services. Because these providers interact directly with end users and deliver a convenient, worry-free overall experience, their business model is typically B2C (business-to-consumer). This model enjoys higher customer stickiness and brand premium, translating into greater valuation and profitability. In contrast, traditional firms focused solely on single-product manufacturing gradually regress to the backend of the solution provider ecosystem, losing direct consumer engagement. Their business models shift from B2C to B2B (business-to-business), with compressed bargaining power and profit margins (Fig. 3).

At the core of this shift is the migration of value creation from the "production side" to the "consumption side." Producers no longer merely consider how to manufacture products efficiently and cost-effectively; they must deeply understand the real

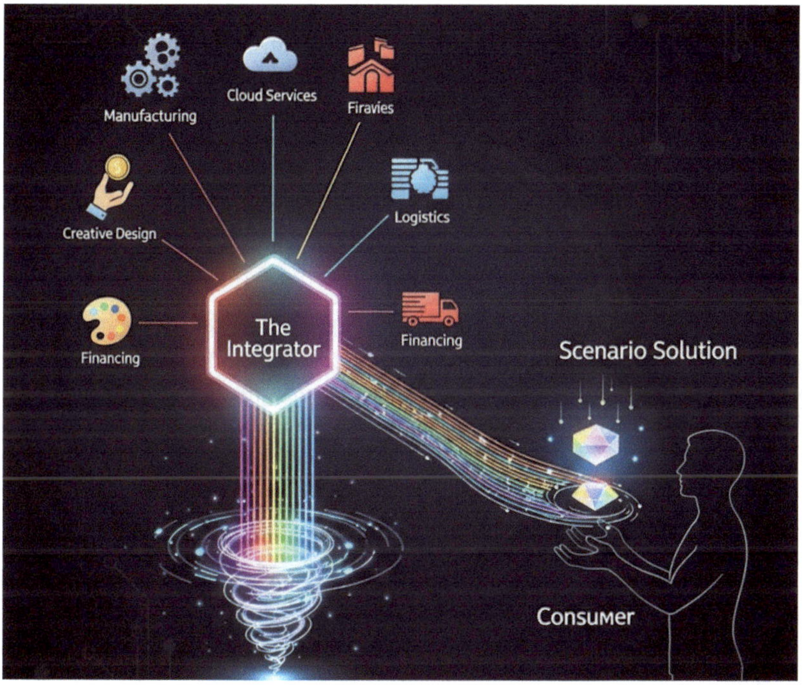


**Fig. 3** Modern business models have shifted from being product-centered to consumer-centered. Solution providers act as central hubs, integrating products and services from various suppliers to deliver a complete "scenario" to consumers. The end customer is no longer served directly by the product manufacturers, but by these solution providers. Because solution providers engage directly with consumers (B2C), they capture higher value and pricing power, while the product manufacturers are relegated to backend B2B operations

needs of consumers and contemplate how to integrate products and services to create seamless, enjoyable experiences. For example, a smart home company delivers not just smart speakers and bulbs, but a fully automated suite covering waking, sleeping, entertainment, and other lifestyle scenarios. This shift liberates companies from single-product profits and allows them to capture value from the additional benefits of offering integrated solutions.

## 4 Industry Disintegration and the Rise of Ecosystems: The Inevitability of Breaking Traditional Boundaries

The next step after "products being replaced by scenarios" is "industries being covered by ecosystems." This represents one of the most profound transformations in today's business world.

Traditionally, industries had clear, fixed boundaries: automotive, steel, real estate, banking, retail, etc. These divisions were based on production stages and product categories, a product of the finely segmented industrial-era specialization. However, as business logic shifts from "products" to "scenarios," these traditional industry boundaries become outdated and fragile.

Take Apple as an example. Which industry does Apple belong to? It manufactures phones, computers, and tablets, making it a hardware company; it develops iOS and macOS, making it a software company; it operates the App Store and Apple Music, functioning as a content platform; it launched Apple Pay, entering fintech; and it is exploring electric vehicles, potentially entering automotive. Apple's success lies not in excelling within a single industry, but in building a massive ecosystem spanning multiple sectors around the core of "user experience."

Within this ecosystem, hardware devices like iPhone, iPad, MacBook, Apple Watch, and HomePod work seamlessly together, while software and services like App Store, iCloud, and Apple Music are tightly integrated. Once users enter this ecosystem, they experience a level of convenience and cohesion that is highly addictive. Behind this experience is Apple's deep integration and reinvention across different "industries." What it offers is not an individual product, but a holistic lifestyle. The power of such an ecosystem lies in its high stickiness. Once a user becomes accustomed to using iMessage on Mac, syncing photos on iPhone, and tracking health data on Apple Watch, switching platforms entails enormous learning costs and experiential loss. Here, competition is no longer between one phone manufacturer and another, but between Apple's ecosystem and the Android ecosystem.

This "ecosystem thinking" is permeating multiple domains. Amazon, starting as an online bookstore, has become a massive ecosystem encompassing retail, logistics (Prime), cloud computing (AWS), and digital media (Prime Video). It not only sells products but locks countless merchants and consumers into its ecosystem via efficient logistics and convenient cloud services, generating strong network effects. Similarly,

Tesla integrates its own supercharging network, battery technology, autonomous driving software, and in-car software updates to build a comprehensive energy and mobility ecosystem. Consumers buy not just a car, but access to a continuously evolving, deeply connected mobility experience. In China, Alibaba's business empire also revolves around a massive ecosystem: from e-commerce platforms (Taobao, Tmall) to payment tools (Alipay), logistics networks (Cainiao) to cloud computing (Alibaba Cloud), and digital entertainment and local services. These seemingly independent businesses are tightly woven together to serve multiple consumer life scenarios, forming a powerful "Alibaba economy."

## 5 Conclusion: Survival Rules in the New Business Era

From the history of computer programming to the evolution of business models, a clear and profound principle emerges: technological advancement and social development ultimately serve to empower humans, simplify complexity, and reduce hardship.

In business, this means shifting focus from "What can I produce?" to "What do consumers need?" Companies clinging to traditional industry boundaries and focusing on single-product performance or price competition are destined to decline, as their "products" can be replaced at any moment by competitors' "scenarios." The companies that survive and prosper will be those that deeply understand consumer needs, prioritize "scenarios" as the core, and integrate cross-industry resources and services to build robust ecosystems.

This is not merely a change in business model, but a revolution in mindset. Entrepreneurs must reassess their commercial landscape, shifting from "producer" to "solution provider" and from "product manager" to "scenario designer."

For any enterprise aiming for success in this new era, transformation is concrete, not abstract, requiring:

- A fundamental shift in thinking: Abandon "product thinking" and embrace "user thinking." From the earliest stages of product development, companies must identify pain points and needs in users' daily lives to define a complete "scenario." For instance, a smart oven company sells not just the oven, but the "effortless baking" scenario, incorporating preset recipes, ingredient delivery partnerships, and community sharing.
- Organizational restructuring: Traditional functional departments (production, sales, R&D) serve "products," whereas "scenarios" demand cross-functional collaboration and integration. Companies need scenario-centered project teams, breaking departmental silos and aligning product, tech, marketing, and service teams to the same user scenario. Haier, for example, promotes a "everyone is a creator" approach, encouraging employees to self-organize micro-teams around user needs.

- Redefinition of core capabilities: Past core capabilities were "manufacturing" and "selling"; future capabilities are "insight" and "integration." Companies must excel in data analysis to understand real user behavior and latent needs, and integrate internal products, third-party services, big data, and AI to create a complete, efficient scenario solution. This capability determines whether a company can escape the red ocean of "product manufacturing" and enter the blue ocean of "scenario creation."

In the consumer-centered era, successful companies will no longer be those producing the best products, but those creating the most compelling scenarios and building the most attractive ecosystems. This is the essential survival rule of the future business world.

## Further Reading

[1] X. Cao, *Strategic Management and Organizational Development*, Springer, 2025.
[2] K. Iansiti and M. Lakhani, *Competing in the Age of AI: Strategy and Leadership When Algorithms and Networks Run the World*, Harvard Business Review Press, 2020.
[3] G. Westerman, D. Bonnet, and A. McAfee, *Leading Digital: Turning Technology into Business Transformation*, Harvard Business Review Press, 2014.
[4] X. Cao, *Modern Business Management*, Palgrave Macmillan, 2025.
[5] R. Adner, *The Wide Lens: What Successful Innovators See That Others Miss*, Penguin, 2012.
[6] M. Jacobides, "In the ecosystem economy, what's your strategy?" *Harvard Business Review*, vol. 97, no. 5, pp. 128–137, 2019.
[7] J. Moore, *The Death of Competition: Leadership and Strategy in the Age of Business Ecosystems*, Harper Business, 1996.
[8] C. Christensen, *The Innovator's Dilemma*, Harvard Business School Press, 1997.
[9] M. Porter and J. Heppelmann, "How smart, connected products are transforming competition," *Harvard Business Review*, vol. 92, no. 11, pp. 64–88, 2014.
[10] H. Chesbrough, *Open Invention: The New Imperative for Creating and Profiting from Technology*, Harvard Business School Press, 2003.
[11] E. G. Carayannis, Ed., *Encyclopedia of Creativity, Invention, Innovation and Entrepreneurship*. New York, NY: Springer, 2013. https://doi.org/10.1007/978-1-4614-6616-1.

# Chapter 12
# Adapting to Change Vs. Responding to Change from Constancy

## 1 Introduction

In the ever-shifting waves of the business world, entrepreneurs are often confronted with a profound dilemma: should they, like chameleons, dance with the environment, emphasizing agility and flexibility through constant adaptation, or should they steadfastly adhere to a set of core principles, responding to change with enduring composure and wisdom? On the surface, the former seems better suited to survive in a rapidly evolving market, appearing as a rule of survival. Yet, when we look beneath the surface and examine the DNA of enduring, cycle-crossing, extraordinary enterprises, we find, unmistakably, that deep within their core flows the logic of "responding to change from constancy." This is not merely a matter of choosing a business strategy; it is a profound thinking paradigm, the roots of which can even be traced back to humanity's philosophical quest for the fundamental nature of the world.

## 2 Origins: The "Atomic" Pursuit in Western Scientific Thought

Every major leap in human civilization, particularly the birth and development of modern Western science, is inextricably linked to a central idea—the desire for ultimate unity in all things and the relentless pursuit of unchanging underlying laws. The seeds of this mode of thinking can be traced back to the Greek philosopher Democritus and his "Atomic Theory." He proposed a groundbreaking concept: the vast complexity of the universe, in essence, is composed of indivisible "atoms." All the differences observed in the world are merely the result of these atoms arranging and combining in various ways within the void (Fig. 12.1).

 
S. Li, *Bridging the Innovation Gap*, Innovation, Technology, and Knowledge Management, https://doi.org/10.1007/978-3-032-22652-5_12

**Fig. 12.1** The ancient Greek philosopher Democritus proposed the theory of atoms

This insight represents a milestone in human cognition. It provides a universal explanatory framework, unifying seemingly unrelated phenomena under a single set of fundamental rules. When confronted with unprecedented new things or phenomena, we no longer need to exhaust ourselves creating a completely new theory for each unique instance; instead, we can apply the known "atomic" principles and their modes of combination to understand, predict, and even transform them. This method of simplifying complexity and governing the many with the one endows science with powerful explanatory, predictive, and practical capabilities. We can clearly observe this in multiple domains: whether it is Einstein dedicating his life to unifying all fundamental forces of nature into a single theory, seeking the ultimate simplicity; or the von Neumann computer architecture, which uses a fixed, universal hardware structure to handle any computable task simply by changing the software program (i.e., the data flow), demonstrating the universality of "unchanging structure, infinite functions"; or even at a more fundamental level, binary logic, which constructs all complex calculations and logical operations using just the simplest symbols, 0 and 1—each of these exquisitely illustrates the immense power of "responding to myriad changes with the unchanging" in both understanding and transforming the world. These are not specific solutions to individual problems; rather, they provide a meta-theory, a meta-structure, which through its own combinations and derivations is sufficient to address countless variations (Fig. 12.2).

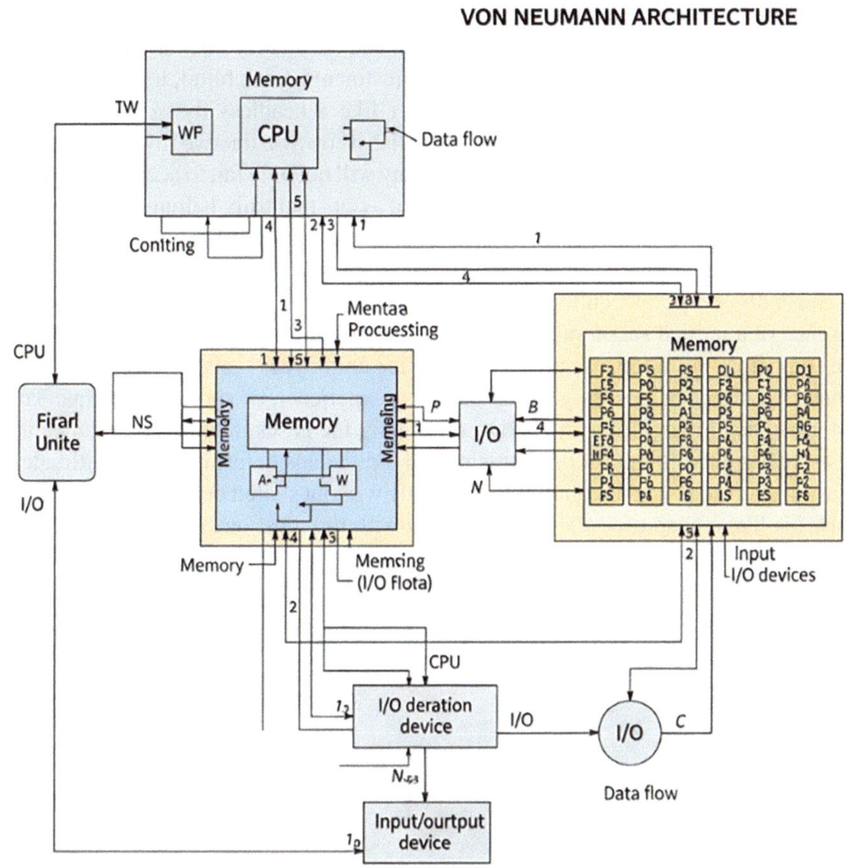


**Fig. 12.2** The von Neumann architecture of computers also pursues the unification of science: using an "unchanging" structure to solve a wide variety of ever-changing problems

## 3 The Entrepreneurial Misstep: When "Adaptability" Loses its Foundation

By applying this profound line of thinking to the context of entrepreneurship, we can deeply understand why pure, rootless "adaptability" often leads to disorientation rather than a clear path forward. In the absence of an internal, solid set of guiding principles and core logic, entrepreneurs who merely react passively and immediately to external changes will see their companies' development trajectories become markedly fragmented and uncertain:

First, a company's market strategy will lose coherence. Every shift in market trends, every innovative move by competitors, and even every fluctuation in macroeconomic data may trigger drastic strategic adjustments. Such blind, logically unsupported shifts cause the company to flounder like a headless fly in the market—constantly busy but ultimately unable to establish its own distinctive rhythm or sustain competitive advantage. Over time, the company will not only fail to accumulate experience but also struggle to crystallize strategic assets that truly belong to it. It is like a fleet without a navigational chart, drifting aimlessly across a vast ocean; even with the fastest ships, it may never reach its intended port (Fig. 12.3).

Secondly, corporate culture tends to become blurred and fragmented. In the absence of a unified set of values, mission, and guiding principles, everyone within the company—from top executives to front-line employees—may act independently when making decisions, relying on personal experience or short-term gains. This inconsistency in cognition and action drastically increases internal communication costs, making it difficult for departments and individuals to form synergy, ultimately causing team cohesion to collapse. A company without shared beliefs and behavioral norms is like a heap of scattered sand; even with the most outstanding talents, it is

**Fig. 12.3** Strategies based on mere adaptability often leave companies at a loss when facing new challenges

hard to realize collective maximum effectiveness. Such internal friction is often more lethal than external competition.

Finally, and most crucially, the company's core competitiveness is difficult to accumulate and solidify. When entrepreneurs excessively chase short-term trends and superficial adaptability, they often disperse their focus, making it challenging to achieve deep technical accumulation, brand building, or model invention in a particular domain. They may pursue AI today, switch to blockchain tomorrow, and dive into a social e-commerce venture the day after. This blind chasing prevents the enterprise from cultivating truly proprietary technological barriers, unique resources, or replicable business models. Ultimately, the company may become nothing more than a floating leaf in the market tide—drifting along and, when the wave recedes, discovering it has nothing left, let alone the capacity to face true "unknowns" and crises. Without an unchanging foundation, every "change" can become a drain rather than a source of growth. It may bring temporary excitement but cannot nurture lasting vitality.

## 4 The "Atomic Theory" of Entrepreneurship: Building an Immutable Inner Drive

Truly successful entrepreneurs master the wisdom of "atomic theory" and construct within their companies a set of "immutable atomic-level logic." This logic acts as the DNA upon which the enterprise depends for survival and growth; all external adaptations are merely expressions or evolutions of this DNA under different circumstances. It provides an anchor for maintaining composure amid unpredictability, ensuring that every decision is effective and directionally sound. These "atoms" typically consist of the following core elements:

First, a clear and grand vision and mission. This represents the fundamental reason for the company's existence and its ultimate destination. It answers the two ultimate questions: "Why do we exist?" and "Where are we headed?" A clear vision and mission are like the initial singularity of the Big Bang, determining the evolutionary direction and ultimate outcome of all organizational "matter." It guides all strategic decisions and provides the team with a firm spiritual pillar and a target for effort, even in the toughest times. It should not fluctuate arbitrarily but possess timelessness and cross-temporal guidance. For example, if a company's mission is "to make learning more efficient," then no matter how technology evolves or user habits change, all product and service inventions will revolve around this core, forming its "immutable atom."

Second, rock-solid core values. These are the fundamental beliefs and ethical guidelines that direct all employee behavior and decision-making. Examples include "customer first," "integrity," "invention-driven," "long-termism," or "teamwork." Core values act as the company's "genes," determining how it manages internal and external relationships, faces opportunities and challenges, and treats employees and customers. They permeate daily operations—from recruitment and training to performance evaluation and reward mechanisms. The stability of core values directly affects the depth of corporate culture. Like the inherent properties of atoms, their essential nature does not change regardless of combinations. When faced with difficult decisions, core values serve as a guiding North Star, helping managers and employees make choices aligned with the company's long-term interests and character.

Third, a unique and self-consistent underlying business logic. Every successful company possesses a clear logic regarding "how to create value, how to capture profit, and how to build competitive barriers." This logic answers the company's most fundamental survival questions. Is it based on delivering exceptional product experiences, disruptive technological invention, highly efficient operational models, or unique brand influence? This underlying business logic is the foundation for the company's market position and the source of its core competitiveness. All business expansions, product iterations, and market strategy adjustments should be valid derivations and implementations of this logic within specific market contexts. For instance, if a company's underlying logic is "use technological invention to reduce costs and provide inclusive services," then all R&D investments and market strategies will revolve around this "atom," rather than randomly entering a high-margin but non-scalable market (Fig. 12.4).

Finally, based on the principles outlined above, a set of universal and flexible management principles and systems must be established. Early-stage startups often lack formal structures, but a maturing enterprise inevitably develops a self-consistent system for incentives, rewards and punishments, decision-making, and communication. This system is not arbitrarily imposed; it is the concretization, institutionalization, and proceduralization of the company's vision, values, and underlying business logic. For instance, if "pursuit of excellence" is a core value, then performance evaluations and promotion mechanisms must be designed around this principle to ensure that

**Fig. 12.4** The stability and guiding role of a company's core principles—as the foundation for all decisions—are akin to atoms in atomic theory. They should remain immutable, while all other company strategies are derived from or composed around them

outstanding performance is promptly recognized and rewarded. Establishing such a system ensures that management no longer depends solely on individual leaders' experience or intuition but forms a replicable, inheritable "algorithm" capable of efficiently addressing daily operational challenges and laying a solid foundation for future scalable growth.

When a company truly possesses this "atomic-level logic," all corporate governance decisions—whether concerning product development directions, marketing strategies, talent recruitment standards, performance evaluation systems, organizational restructuring, or crisis response plans—become applications and extrapolations of this unified theory in specific contexts. Even when confronted with unprecedented market upheavals or industry reshuffles, entrepreneurs can return to these fundamental "atoms," analyzing problems and seeking solutions from core principles rather than succumbing to panic and disorder. This intrinsic stability and certainty serve as the ballast that allows a company to maintain its course amid external uncertainties.

## 5 Conclusion: Anchoring the Unchanging amid Change, Embracing Change within the Unchanging

Thus, the path to entrepreneurial success is not about choosing between "adapting to every change" and "responding to all change with constancy," but about embracing a constantly changing market within the framework of an unchanging underlying logic (Fig. 12.5).

**Fig. 12.5** Rooted in the unchanging, embracing all that changes

Entrepreneurs should, like scientists in pursuit of the truths of the universe, dedicate themselves to deeply reflecting on and defining their company's "atoms"—the core vision, values, underlying business logic, and the derived management principles that constitute the enterprise's life force. This "unchanging core" provides the company with powerful explanatory, predictive, and actionable guidance. It allows the enterprise, when facing a complex and ever-changing market environment, to maintain a clear sense of direction and strategic steadiness, effectively resisting short-term temptations and the risks of blindly following trends.

At the same time, this "unchanging" logic is by no means rigid. It provides a solid foundation and clear boundaries for genuine "adaptability." Guided by these core "atoms," a company can flexibly adjust its tactics: rapidly iterate products, optimize marketing channels, reorganize structures, and embrace waves of new technology. These "changes" are no longer aimless reactions, but strategic optimizations and adaptations centered on core objectives. They are new combinations and forms of the atoms in different environments, rather than alterations of the atoms themselves.

Ultimately, exceptional entrepreneurs are those who deeply understand and practice this "atomic theory" wisdom. They recognize that only by firmly anchoring the unchanging core amid change can they master the forces of transformation, turning seemingly chaotic market challenges into effective applications of their "unified theory" and opportunities for sustained growth, ultimately achieving enduring success in the fierce arena of business competition.

## Further Reading

[1]. P. Drucker, *Management Challenges for the 21st Century*, Harper Business, 1999.
[2]. X. Cao, *Modern Business Management*, Palgrave Macmillan, 2025.
[3]. J. Collins, *Built to Last: Successful Habits of Visionary Companies*, Harper Business, 1994.
[4]. C. Handy, *The Age of Paradox*, Harvard Business School Press, 1994.
[5]. X. Cao, *Strategic Management and Organizational Development*, Springer, 2025.
[6]. N. Taleb, *Antifragile: Things That Gain from Disorder*, Random House, 2012.
[7]. M. Tushman and C. O'Reilly, *Lead and Disrupt: How to Solve the Innovator's Dilemma*, Stanford Business Books, 2016.
[8]. H. Mintzberg, *The Rise and Fall of Strategic Planning*, Free Press, 1994.
[9]. J. Kotter, *Leading Change*, Harvard Business School Press, 1996.
[10]. C. Argyris and D. Schön, *Organizational Learning II: Theory, Method, and Practice*, Addison-Wesley, 1996.

# Chapter 13
# Monetization Breakthroughs for Researchers: Turned: Entrepreneurs

## 1 Introduction

In the complex ecosystem of business, research and development (R&D), production, and sales form a complete chain that takes a product from concept to the realization of its commercial value. These three links are tightly interwoven, mutually dependent, and collectively determine the success of a business as well as the lifecycle of a company. However, entrepreneurs with different backgrounds and experiences exhibit significant variations in their depth of understanding, resource allocation, and control over these three core segments, which directly affects their entrepreneurial paths and likelihood of success.

Take, for example, researchers who have long been immersed in academia and laboratory work. They usually possess unparalleled expertise in R&D. They can deeply understand technical principles, tackle scientific challenges, drive cutting-edge inventions, and design disruptive product prototypes. During the process of translating research outcomes into actual products, they might have some exposure to small-scale production, such as prototype fabrication or lab-level trial runs. Yet, when it comes to large-scale, standardized, cost-optimized industrial production, and—most critically—market commercialization and product sales, researchers often display a relative lack of practical experience and systematic knowledge. This constitutes a prominent and frequently underestimated weakness in their entrepreneurial journey.

This cognitive gap sharply contrasts with entrepreneurs from other backgrounds. For instance, an experienced Chief Technology Officer (CTO) may also have deep technical understanding, but their core strength often lies in integrating technology with supply chain management and production process optimization, excelling at converting technical blueprints into mass-producible, high-quality products. Consequently, they have a more sophisticated grasp of the production segment but may feel less familiar with large-scale, direct-to-market sales and consumer engagement.



S. Li, *Bridging the Innovation Gap*, Innovation, Technology, and Knowledge Management, https://doi.org/10.1007/978-3-032-22652-5_13

In even starker contrast, a seasoned sales director's core competency lies in accurately sensing market trends, deeply understanding customer needs, building robust channel networks, and executing highly effective sales strategies. Such an individual is intimately familiar with every aspect of the sales process, possesses a general understanding of production workflows, but may be relatively less knowledgeable about underlying technical principles or cutting-edge scientific breakthroughs.

Yet one indisputable and critical truth remains: the sales segment is the ultimate gateway through which products are converted into actual revenue—it is the final step in realizing commercial value. Prior investments in R&D and production, no matter how much wisdom, effort, or advanced technical performance they embody, cannot achieve a transformation from "things" to "money" if the product cannot effectively reach consumers and drive transactions. High-tech, high-investment products that fail to successfully enter the market remain trapped at the level of potential value, and all prior investment becomes sunk cost (Fig. 13.1).

This cognitive bias often leads researcher-entrepreneurs into the fallacy of "product determinism," the belief that "if I develop product X, sales will naturally

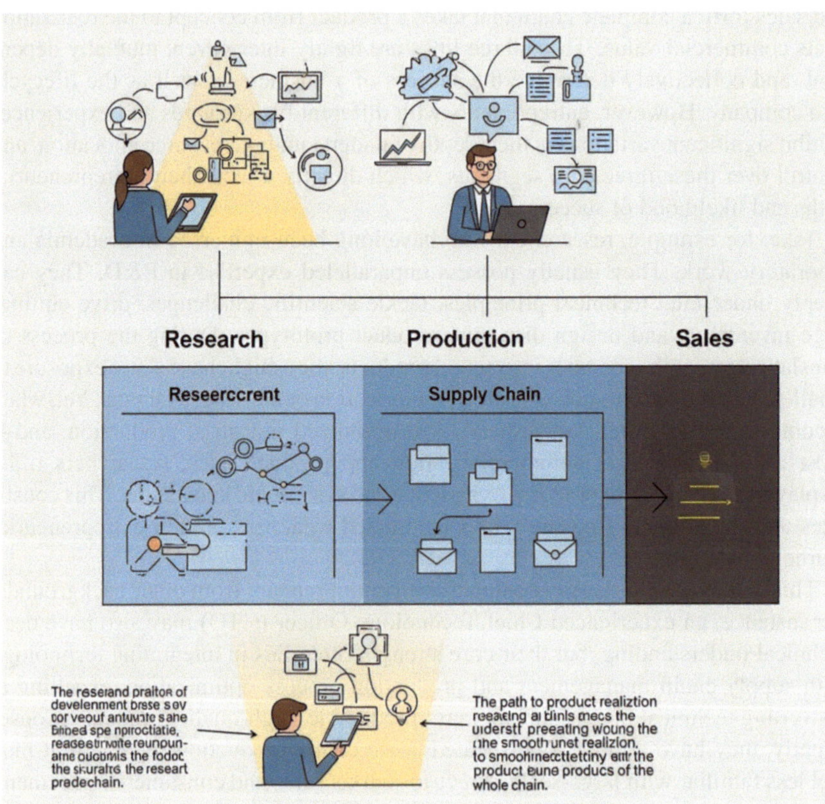


**Fig. 13.1** The R&D–Production–Sales chain: the blind spot of researcher entrepreneurs

follow, and the market will come to me." This mindset usually stems from the purity of scientific work—a relentless pursuit of technical breakthroughs and performance metrics—leading them to assume that the intrinsic value of the product alone can overcome all market barriers. However, harsh reality repeatedly proves otherwise: once the product reaches the market, the inevitable question arises—how will it be sold? Addressing this goes far beyond merely finding buyers; it encompasses market positioning, target customer segmentation, channel construction, brand development, pricing strategies, marketing campaigns, customer relationship management (CRM), and both pre-sale and post-sale services—a complex and highly dynamic array of commercial activities. Only by overcoming this obstacle, conquering the "last mile" of sales, can researchers achieve a complete commercial cycle, transforming the potential value of their scientific achievements into tangible economic returns.

## 2 The Essence of Sales: A Deep Analysis of Brand and Market Forces beyond Rational Consumption

Some R&D personnel may hold an idealized view: that consumers are always rational, making optimal choices based on a product's performance, quality, and price. Therefore, as long as a product is excellent and competitively priced, it should naturally succeed in the market. However, actual consumer behavior is far from so straightforward. Consumers are often "boundedly rational" and, in many cases, are strongly influenced by non-rational factors such as emotions, herd behavior, brand stories, social attributes, trust, habits, information asymmetry, and cognitive biases (Fig. 13.2).

The market offers abundant examples: certain well-known brands' products may not be technically superior or cost-effective, yet thanks to strong brand influence, market recognition, emotional connection, and mature marketing strategies, they can consistently top sales charts and command a market share and premium far exceeding their "pure technical value." For instance, in the luxury goods sector, a product's value is largely determined not by raw materials or production costs, but by its brand history, cultural connotations, scarcity, and significance as a social status symbol. In the fast-moving consumer goods (FMCG) sector, consumers may prefer familiar, trusted, and heavily advertised brands, even if other products offer better cost-performance ratios.

A closer analysis shows that consumers' purchase decisions are not based solely on objective considerations of functionality and price; they are also heavily influenced by perceived value. This perceived value includes not only a product's functional utility but also many ancillary attributes such as brand image, service experience, and social recognition. Even if a product is technically superior, it will struggle to convert into sales if the market does not understand its value, does not trust its performance, or faces high acquisition costs (including purchase price, learning costs, and time costs). For example, a powerful professional software with a steep learning curve may

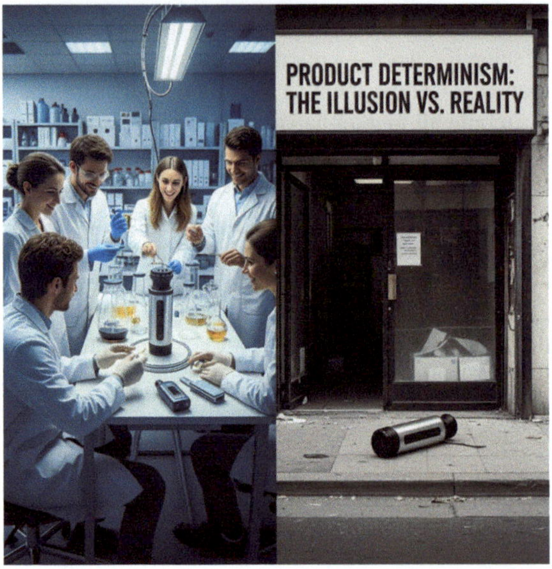


**Fig. 13.2** The illusion and harsh reality of product determinism

fail to achieve broad adoption. Information asymmetry is another important factor: ordinary consumers often lack the expertise to objectively evaluate the technical merits of high-tech products and therefore rely more on brand reputation, expert endorsements, or social media reviews.

This fully demonstrates that technical performance or price advantage alone is no longer sufficient to guarantee commercial success. Brand, marketing, and channel development play a decisive role in modern competitive markets: together they shape a product's market competitiveness and consumers' perceived value, and ultimately determine whether it can be monetized. Brand is more than a name or logo; it is the composite expression of corporate reputation, product quality, and unique value. Marketing is the art of communicating that value effectively to target audiences and stimulating purchase desire. Channel development ensures that the product can reach consumers efficiently and conveniently. For researcher-entrepreneurs, recognizing this is the first step in transforming their commercial mindset and the key to formulating effective business strategies (Fig. 13.3).

This presents a new strategic challenge for scientists-turned-entrepreneurs: how to minimize their relative weakness in sales while fully leveraging their overwhelming strength in research and development. A viable and strategically intelligent approach is to target niche sectors that place minimal emphasis on sales but extremely high—even disruptive—demands on R&D capability. This "playing to one's strengths" strategy aims to maximize the value of scientific expertise, allowing the "technology is king" philosophy to manifest meaningfully in selected markets and thus achieve faster and more effective commercial realization.

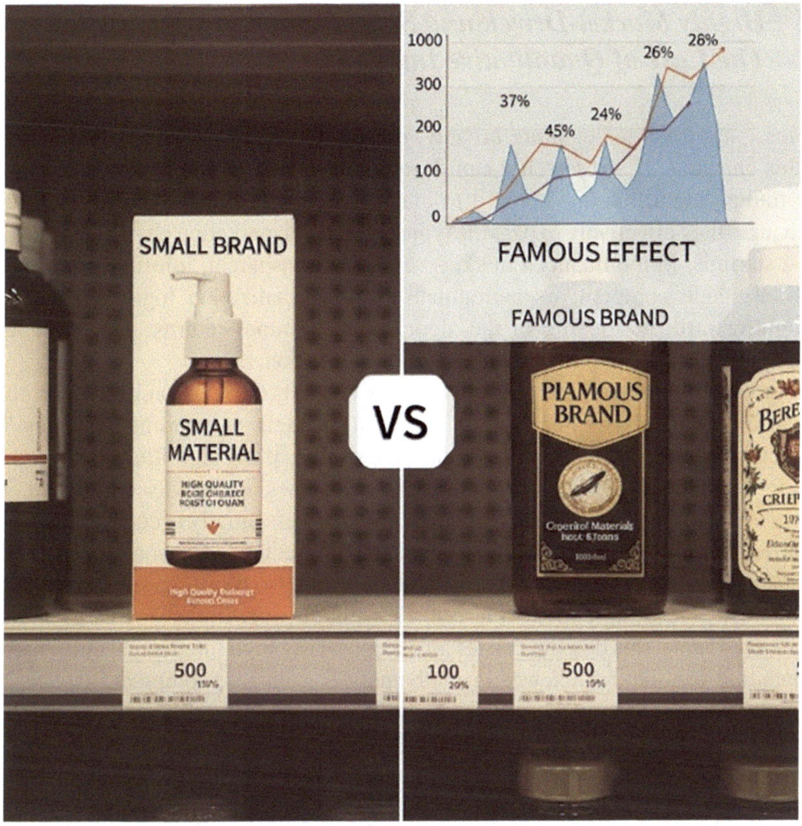


**Fig. 13.3** The "product determinism" assumption does not always hold true. In some cases, well-known branded products may be more expensive and not necessarily superior in performance compared to lesser-known alternatives, yet still achieve stronger sales due to the power of brand influence

## 3 Selecting the Ideal Battlefield: The Intersection of Market Forces, Competition, and Supply-Demand Imbalance

Where, then, do these ideal sectors exist? Through careful analysis of industrial characteristics, we can identify two typical types of sectors that meet these criteria. Their common underlying logic is a highly market-driven demand side, intense competition, and a structural imbalance where demand far exceeds supply. Such industries typically have a strong intrinsic demand for technological invention, while high technical and knowledge barriers make it possible for researchers with core technologies to establish differentiated advantages.

## *3.1 Highly Market-Driven and Sales-Competitive Industries: The Case of Quantitative Investing*

Professional trading—or more broadly, quantitative finance—is a prime example of this category. If a researcher can develop an advanced and profitable quantitative trading algorithm and apply it to markets such as equities, futures, or foreign exchange, they effectively bypass the typical sales and marketing challenges faced by most startups. In the financial market—a highly transparent, information-efficient, and sales-side competitive environment—commercialization logic is direct and straightforward: the quality of the algorithm determines returns, and profit itself is the purest and most immediate form of monetization.

Here, the researcher's R&D ability directly converts into economic value, without the need for marketing campaigns, distribution channels, or branding strategies. The financial market's instant feedback loop ensures that strong algorithms are rewarded almost immediately through profits, while weak ones are rapidly eliminated. The "sales" work of a scientific entrepreneur in this space essentially becomes a process of continuous optimization and performance improvement. Furthermore, the scalability of quantitative strategies allows successful algorithms to be replicated and expanded efficiently, generating exponential returns without proportional increases in sales effort. Of course, this domain carries an exceptionally high intellectual entry barrier, demanding top-tier proficiency in mathematics, statistics, computer science, and financial theory.

## *3.2 "Boom" Industries: Where Demand Overwhelms Supply*

Another strategic path lies in identifying and entering industries undergoing explosive growth, where market demand far outstrips existing supply capacity. These sectors exhibit strong structural demand imbalances, meaning that any capable provider of relevant technologies or products—regardless of marketing sophistication—can achieve rapid monetization (Fig. 13.4).

Historical examples abound:

- In the early 2000s, search engine technologies such as Google rose swiftly after the dot-com crash by meeting urgent information retrieval needs.
- In the 2010s, the mobile internet and the app ecosystem created a surge of opportunity where functionality mattered more than branding.
- In recent years, artificial intelligence algorithms, new energy vehicle battery technologies, and biomedical breakthroughs such as mRNA vaccines and gene-editing tools have shown similar "supply creates value" characteristics.

In these rapidly emerging markets, the question of "Do you have it?" often outweighs "Is it the best?"—as long as the product satisfies essential functionality,

**Fig. 13.4** Playing to one's strengths: targeting sectors with high R&D barriers and low sales friction

it can capture market share rapidly, attract capital interest, and even begin forming early-stage industry barriers.

However, in rapidly emerging industries, a "winner-takes-all" phenomenon often emerges, posing significant challenges for late entrants or non-leading firms. Despite overall market demand exceeding supply, demand-side conservatism, obsession with "optimal" performance, or blind loyalty to leading brands can lead customers to pay high premiums for top-tier products, rejecting diversity even when alternative suppliers offer competent solutions.

This concentration effect can arise from several underlying mechanisms:

1. Network Effects: The value of a product or service increases with the number of users (e.g., social media platforms, operating systems, instant messaging apps). Once a product dominates the market, strong user stickiness makes it extremely difficult for newcomers to break through.
2. High Switching Costs: The costs for customers to switch from one product or service to another (including data migration, retraining, and ecosystem compatibility). For example, enterprise software or cloud computing services, once deeply integrated, are costly and risky to replace.
3. Proprietary Standards and Ecosystems: Leading firms may establish proprietary technologies or build comprehensive ecosystems that effectively lock customers into their platforms.
4. Economies of Scale: Large-scale production or service delivery leads to cost advantages, allowing dominant players to set price barriers.
5. Brand Trust and Safety Preference: In critical industries such as medical devices, aerospace components, or financial systems, buyers prioritize reliability and safety, favoring established brands even at higher prices.

**Fig. 13.5** Quantitative investment is also a research-intensive, sales-light industry. If researchers develop superior algorithms, they can directly generate returns without the need for additional sales efforts

6. Regulatory Barriers: In highly regulated sectors like biotechnology and energy, leading companies often invest heavily in compliance and approvals early on, gaining first-mover advantages that are hard to replicate.

Therefore, when entering a fast-growing "hot" industry, scientific entrepreneurs must carefully evaluate the market structure and potential winner-takes-all risks. Success depends not only on technological breakthroughs but also on strategic positioning—finding unique differentiation or niche entry points to avoid homogeneous competition. This might involve focusing on specific vertical segments, adopting innovative business models, or pursuing open collaboration strategies to carve out a sustainable foothold (Fig. 13.5).

## 4 Strategic Essence: Combining Fully Marketized Demand with Scarce Supply Advantages

By synthesizing the in-depth analysis of the two typical cases above, we can distill the common characteristics of ideal entrepreneurial tracks for researchers: a highly marketized demand side (where consumer or enterprise client choice mechanisms are robust and active, pursuing maximum value), sufficient market competition (where products and services can circulate freely and information is relatively transparent), and demand forces that far exceed supply capacity (markets exhibit a strong desire for innovative technologies or products, with high willingness to pay a premium to solve pain points). In such a market environment, technological and product excellence can directly drive demand, significantly reducing reliance on traditional sales channels

**Fig. 13.6** Robotics and artificial intelligence are among the latest investment hotspots. These industries are currently experiencing a stage of technology undersupply. Due to the high number of demand-side players, technology providers in these fields often do not need exceptional sales skills to successfully connect with demand and achieve technology monetization

and accelerating monetization. In these scenarios, the product itself becomes the best "salesperson." (Fig. 13.6)

Specifically, these industries and segments include, but are not limited to:

1. High-end industrial-grade core components or materials: These products are the "crown jewels" of the industrial sector, with extremely high technical barriers and often requiring years of fundamental research and applied validation. Examples include semiconductor manufacturing (high-purity silicon wafers, EUV photoresists, specialty gases, high-end target materials), aerospace (lightweight high-strength aerospace alloys, high-temperature ceramic matrix composites, high-performance carbon fiber composites), high-end medical devices (biodegradable implant-grade biomaterials, ultra-precision transmission components in minimally invasive surgical robots, high-resolution medical imaging sensors), and new energy vehicle power batteries (new cathode and anode materials, solid-state electrolytes, core chips for battery management systems). If researchers can develop breakthrough key materials or core components with globally leading, unique, and superior performance, their scarcity, irreplaceability, and significant performance advantages will make them highly sought-after by downstream manufacturers (typically large industrial enterprises). These products are often sold directly to B2B clients, who prioritize technical specifications, product reliability, compliance standards, and practical effectiveness rather than brand marketing gimmicks. Once a product passes strict industry standard testing and client validation, demonstrating significant advantages, the market will actively seek collaboration, and the sales process focuses more on technical verification, business negotiation, and long-term relationship building rather than broad marketing.

2. Enterprise-level SaaS and deep-tech software: These solutions are not simple tools but professional-grade solutions designed for complex business scenarios. They leverage algorithms, data analytics, and artificial intelligence to solve core enterprise pain points, significantly improve efficiency, or create new value. Examples include data analytics and predictive maintenance platforms for industrial IoT (IIoT), AI-based supply chain optimization and smart inventory management software, or simulation and decision-support tools for specific industries (such as drug molecule screening and optimization platforms in biopharmaceutical R&D, real-time complex fraud detection systems in financial risk management, autonomous vehicle simulation and verification tools, and climate modeling or environmental monitoring big data analysis). Once these products demonstrate real value creation, significant cost reduction, or high ROI for clients, enterprise customers actively seek collaboration and spread awareness through word-of-mouth, industry exhibitions, and professional media. While sales cycles may be long, the essence of selling is solution-and value-driven rather than pure promotion, and once clients are acquired, retention is high.
3. Innovative medical diagnostic technologies or devices: The healthcare sector has a perpetual demand for innovative technologies, especially those that save lives, improve patient quality of life, or significantly reduce healthcare costs. Examples include high-precision non-invasive early cancer detection technologies (such as liquid biopsy based on circulating tumor DNA, multimodal AI imaging diagnostic systems), breakthroughs in genetic sequencing for hereditary disease screening or personalized medicine, or targeted treatments for specific diseases (such as CAR-T cell immunotherapy, AI-based drug discovery platforms, novel minimally invasive surgical robots). Once these technologies pass rigorous clinical validation, regulatory approval, and demonstrate significant advantages, hospitals and patients become active buyers. Markets show extremely rigid demand and strong willingness to pay for life-saving or quality-of-life-enhancing technologies, and the sales process is more based on efficacy, safety, clinical data, and professional medical promotion.
4. Professional consulting services in specialized fields (based on algorithms or data models): These services are usually provided by experts with deep research backgrounds, using advanced algorithms, big data analytics, and domain knowledge to deliver highly customized solutions. Examples include optimizing high-frequency trading strategies and building risk management models for financial institutions, AI-based production process optimization and intelligent scheduling/quality control solutions for manufacturing, precise pollution source tracking and remediation models for environmental protection, or smart traffic flow and energy management solutions for urban planning. These services leverage the researcher's profound capabilities in data analysis, modeling, and algorithm development, and their results directly enhance client revenue, reduce costs, or solve complex problems. Successful cases quickly build reputational capital and bring follow-up business, with sales rooted in professional trust and tangible client value rather than broad market promotion.

## 5 Conclusion and Outlook: Cognitive Transformation and Ecosystem Building for Research Entrepreneurs

For researchers driven by technological dreams, entrepreneurial success is not about being a "jack-of-all-trades" but depends on a deep understanding of core strengths and a clear, strategic avoidance of weaknesses in the commercial chain, especially the sales segment. By precisely targeting tracks where demand is highly marketized, competition is sufficient, and supply exhibits significant scarcity or technical barriers, researchers can maximize their dominant R&D advantages, accelerate technology monetization, and ultimately realize their commercial ambitions.

However, this "play to strengths and avoid weaknesses" strategy does not imply entirely neglecting sales; rather, it represents a more sophisticated form of selling. Researchers still need to cultivate basic market sensitivity, understand real client needs, and learn to translate complex R&D outcomes into easily comprehensible commercial value propositions. Even in technology-driven tracks, attention must be paid to the "minimum viable product (MVP)" concept—delivering core functionality quickly and efficiently, gathering early user feedback, and iterating rapidly based on that feedback. This customer-centric, iterative optimization mindset is crucial to entrepreneurial success. Additionally, sales can also involve market education—introducing disruptive technologies requires effort to educate potential clients and the industry at large about the technology's value and application prospects.

More importantly, researchers need a profound cognitive shift: moving from a purely technology-driven approach to a dual focus on technology and market. This entails not only asking "What can I make?" but also "What does the market truly need?" and "How can my technology be converted into market value most efficiently?" Researchers must step out of the lab, deeply engage with markets and clients, and integrate market insights throughout the R&D process.

Building a complementary entrepreneurial team is equally critical. Research teams should actively recruit partners with experience in marketing, sales, operations, finance, and legal affairs to offset weaknesses outside of R&D, forming a multi-dimensional, high-efficiency entrepreneurial matrix. In high-R&D, deep-tech fields, effective intellectual property (IP) protection and management are key to securing long-term commercial value from core technologies. Filing patents, copyrights, and trademarks builds robust IP barriers, protecting invention while attracting investment and enhancing enterprise valuation.

Finally, research entrepreneurship is rarely a solo endeavor. Actively constructing an ecosystem—collaborating with upstream and downstream enterprises, research institutions, government agencies, and even competitors—is an effective means of rapidly translating technology and scaling markets. Examples include partnering with large corporations for technology validation and market deployment, or establishing industry alliances to set standards. Only by organically combining rigorous scientific spirit, acute market insight, excellent commercial execution, and strategic resource integration can research entrepreneurs truly navigate the commercial tide, conquer the final hurdle from "product" to "profit," and create a business legacy for technology innovators.

## Further Reading


1. S. Shane, *Academic Entrepreneurship: University Spinoffs and Wealth Creation*, Edward Elgar, 2004.
2. X. Cao, *Modern Business Management*, Palgrave Macmillan, 2025.
3. H. Etzkowitz, *The Triple Helix: University–Industry–Government Invention in Action*, Routledge, 2008.
4. R. Florida, *The Rise of the Creative Class*, Basic Books, 2002.
5. X. Cao, *Strategic Management and Organizational Development*, Springer, 2025.
6. M. G. Colombo and L. Grilli, "Founders' human capital and the growth of new technology-based firms: A competence-based view," *Research Policy*, vol. 34, no. 6, pp. 795–816, 2005.
7. H. Chesbrough, *Open Business Models: How to Thrive in the New Invention Landscape*, Harvard Business School Press, 2006.
8. E. Ries, *The Lean Startup*, Crown Business, 2011.
9. S. Blank, *The Startup Owner's Manual*, K & S Ranch, 2012.
10. J. Roberts and D. Malone, *Academic Spin-Offs and Technology Commercialization*, Edward Elgar, 2021.

# Chapter 14
# Scientific Thinking Vs. Engineering Thinking: The Twin Wings of Corporate Strategic Planning

## 1 Introduction

In today's complex, ever-changing, and increasingly competitive business environment, corporate leaders face unprecedented challenges. It is akin to a captain navigating uncharted waters—requiring not only a clear sense of direction to ensure the company's long-term course is correct, but also efficient navigation strategies to cope with the rapidly shifting market waves. In this voyage, scientific thinking, with its profound pursuit of fundamental truths, and engineering thinking, with its pragmatic approach to solving real-world problems, together form the indispensable twin wings of corporate strategic planning and execution, driving enterprises toward sustainable development, continuous invention, and ultimately, excellence (Fig. 1).

This article will delve into the core principles and essential differences of these two modes of thinking, as well as their specific manifestations in corporate strategic planning and daily operations. More importantly, we aim to elucidate how these two seemingly divergent yet actually complementary modes of thought can be organically integrated, forming a systematic and powerful corporate management philosophy that enables enterprises to anticipate opportunities, execute efficiently, and ultimately achieve ambitious long-term goals.

## 2 Scientific Thinking: Deep Insight and Long-Term Consideration

At its core, scientific thinking is characterized by a relentless pursuit of "truth-seeking." It emphasizes the steadfast quest for the fundamental nature of things and universal laws. No matter how complex the challenges or difficulties, it demands persistent and thorough exploration until the very root of the problem and the ultimate truth are reached. When applied to corporate strategic planning, this means that we



S. Li, *Bridging the Innovation Gap*, Innovation, Technology, and Knowledge Management, https://doi.org/10.1007/978-3-032-22652-5_14

**Fig. 1** Corporate leaders not only need a clear sense of direction to ensure the company's long-term development stays on the right course, but also require efficient navigation strategies to respond to rapidly changing market waves. In this journey, scientific thinking's profound pursuit of fundamental truths, together with engineering thinking's pragmatic solutions to real-world problems, form the indispensable twin wings of corporate strategic planning and execution

cannot merely focus on addressing surface-level phenomena or short-term problems; instead, we must adopt a forward-looking and penetrating approach to uncover the underlying logic and driving factors of operations, laying a solid foundation for the company's long-term development.

## 2.1 The Relentless Pursuit of Truth and Fundamentals

The essence of scientific thinking lies in its repeated questioning of "why." It is not satisfied with merely knowing "what" or "how," but seeks to deeply understand the underlying mechanisms and universal laws governing events. This mode of thinking requires us to disentangle complex business phenomena, extracting principles that are both universal and enduring (Fig. 2).

In the business context, the "truth" we refer to is not absolute philosophical truth, but rather the fundamental laws that shape markets, industries, consumer behavior, and technological evolution. This includes the essence of user value creation, the true sources of competitive advantage, the S-curve patterns of technological development, and the intrinsic drivers of economic cycles, among others. Scientific thinking urges us not to be deceived by superficial prosperity or short-term market fluctuations, but to consistently strive to see through phenomena to grasp their underlying essence.

The pursuit of these "truths" is often a long and arduous process, requiring significant investment, repeated experiments, rigorous validation, and sometimes multiple failures. For enterprises, this means that when conducting foundational research, tackling core technologies, or exploring entirely new business models, sufficient

**Fig. 2** Scientific thinking repeatedly asks "why," refusing to be satisfied with merely understanding "what" or "how," and instead delves into the underlying mechanisms and universal laws behind events. In corporate management, a deep reflection on causal relationships and management strategies enables leaders to gain profound insights

patience, and strategic discipline are required to avoid abandoning efforts due to a lack of immediate returns. This embodies a spirit of "persistent exploration."

Ultimately, scientific thinking seeks to "reach the root of the problem and the end of truth." This means that when analyzing problems, one should not merely address the surface-level "pain points," but trace back to their underlying causes. For example, if a company experiences a decline in product sales, engineering thinking may quickly adjust marketing strategies or pricing, whereas scientific thinking encourages an in-depth analysis of changes in consumer behavior, iterations of competing products, and shifts in the macroeconomic environment to uncover whether there are more universal patterns at play. Only this exploration of the root causes can provide truly meaningful and potentially disruptive solutions for the enterprise.

## *2.2 Deep Manifestations in Corporate Strategy*

Scientific thinking provides enterprises with a powerful intellectual tool for long-term development, ensuring that strategic decisions are profound, forward-looking, and sustainable.

First, in terms of industry and market insights, applying scientific thinking means that enterprises no longer settle for simple analyses of macro-level data such as current market share or growth rate. Instead, it requires delving into industry evolution patterns, understanding lifecycle stages from emergence, growth, and maturity to decline, and identifying critical success factors at each stage. For instance, a deep analysis of the "winner-takes-all" effect in the Internet industry, or a study of the market drivers for the new energy vehicle sector after subsidy reductions, represents a search for the "permanent truths" behind industry development. This deep understanding enables companies to anticipate future trends rather than chase short-term fads. To achieve this, enterprises may build market models and theoretical frameworks—not merely collecting data, but attempting to construct models that explain market behavior, consumer choices, and competitive dynamics. Through model simulations, companies can understand causal relationships among variables and more accurately predict market trends and consumer responses. For example, when entering an emerging market, a company may study not only demographics and spending patterns but also the cultural, social, and economic contexts that influence behavior, thereby crafting a market entry strategy tailored to local characteristics.

The practice of such thinking is evident in fields like AI and biotechnology. Companies such as Google and DeepMind invest heavily in fundamental research in artificial intelligence, exploring the frontiers of deep learning and reinforcement learning. While these investments may not yield immediate financial returns, the pursuit of the "end of truth" in technology positions them strategically when AI waves arrive. Similarly, large biopharmaceutical companies invest long-term in gene editing and cell therapy technologies based on a deep understanding of life sciences.

Second, in core technology and product development, the role of scientific thinking is even more pronounced. It encourages companies to shift their R&D focus from short-term product iteration to long-term foundational research and core technological breakthroughs, thereby creating technological moats that are difficult to replicate. This requires long-term investment in foundational research—just as Bell Labs contributed to transistors, lasers, and communication theory through sustained, pure scientific research. Modern enterprises may establish dedicated R&D departments or invention labs, encouraging engineers and scientists to explore beyond current product lines and undertake broader, more fundamental technological research. Companies should pursue breakthroughs in technological principles, not merely integrate or apply existing technologies, aiming for fundamental advances in materials science, algorithm optimization, and energy efficiency. In new energy battery research, for instance, inventions focus not only on capacity improvements but also on electrochemical reaction mechanisms and material structures. Semiconductor companies like TSMC and Intel invest extensively in semiconductor physics, materials science, and quantum mechanics to continually advance Moore's Law and lead the industry. Aerospace research into new composite materials and high-temperature alloys also demonstrates the foundational importance of understanding "unchanging" material properties.

Third, in business model invention, scientific thinking manifests as a profound insight into the core logic of value creation rather than simple imitation or superficial reform. This includes deconstructing the value chain and ecosystem, examining not only the company's profitability but also how different participants coordinate, allocate value, and identify new opportunities for value creation. The success of platform economy models lies in a deep understanding of supply-demand matching efficiency and the essence of network effects. Companies also need to explore the underlying reasons for sustainable profitability: Is it technological monopoly, brand premium, economies of scale, or unique customer relationship management? Scientific thinking helps strip away superficial phenomena to uncover these deeper causes, forming the basis for sustainable business models. Subscription and sharing economy models exemplify this. Subscription models reflect profound insights into changes in consumer behavior, content consumption habits, and the shift from ownership to access. The rise of the sharing economy is based on understanding asset utilization, idle resources, and interpersonal efficiency. The success of these models stems from scientific reflection on business essence and value creation logic.

Finally, scientific thinking profoundly influences organizational culture and values. It encourages enterprises to uphold enduring core values and corporate spirit, which remain guiding principles regardless of external changes. This involves building a principle-based decision-making system rather than relying on short-term goals or personal preferences. For example, a company emphasizing "customer first" will prioritize customer interests under any circumstance—an embedded corporate truth. Scientific thinking also fosters a culture of learning and exploration, cultivating employees' critical thinking, curiosity, and continuous learning so that everyone acts like a "scientist," constantly questioning, verifying, and seeking better solutions. Google's "Don't be evil" and Amazon's "customer obsession" exemplify such cultures. These core values are not empty slogans but guiding truths in product development, market expansion, and talent acquisition. These enduring values help companies maintain competitive advantage and social influence amid fierce market competition.

## 2.3 *Resisting Short-Termism: Lessons From Chinese and Western Medicine*

The original comparison between Chinese and Western medicine provides a profound lesson for understanding the importance of scientific thinking. It points out that Chinese medicine "from its inception sought to solve problems," but because "the theory was never mature initially," efforts focused on "using weak theory to solve problems," resulting in "no one deeply and thoroughly studied the mechanism of the theory itself." Consequently, "the foundation was not solid," and it "could not ultimately solve practical problems." This warns that if a company focuses solely on short-term problem-solving while neglecting research into core theories and underlying mechanisms, its "engineering" lacks vitality and cannot achieve sustainable development.

In contrast, Western medicine's progress comes from scientists' "less utilitarian" approach. They delve into cell biology, molecular biology, and physiology, "constantly pursuing the truth of problems." This pure pursuit of truth strengthens the theoretical system, "making the path to problem-solving ever wider."

The strategic lesson for enterprises is clear: in a competitive environment, if a company invests all its energy too early in application-level solutions while neglecting foundational research, core technological breakthroughs, and the deep logic of business models, its "engineering" will be mere stopgap fixes, lacking resilience, and unable to tackle deeper challenges. Long-term competitiveness is built on a solid, in-depth scientific foundation.

## 3 Engineering Thinking: Efficiency and Pragmatic Practice

Unlike the grandeur and depth of scientific thinking, engineering thinking emphasizes "solving problems." Rooted in science but not limited to a single discipline, it centers on pragmatism and aims to resolve issues within given constraints. This thinking is practical and flexible—statistically valid empirical formulas may be used even without absolute scientific proof. Engineering thinking seeks "the shortest effective path," is accountable only for results and tasks, and ensures efficient implementation of strategy, rapid business growth, and precise task completion.

### *3.1 Problem-Solving and Pragmatism*

The essence of engineering thinking is a goal-oriented practical philosophy. It focuses on how to efficiently convert resources into outputs and solve real-world problems.

First, "solving problems" is both the starting point and endpoint. Whether facing technical difficulties, market bottlenecks, or operational inefficiencies, engineering thinking prioritizes feasible solutions. Unlike scientific thinking, it does not obsess over theoretical perfection but emphasizes practical effectiveness.

Second, "pragmatism" is its core principle. Engineering thinking does not seek absolute theoretical completeness or perfect elegance, but prioritizes achieving results under real-world constraints such as time, cost, and available resources. As the original text emphasizes, "even empirical formulas without scientific proof, if statistically consistent with experimental data, are commonly used methods." This demonstrates engineering thinking's flexibility and pragmatism.

Third, the goal of solving problems within a given timeframe is a defining feature. Projects have clear deadlines, tasks have strict schedules. Engineering thinking requires making optimal decisions within a limited window to achieve objectives at minimal cost—reflecting its emphasis on pragmatism and efficiency.

Finally, engineering thinking does not get "stuck on a single science." Engineering is inherently interdisciplinary. To solve specific problems, engineers may draw from physics, chemistry, computer science, materials science, and even psychology. As long as the problem is solved, no single theoretical system is prioritized. In enterprises, this manifests as encouraging cross-departmental collaboration to approach complex problems from multiple perspectives (Fig. 3).

**Fig. 3** Engineering thinking is a goal-oriented practical philosophy. It focuses on how to efficiently convert resources into outputs within a given timeframe and address real-world problems

## 3.2 *Efficient Implementation in Business Operations*

Engineering thinking permeates all aspects of daily business operations and serves as the cornerstone for improving efficiency, achieving goals, and tackling challenges.

Engineering thinking plays a central role in project management. It emphasizes clearly defining task objectives and timelines at the project's outset, specifying *What* needs to be done, *When*, *How Much* resource is required, and *Who* is responsible. For instance, when launching a new product, the functional list, performance metrics, and release date must be clearly defined and broken down into actionable tasks. To improve efficiency, companies often adopt lean processes and agile iteration, splitting large projects into small, deliverable cycles for rapid feedback and continuous improvement. This approach mitigates the risks of trying to do everything at once and ensures timely adjustments, increasing project success rates.

In resource-constrained scenarios, engineers optimize resources and select paths by weighing cost, efficiency, and risk to choose the "fastest and most accurate" solution. For example, in software development: should a company build in-house or use open-source components? Should it aim for peak performance immediately or first meet core functionality? These decisions reflect engineering thinking. Tools like OKR (Objectives and Key Results) and lean manufacturing exemplify this mindset. OKRs focus on clear goals and measurable key results, demonstrating engineering thinking in strategy execution. Lean production maximizes efficiency by eliminating waste and optimizing workflows, emphasizing engineering management of the production process.

Engineering thinking is equally crucial in marketing and sales, focusing on efficiently acquiring customers, improving conversion rates, and achieving revenue targets. This entails data-driven marketing decisions rather than blind spending. Techniques like A/B testing, channel effectiveness analysis, and user behavior tracking allow companies to quantify marketing performance and quickly adjust strategies. For example, testing different ad copies or channels helps identify the highest ROI. Sales processes are standardized and optimized by breaking them into measurable steps—lead identification, initial contact, needs analysis, proposal presentation, objection handling, and closing—improving overall conversion. Given that marketing and sales often have quarterly or annual targets, engineering thinking emphasizes short-term results and efficiency, focusing on maximizing revenue "within the given timeframe," even if it involves using heuristics or temporary tactics. Precision digital marketing and optimized conversion funnels are practical examples: platforms allow targeted ad delivery and real-time monitoring, enabling teams to adjust strategies swiftly, while optimized sales funnels enhance customer conversion rates.

Engineering thinking manifests in a relentless pursuit of efficiency, cost reduction, and risk management. Lean operations and process automation identify and eliminate waste—like inventory backlogs, transport delays, or overproduction—to minimize costs. Automation improves operational efficiency and accuracy, while supply chain flexibility and resilience ensure the ability to handle disruptions (e.g., raw material shortages, logistics interruptions). This requires engineering-based design and stress testing of all supply chain components. Data-driven decision-making is also essential: analytics tools monitor inventory, production progress, and delivery efficiency in real time, enabling rapid optimization. Amazon's logistics system and Toyota's production model exemplify this approach. Amazon's global logistics network leverages sophisticated algorithms and automation to maximize efficiency, while Toyota's lean manufacturing improves production efficiency and quality through continuous improvement and zero-inventory management.

Engineering thinking emphasizes risk avoidance and rapid mitigation. It begins with identifying and assessing risks—project, market, financial, and operational—then developing contingency plans and response protocols to minimize losses. This approach prioritizes short-term technical problem-solving over long-term research, ensuring rapid solutions in emergencies. For example, information security teams establish multi-layered defenses and conduct regular drills, while finance departments use cash flow forecasting and hedging tools to prevent liquidity crises, maintaining business continuity within tight time constraints.

### *3.3 Emphasizing Efficiency and Risk Control: Calculating the "Economic Equation"*

The core of engineering thinking is calculating the "economic equation": maximizing returns while minimizing risks within a given timeframe. This pragmatic mindset encourages leveraging external resources and proven solutions.

Under this approach, companies often favor "borrowing" and "integration." When time and resources are limited, engineering thinking suggests outsourcing, purchasing, or strategic partnerships to leverage mature technologies, products, or services for faster outcomes. For example, building a customer service system may be more efficiently achieved by purchasing an existing CRM or partnering with a specialized service provider than developing one from scratch.

At the same time, engineering thinking balances efficiency with risk avoidance. When evaluating multiple solutions, it considers speed, precision, and potential risks, selecting paths that minimize risk across technical, market, and operational dimensions.

Moreover, engineering thinking promotes short-cycle technical problem-solving. Unlike scientific thinking, which focuses on long-term foundational research, engineering thinking emphasizes resolving specific technical challenges within project timelines. This approach is common in fast-iterating, technology-driven businesses. For instance, quickly validating a new business model through partnerships, acquisitions of small teams, or limited market tests is preferred over full-scale, in-house development. This "small steps, rapid testing" strategy vividly illustrates the essence of engineering thinking (Fig. 4).

# 4 Scientific and Engineering Thinking: Dialectical Unity and Integrated Application

Scientific thinking and engineering thinking are not opposing extremes; rather, they complement each other and form the dual wings of corporate strategy. Successful companies, without exception, understand how to flexibly switch between and skillfully integrate these two modes of thinking depending on different time horizons and task characteristics.

## *4.1 Complementary Strategic Wings*

We can liken scientific thinking to a company's "navigation system." It guides the direction and corrects the course, ensuring the company moves toward the "truth" and is not distracted by the temptations of short-term gains. Engineering thinking, on the other hand, functions like the company's "propulsion system." It provides thrust and optimizes efficiency, ensuring the company can reach its destination quickly and accurately.

The most apparent manifestation of this relationship is scientific thinking at the strategic level and engineering thinking at the execution level. During strategic planning, a company must rise above daily operations, apply scientific thinking to conduct deep analysis, understand industry fundamentals, and anticipate future trends, thereby constructing a grand blueprint. Once the strategic direction is clear,

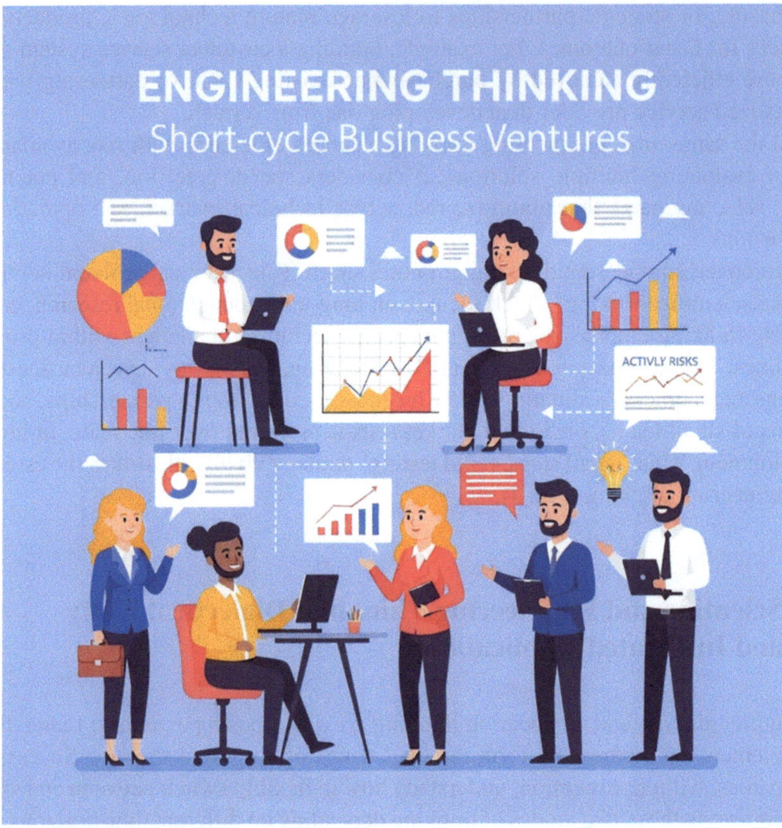


**Fig. 4** Engineering thinking focuses on delivering results, taking responsibility for the outcomes and overall gains. It often does not concern itself with *how* the goal is achieved, but emphasizes completing it within the designated timeframe with minimal risk, ensuring successful delivery

execution requires switching to engineering thinking: using pragmatism and result-oriented principles to translate the strategic blueprint into concrete projects and tasks and drive them forward efficiently.

On a deeper level, science and engineering nurture each other in a spiraling upward relationship. Scientific research provides a solid theoretical foundation and new possibilities for engineering practice, preventing blind trial and error. Meanwhile, practical engineering experience and the new problems it uncovers inspire further scientific exploration, leading to theoretical refinement and breakthroughs. This virtuous cycle allows companies to continuously deepen their understanding in practice and to execute more efficiently under the guidance of knowledge.

## 4.2 Task Layering and Matching Thinking Modes

The wisdom of corporate management lies in recognizing the nature of different tasks and matching them with the most suitable mode of thinking.

For tasks that require solving problems within a given time frame, engineering thinking should dominate. For example:

1. New product launches: Clear launch dates, feature lists, and sales targets require engineering thinking to coordinate R&D, production, marketing, and sales, ensuring the product is delivered on time, with quality and quantity as planned.
2. Quarterly performance sprints: Short-term objectives like boosting revenue or profit margins demand marketing and sales teams to apply engineering thinking, using precise campaigns, sales strategy adjustments, and client visit plans to efficiently achieve goals.
3. Specific technical problem-solving: Production line failures or software bug fixes require engineers to quickly diagnose the issue, analyze the root cause (without necessarily delving to the extreme), and provide rapid solutions to restore normal operations.
4. Organizational adjustments: Layoffs or restructuring within a specific time window to respond to market changes or improve efficiency also necessitate engineering thinking, with clear plans, processes, schedules, and risk management.

In these situations, pragmatism, result orientation, and efficiency are the core principles. The philosophy of "it doesn't matter if it's a white cat or a black cat, as long as it catches mice" guides the company to quickly select the most effective solution, avoiding over-analysis and decision paralysis.

Conversely, for tasks without immediate time pressure but critical to long-term competitiveness, scientific thinking should dominate. This includes:

1. Corporate universities and talent development systems: Aimed at long-term skill and holistic employee development, requiring deep study of learning theories and talent development patterns to design scientific curricula and growth paths.
2. Corporate culture and value propagation: A long-term process that requires continuous investment and practice to embed core values into employee behavior, leveraging organizational behavior and psychology.
3. Long-term R&D projects: Focused on breaking core technology bottlenecks and securing future advantages, requiring teams with autonomy and patience to pursue "truth" without being constrained by short-term benefits.
4. Employee personal growth and hobbies: Encouraging knowledge accumulation and intellectual exploration when no immediate deliverables exist, fostering deep understanding.

These seemingly "non-utilitarian" investments form the theoretical foundation and invention source for solving complex engineering problems in the future. In this context, companies do not emphasize quick wins and disdain superficial understanding, because such investment is the foundation for executing engineering tasks

**Fig. 5** Modern management requires leaders to master both scientific and engineering thinking, achieving a balance between short-term deliverables and long-term value for the enterprise

efficiently and accurately—without a solid theoretical guide, rapid and precise execution becomes extremely difficult (Fig. 5).

## *4.3 The Art of Dynamic Balance Between Depth and Speed*

In practice, finding a dynamic balance between the depth of scientific thinking and the speed of engineering thinking is both an art of management and a continuous challenge. Overemphasizing either side can have negative consequences.

If a company leans too heavily toward engineering, focusing solely on efficiency while neglecting scientific thinking, it may fall into a "treat the symptom, not the cause" trap. Without long-term accumulation of understanding of fundamental principles and theoretical foundations, the enterprise risks losing core competitiveness, failing to respond to deep market changes, or even making strategic errors in technology choices. As mentioned in the text regarding traditional Chinese medicine, if problem-solving is emphasized while the theoretical foundation is weak, the problems cannot be truly solved.

Conversely, if a company leans too heavily toward science, indulging in theoretical perfection and endless exploration while neglecting implementation and execution, it may result in "armchair theorizing," detached from market realities. For example, highly advanced technologies may be developed, but without considering market demand and cost, they ultimately cannot be commercialized.

Therefore, seeking balance is crucial. This requires a series of strategies:

1. **Establish collaboration between invention labs and product departments.** Invention labs can focus on long-term, foundational research (scientific thinking), while product departments are responsible for rapidly turning mature technologies into market-ready products (engineering thinking). Effective communication channels and conversion mechanisms must exist between the two.
2. **Enhance communication between R&D and marketing teams.** While conducting scientific exploration, R&D teams should regularly communicate with marketing to understand market needs and pain points, ensuring research directions have commercial value. Conversely, marketing teams should understand the limitations and potential of technological developments to avoid unrealistic demands.
3. **Implement differentiated performance evaluation systems.** For foundational research teams, assessment cycles can be longer and focus on invention and breakthroughs; for product development and operations teams, performance evaluations should emphasize achieving short-term goals and efficiency.
4. **Leadership plays a critical role.** Leaders must have insight to recognize the nature of different tasks and switch thinking modes according to context, guiding team members to adopt the appropriate mode. They act as both integrators and practitioners of the two thinking approaches.

## *4.4 The Key Role of Organizational Culture and Leadership*

The deep integration of scientific and engineering thinking must ultimately be reflected in organizational culture and leadership.

Companies need to foster a culture that encourages both deep thinking and exploration while emphasizing efficient execution and results. This can be achieved through internal knowledge-sharing platforms that allow employees to share research outcomes and practical experiences. Additionally, a "fail-fast" culture should be promoted, permitting mistakes in new explorations but requiring rapid iteration and lessons learned.

Leaders serve as integrators and practitioners of the two thinking modes. They must possess strategic foresight, using scientific thinking to anticipate the future and craft a grand blueprint for the company. Simultaneously, they need strong execution capabilities, applying engineering thinking to break strategy into actionable tasks and ensure efficient implementation. Leaders should also empower teams by delegating authority to enable efficiency in engineering tasks, while providing resources and platforms to support scientific exploration. Ultimately, leaders act as communicators and bridges, fostering understanding and collaboration across R&D, marketing, operations, and other functional departments, breaking down silos, and maximizing overall organizational effectiveness (Fig. 6).

**Fig. 6** Organizational culture and leadership are key to ensuring that scientific and engineering thinking complement each other effectively within the enterprise

# 5 Practical Pathways to Building an Outstanding Enterprise

Integrating scientific thinking and engineering thinking into corporate practice is not achieved overnight; it is a systematic construction process. It involves multiple dimensions, including strategic framework, execution system, knowledge management, and talent development.

## *5.1 Scientific Construction of Strategic Framework*

The formulation of corporate strategy should be as scientific as possible to ensure its foresight and correctness.

First, in the initial stage of strategy formulation, thorough research and data analysis should be conducted. This means investing substantial resources in market research, consumer behavior analysis, and competitor analysis, while leveraging big data, artificial intelligence, and other tools for deep mining and pattern recognition. This is a typical application of scientific thinking—extracting patterns and insights from large amounts of data.

Second, apply systems thinking and model construction. View the enterprise as a complex system and understand the internal connections and interactions between elements. Construct strategic models such as the value chain model, Five Forces model, SWOT analysis. These are not only tools but frameworks that help structure thinking and conduct scientific analysis. For example, when considering entry into a new market, one should not only consider market size but also analyze entry barriers, potential competitors, and suppliers' bargaining power to form a comprehensive scientific evaluation.

Third, scenario planning and uncertainty management are essential. Scientific thinking acknowledges that the future is full of uncertainty. Through scenario planning, predict multiple possible future scenarios and develop corresponding response strategies for each scenario. This helps enterprises maintain strategic flexibility in the face of uncertainty, avoiding being trapped by a single incorrect forecast.

Finally, adhere to scientific hypotheses and verification. Treat strategic choices as a series of scientific hypotheses and validate them through small-scale trials or pilot projects. This "hypothesis–experiment–validation–iteration" loop is the core application of scientific methodology at the strategic level.

## *5.2 Engineering Implementation of Execution Systems*

Even the most perfect strategy requires efficient execution to be realized. Engineering thinking plays a key role here.

First, establish efficient project management processes. Whether it is new product development, marketing campaigns, or internal process optimization, a clear project charter, detailed work breakdown structure (WBS), defined milestones, and responsible persons are required. Using engineering management methods such as Agile and Scrum ensures that projects are completed on time, on quality, and within budget.

Second, establish result-oriented performance assessment and incentive mechanisms. Break down strategic goals into measurable KPIs (Key Performance Indicators) and link them to employees' compensation and promotion. This motivates employees to focus on goals and improve efficiency through engineering thinking. At the same time, it is necessary to guard against overemphasis on short-term indicators at the expense of long-term value.

Third, optimize resource allocation. Accurately identify the resources required for each task (human, financial, technical, time) and allocate them efficiently. When resources are limited, prioritize core tasks and leverage external resources to ensure high efficiency.

Furthermore, encourage trial-and-error and rapid iteration. In highly uncertain areas, engineering thinking promotes small-step rapid testing. Using rapid prototypes and user testing helps identify issues early and correct them promptly, reducing trial-and-error costs. This "fail–learn–improve" cycle vividly embodies engineering efficiency.

Finally, promote digitalization and automation. Introduce digital tools and automated processes to enhance operational efficiency. For example, using CRM systems to optimize customer management, SaaS tools to enhance team collaboration, and automation robots for repetitive tasks are all applications of engineering thinking in technology.

## *5.3 Knowledge Management and Experience Accumulation Loops*

Integrating scientific and engineering thinking also requires establishing a comprehensive knowledge management system to facilitate knowledge flow and experience accumulation.

This includes digitizing and modeling engineering practices. Collect, organize, and analyze data from daily operations and project practices to extract patterns and rules. For example, marketing data can optimize ad placement models, and production data can improve quality control algorithms. These practice-derived data and models can serve as starting points for new scientific research or directly guide future engineering practice.

At the same time, establish knowledge-sharing platforms. Encourage knowledge sharing across departments and hierarchies. Through internal forums, seminars, and knowledge repositories, employees' personal experience and professional knowledge can be transformed into collective organizational wisdom. This helps avoid repeated mistakes and accelerates the dissemination and application of new knowledge.

Regular reviews and summaries are also crucial. Not only should project results be evaluated, but the reasons for success and failure should be analyzed in depth to extract lessons learned. This process transforms engineering practice into scientific cognition, helping enterprises better understand why success or failure occurred and guiding future strategy and execution.

Finally, emphasize patent and intellectual property management. Protect innovative achievements obtained from scientific exploration and engineering practice through patents, copyrights, etc., turning them into intangible assets and core competencies.

## 5.4 Talent Development and Internalization of Thinking

Ultimately, the integration of scientific and engineering thinking must be reflected in talent development and individual cognitive shaping within the enterprise.

Enterprises need to cultivate critical thinking and systems thinking (scientific thinking). Encourage employees to question assumptions, think critically, and analyze problems thoroughly at both macro and micro levels. This can be achieved through training, workshops, and challenging assignments to enhance employees' cognitive depth.

Simultaneously, cultivate problem-solving skills, execution capability, and result orientation (engineering thinking). Emphasize hands-on ability and the capacity to solve practical problems. By assigning responsibilities, providing practical opportunities, and setting clear goals, employees' execution ability, sense of responsibility, and accountability can be developed.

Moreover, fostering interdisciplinary talent is crucial. Encourage employees to expand knowledge boundaries and learn methods from different fields. Talents with hybrid knowledge backgrounds can better bridge science and engineering, enabling cross-disciplinary invention. For example, a product manager who understands both technology and market, or a strategy analyst who understands both finance and business.

Establishing mentorship systems and learning organizations is an effective way to promote this integration. Through guidance from experienced staff, new employees can learn and master these two thinking modes. Build the enterprise into a continuous learning organization, allowing knowledge and experience to flow and accumulate internally.

Finally, establish a sound incentive mechanism to encourage invention and practice. Reward employees who achieve breakthroughs in scientific exploration and teams that efficiently solve problems in engineering practice. Make employees recognize that both deep theoretical work and hands-on practice are key to enterprise success.

## 6 Conclusion

In an increasingly competitive and uncertain business environment, enterprises seeking sustainable leadership must learn to organically combine the profound insights of scientific thinking with the execution efficiency of engineering thinking. Scientific thinking equips enterprises with strategic steadiness to see through the fog and perceive the essence, allowing them to stand taller and see farther, ensuring the correctness and longevity of development direction; engineering thinking ensures that enterprises can act efficiently, respond quickly to the market, and turn grand blueprints into tangible results.

Only by integrating these two thinking modes and internalizing them into corporate culture, management practices, and every employee's actions, can enterprises truly build an indestructible strategic fortress. In this process, enterprises will no longer blindly drift with the current but can plan the future with scientific rigor and execute with engineering pragmatism, ultimately remaining invincible in a constantly changing market while achieving continuous invention and excellence.

So, in the challenges you face, which problems require deep exploration with scientific thinking, and which are better suited for efficient resolution with engineering thinking? We look forward to your reflection and practice.

## Further Reading

[1] D. Schön, *The Reflective Practitioner: How Professionals Think in Action*, Basic Books, 1983.
[2] X. Cao, *Strategic Management and Organizational Development*, Springer, 2025.
[3] H. Simon, *The Sciences of the Artificial*, MIT Press, 1969.
[4] X. Cao, *Modern Business Management*, Palgrave Macmillan, 2025.
[5] T. Kuhn, *The Structure of Scientific Revolutions*, Univ. of Chicago Press, 1962.
[6] K. Popper, *The Logic of Scientific Discovery*, Routledge, 1959.
[7] D. Norman, *The Design of Everyday Things*, Basic Books, 2013.
[8] P. Checkland, *Systems Thinking, Systems Practice*, Wiley, 1981.
[9] H. Mintzberg, *The Nature of Managerial Work*, Harper & Row, 1973.
[10] J. March, "Footnotes to organizational change," *Administrative Science Quarterly*, vol. 26, no. 4, pp. 563–577, 1981.
[11] S. Li, *Haircutting Robots*, Switzerland: Springer, 2025.
[12] E. G. Carayannis, Ed., *Encyclopedia of Creativity, Invention, Innovation and Entrepreneurship*. New York, NY: Springer, 2013. doi:https://doi.org/10.1007/978-1-4614-6616-1.

# Chapter 15
# Persist or Adapt: How to Choose When Direction is Unclear

## 1 Are You Upholding Your Beliefs, or just Being Stubborn?

In today's era of information overload and rapid pace, choice anxiety has become a widespread phenomenon in society. Almost every day, we find ourselves standing at countless "crossroads," facing an overwhelming amount of information, complex options, and the accumulation of multiple tasks (multi-tasking), all while our minds wrestle with a persistent question: should we continue along the path before us, or decisively adapt and take a new route? The difficulty of this choice is not merely a personal issue—it is an inevitable outcome of societal and even epochal developments.

Cognitive science tells us that human cognitive resources are extremely limited and scarce. When confronted with large volumes of information and decisions, the brain rapidly depletes its finite attention and judgment capacity, leading to what is known as "decision fatigue"—the more complex the choice, the easier it is to fall into endless anxiety and procrastination. At such times, without an efficient "judgment mechanism," we are prone to repeated internal friction, wasting time and impairing efficiency (Fig. 1).

Therefore, the three simple yet profound self-inquiry questions introduced at the beginning of this chapter are precisely designed to help you quickly clarify your thinking and conserve cognitive resources:

- **Is this endeavor building a valuable system?**

  When you invest time and energy in something, ask yourself: is this a mechanism for long-term accumulation? Examples include research methodologies, writing systems, professional skills, or networks of contacts. Truly valuable systems are not built overnight; they are the result of persistent, continuous effort. If the answer is yes, then the significance of persistence becomes obvious.

- **If today were the first day, would I choose to start this again?**



S. Li, *Bridging the Innovation Gap*, Innovation, Technology, and Knowledge Management, https://doi.org/10.1007/978-3-032-22652-5_15

**Fig. 1** Are you upholding your beliefs, or just being stubborn?

This question helps avoid the sunk cost fallacy. Sunk costs refer to past investments of time and resources that, even when the current situation is unfavorable, lead us to cling to continuing merely because of what we've already spent. If you wouldn't start this now from scratch, you are likely being trapped by past sunk costs.

- **Am I avoiding pain, or seeking a better opportunity?**

When considering adaptation, it is crucial to distinguish your true motivation. Are you giving up due to temporary fatigue, anxiety, or frustration, or have you calmly assessed that adjusting your approach could bring greater opportunity and growth? The former is emotion-driven and unlikely to produce substantive change; the latter reflects rational decision-making and often leads to qualitative leaps.

These three questions may seem simple, but they contain deep psychological mechanisms and principles of behavioral economics. Mastering them can not only free you from indecision but also enable you to make mature and rational choices swiftly in complex environments.

Persistence and adaptation are among life's most complex and critical choices. In moments of difficulty, two voices often vie within us: one urging, *"Keep going; the breakthrough might be just ahead,"* and the other whispering, *"Abandon this path and seek a new direction."* This tug-of-war manifests not only in personal life but also permeates scientific research, business development, and even the progress of civilization.

## 2 Is Great Persistence Really About Willpower?

To many people, persistence seems to be simply about strong will—the ability to press on without giving up, no matter the obstacles. Yet, a deeper examination of truly great persistence reveals that it is far more complex and profound than mere "endurance."

Physicist Chen-Ning Yang once shared a thought-provoking story: in the mid-twentieth century, the physics community faced the immense challenge of constructing a fundamental particle gauge theory. They required a new mathematical language to describe the complex structures they were observing. Remarkably, decades earlier, mathematicians had already developed a comprehensive theoretical framework—fiber bundles—which turned out to be exactly the tool physicists needed. At the time, differential geometry was regarded as a "useless" and esoteric branch of mathematics. Yet, because a group of researchers persisted in exploring it for decades, it eventually became the key to unlocking a new frontier in physics.

Shiing-Shen Chern, one of the greatest differential geometers of the modern era, embarked on his studies in this field with uncertainty. He did not know the ultimate significance of his work; he simply found it "interesting" and "structured," and so he persisted. No one could have predicted that this seemingly aimless and "useless" pursuit would, decades later, become a cornerstone for advancing the natural sciences (Fig. 2).

This history teaches us that true perseverance is not merely about "gritting your teeth" with sheer willpower; it is often an investment in long-term value, a patience that quietly cultivates in the shadow of unseen results. At the same time, we must recognize that such perseverance involves a genuine love for one's interests and a deep

**Fig. 2** The essence of perseverance: Vision and reflection

appreciation for the knowledge system itself. Another example is Alan Turing, whose early explorations in artificial intelligence were likewise marked by persistence amid loneliness and doubt, even though society and technology at the time were not ready to embrace the field. His perseverance was deliberate and patient—acknowledging present difficulties while always holding onto the possibilities of the future.

However, perseverance is by no means unconditional stubbornness. Behavioral economics points out that humans are naturally inclined toward immediate gratification, which causes many to struggle with temporary setbacks or low returns when pursuing long-term goals. True perseverance requires escaping this short-sighted trap, cultivating "strategic patience," and being willing to endure present uncertainties and hardships for the sake of enormous future value. Perseverance is a strategic choice, not blind obstinacy.

More importantly, great perseverance includes tolerance for mistakes and reflection. Blindly persisting can trap one in path dependency, becoming an obstacle to success. Only through continuous reflection and willingness to correct deviations can perseverance be truly wise. In other words, great perseverance is flexible—a dynamic adjustment guided by long-term goals rather than rigidly holding on.

In conclusion, the essence of perseverance is not merely willpower; it is strategic patience with foresight, a steadfast pursuit of inner passion and long-term value, combined with the capacity for reflection and adjustment. Only in this way can perseverance become a solid cornerstone for success, rather than an obsession leading astray.

## 3 True Adaptability is Far from Simply Giving up

Adaptability is often misunderstood as compromise, surrender, or even weakness, but the reality is quite the opposite. True, wise adaptability is a deep understanding of reality, a rational reallocation of resources and opportunities, and the courage and capability to seek optimal solutions in a constantly changing environment. Psychologist Spencer Johnson, in his management fable *Who Moved My Cheese?*, vividly illustrates humanity's instinctive resistance to change and path dependency through the story of two little mice and two little people. Some cling stubbornly to the lost "cheese," trying to regain past stability through persistence; others quickly adjust their mindset, "put on their running shoes," and actively seek new opportunities. Ultimately, the latter reap new resources and growth, while the former fall into prolonged loss and stagnation (Fig. 3).

Behind this kind of flexibility lies a profound psychological mechanism: humans' fear of the unknown and reliance on stability make adaptability no easy feat. Especially when facing endeavors in which one has already invested considerable time and emotion, flexibility often triggers the sunk cost fallacy—people find it difficult to let go of past investments even when the path ahead is clearly unpromising. Rational flexibility requires overcoming this psychological barrier, recognizing opportunity

**Fig. 3** Persistence and Adaptability, Resilience and Growth, Have Always Been Central Themes in Our Lives

costs, abandoning paths that no longer serve one's development, and redirecting limited time and energy toward directions with greater potential.

Real-world cases demonstrate that many famous companies' successes exemplify such adaptability. Slack, originally an internal tool for a game development team, pivoted strategically to become a globally recognized collaboration platform. Shopify transformed from a surfboard e-commerce business into a leading global e-commerce platform. Instagram started as a location check-in app and became the world's largest photo-sharing community. These successes were not accidental; they were achieved by facing reality honestly, boldly adjusting direction, and redefining themselves. In the fiercely competitive business world, clinging rigidly to the initial positioning often leads to being surpassed by more agile competitors.

Flexibility is a rational choice and a smart way to manage one's resources. It requires continuously observing environmental changes and adjusting strategies accordingly, rather than being confined by rigid thinking. It is not avoidance of challenges, but recognition of reality's uncertainty, using path adjustments to achieve better long-term outcomes.

However, flexibility does not imply frequent abandonment or indecisive wavering. Truly effective flexibility is based on deep analysis and self-awareness, not emotional reactions. Only when adaptability becomes a mature strategy, combined with accurate assessment of one's abilities and the environment, can it produce qualitative leaps.

Flexibility is far from mere compromise; it is a highly rational dynamic adaptation—a continuous optimization of choices in an ever-changing world. It requires courage, wisdom, and stands as another vital path to success.

## 4 The Analogy of Choice Mechanisms—a Robot in a Maze

Life's decisions often leave us perplexed, much like a robot searching for an exit in a complex maze. In computer science, this problem is abstracted as a graph search problem: how to move from a starting point through a series of state transitions to ultimately reach a target state. Different search strategies reflect the various ways we think and act when faced with life choices.

A classic strategy is breadth-first search, which emphasizes exploring all paths broadly before delving deeply into any single one. Applied to life decisions, this resembles the early exploration phase—such as entering the workforce or experimenting with multiple interests and directions. This period is characterized by incomplete information, diverse opportunities, and high uncertainty. Breadth-first strategy advises us not to rush into deep commitment to a single path, but to first "see the whole picture" and try multiple possibilities, increasing the likelihood of discovering unexpected opportunities.

In contrast, depth-first search focuses on thoroughly exploring one path until encountering a barrier or reaching the goal before backtracking. Depth-first is often suited to stages where goals are relatively clear, and one possesses strong conviction and long-term focus. For example, a researcher who has chosen a research direction will persistently explore it despite difficulties and bottlenecks, until fully understanding its potential and challenges. Depth-first reflects focus, perseverance, and the power of long-term accumulation.

In reality, purely breadth-first or depth-first strategies are insufficient for navigating complex, dynamic environments. Heuristic algorithms, such as A* search, combine the advantages of both approaches, using "heuristic information"—estimates of distance to the goal—to guide the search more efficiently. In life, heuristic information consists of our cognition, experience, intuition, and external inputs. It helps us quickly identify the most promising directions among numerous options, avoiding blind and prolonged trial-and-error (Fig. 4).

However, the effectiveness of heuristic algorithms heavily depends on the accuracy of the heuristic information. When our cognitive biases, overconfidence, or confirmation bias interfere with judgment, heuristics can mislead us, resulting in

**Fig. 4** The problem of a robot finding the exit in a maze is analogous to how we search for solutions to problems and navigate the maze of life. There are well-established scientific conclusions on how a robot can find its way out of a maze. Referencing these scientific findings can provide significant guidance and insights for how we approach and solve problems

poor path choices. This reminds us that, in addition to relying on existing knowledge and experience, we must maintain cognitive openness and engage in reflection to avoid falling into mental traps.

Beyond these deterministic search methods, life also requires a certain degree of randomness and exploratory mechanisms. Analogous to stochastic optimization algorithms such as Simulated Annealing, occasionally letting go and engaging in "exploratory trials" can lead to unexpected breakthroughs. Life's "trial-and-error" and serendipitous discoveries often arise from this nonlinear, random exploration.

Through the maze-search analogy, we can see that different life stages and environmental conditions call for different decision-making strategies. Early on, broad exploration is needed to build a cognitive foundation; in the mid-stage, deep specialization is required to accumulate core competencies; at critical moments, heuristic judgment—combined with experience and intuition—guides wise decisions; and when necessary, one must accept uncertainty and random exploration, embracing change and opportunity.

This analogy is not only technical but also offers insights into life cognition. The art of choice is neither mere persistence nor blind flexibility; it is the dynamic adjustment of strategy according to one's environment and cognitive state, responding flexibly to complex situations. Understanding this allows us to better navigate life's "maze-like robot," step by step finding our own exit (Fig. 5).

**Fig. 5** Cognition Determines the Path: Establishing an Appropriate Judgment System Is Crucial

## 5 Cognition Determines the Path—How to Build Your Judgment System

The complexity of making choices largely stems from the limitations of our cognition and the incompleteness of information. Cognitive resources themselves are scarce, yet we live in a world overflowing with information and rapid changes. Establishing an effective judgment system in such an environment has become a challenge that everyone must confront. As Zhang Yiming once pointed out, the key to accomplishing something lies in one's understanding of it. In other words, cognition determines the path, shapes the quality of decisions, and ultimately directs the course of the future.

So how do we construct such a cognitive model? First, a cognitive model must be dynamically updated. We cannot treat our cognition as a fixed truth; instead, we must continuously absorb new knowledge and embrace new information. This is especially crucial in today's era, where technological and market changes occur at breakneck speed and past experiences that were once effective may become obsolete almost instantly. Continuous learning and expanding the boundaries of our cognition are fundamental to maintaining sharp judgment (Fig. 6).

Second, cognitive diversity is equally crucial. A perspective confined to a single domain is often limited and prone to the "frog in the well" dilemma. Engaging in cross-disciplinary learning and integrating ideas from different fields can spark innovative thinking and broaden the dimensions of judgment. Much like "cross-boundary integration" in entrepreneurship, this approach allows us to view problems from multiple angles, avoid cognitive biases, and improve the quality of decision-making.

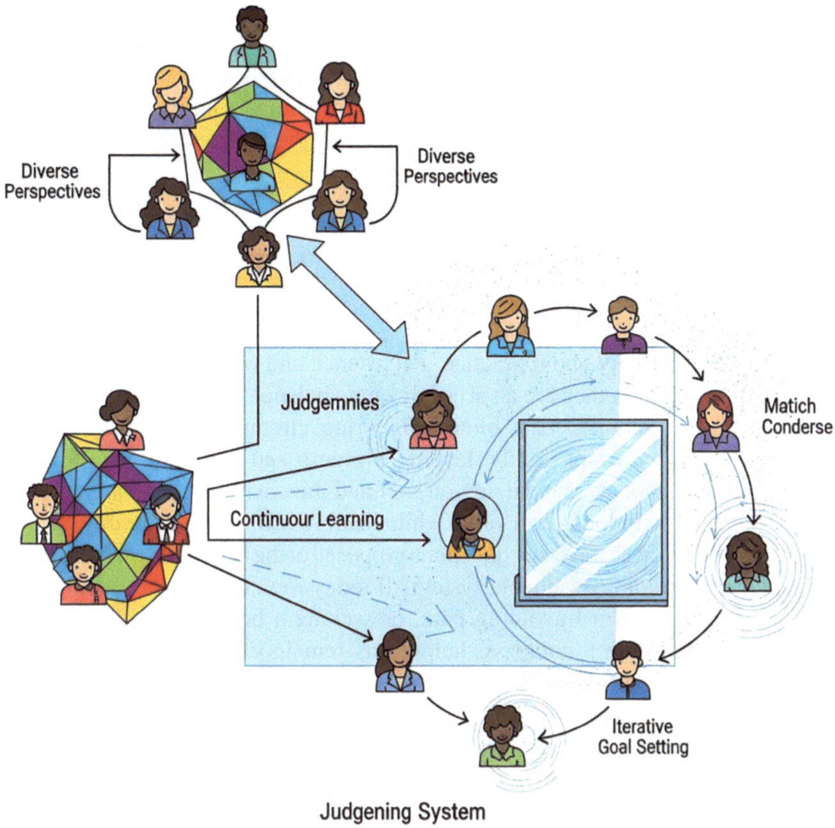


**Fig. 6** Cognition Determines the Path: Establishing a Well-Defined Judgment System Is Crucial

Furthermore, regular reflection and review are essential components in building a cognitive model. Without reflection, actions tend to fall into inertia, repeating past mistakes. By reviewing previous decisions, we can not only summarize lessons learned but also correct cognitive biases and adjust future decision-making directions. This habit of reflection serves as an accelerator for enhancing cognitive wisdom.

Additionally, setting "experimental goals" rather than one-time terminal goals is a practical method for establishing a judgment system. The real world is complex and ever-changing, and grand objectives are rarely achievable all at once; attempting to do so can easily lead to frustration. Applying a concept similar to the "Minimum Viable Product" (MVP) in entrepreneurship, goals can be broken down into small, short-term executable targets, allowing rapid trial-and-error and adjustment. This both accumulates experience and enables flexible responses to external changes. Such "iterative thinking" makes our choices more scientific and resilient.

By continuously updating knowledge, incorporating diverse inputs, reflecting and reviewing, and iterating on goals, we construct a highly adaptive cognitive model.

This model not only helps us make more accurate judgments about the present situation but also provides strategies for coping with future uncertainties. It allows us to make more mature and wiser decisions between "persistence" and "adaptation."

In summary, cognition forms the foundation of choice. Only by establishing a scientifically sound judgment system can we navigate the complex and ever-changing maze of life, progressing further and more securely.

## 6 Conclusion

Choice is both an ability and a practice. Persistence and adaptation are not simply opposing forces; rather, they are an art of dynamic balance in a constantly changing environment. We cannot persist blindly, ignoring circumstances and situational changes, nor can we adapt lightly, lacking firmness and direction. Truly mature decision-making involves recognizing oneself and the environment clearly, making choices that align with long-term value while flexibly responding to reality.

Here, we return to the three key questions proposed at the beginning of this chapter: Is this endeavor building a valuable system? If today were the first day, would I still choose to pursue it? Am I avoiding pain, or seeking a better opportunity? These three questions act like a compass, helping us remain clear-headed and rational amid complex and overwhelming choices. They are not rigid judgment rules but a framework guiding us to clarify our true intentions and weigh pros and cons.

It is this rationality and self-reflection that enable us to rise above emotional interference, escape the trap of sunk costs, and ultimately form a stable yet flexible "Persistence vs. Adaptation" mechanism. It allows us to move forward through the fog, not stalling due to uncertainty, nor giving up easily in temporary difficulties.

A mature life does not consist of making perfect choices, but of maintaining forward momentum and inner confidence even in the face of the unknown and risks. The essence of choice lies in the process itself—a discipline of cognition, patience, and adaptive wisdom. Only in this way can we continue to explore, grow, and ultimately reach the bright horizon that belongs to us.

## Further Reading

1. D. Kahneman, *Thinking, Fast and Slow*, Farrar, Straus and Giroux, 2011.
2. X. Cao, *Modern Business Management*, Palgrave Macmillan, 2025.
3. C. Heath and D. Heath, *Decisive: How to Make Better Choices in Life and Work*, Crown Business, 2013.
4. X. Cao, *Strategic Management and Organizational Development*, Springer, 2025.
5. J. March, "Exploration and exploitation in organizational learning," *Organization Science*, vol. 2, no. 1, pp. 71–87, 1991.
6. D. Ariely, *Predictably Irrational: The Hidden Forces That Shape Our Decisions*, HarperCollins, 2008.

7. J. Collins, *Good to Great*, Harper Business, 2001.
8. C. Christensen, *How Will You Measure Your Life?*, Harper Business, 2012.
9. N. Taleb, *The Black Swan: The Impact of the Highly Improbable*, Random House, 2007.
10. P. Drucker, *Managing for Results*, Harper & Row, 1964.
11. S. Li, *Haircutting Robots*, Switzerland: Springer, 2025.

## Further Reading

# Chapter 16
# The Wisdom of Maritime Civilization—Complementary Balance and the Survival Laws of Modern Entrepreneurial Teams

## 1 Introduction

Imagine the ancient Aegean Sea—a vast expanse of shimmering blue waters dotted with countless islands. The inhabitants of these islands did not serve a single monarch, nor did they possess the kind of wide, flat mainland territories that could easily be conquered. They navigated their modest boats through the sea breeze, journeying from one island to another for fair and voluntary trade. On one island, you might buy olive oil; on another, sell pottery. And if a merchant attempted deceit or offered an unfair price, you could simply sail to the next island—for choices were everywhere.

Each island stood as an independent, well-defended fortress. Even the mightiest city-state found it difficult to impose its will by force or to trample another island underfoot. It was within this unique geographical context that a maritime civilization arose—one that emphasized market economy and democracy, founded upon a naturally evolved system of complementary balance and mutual restraint (Fig. 1).

This relationship bears a striking resemblance to the modern business world—particularly to the ecosystem of startup companies. Entrepreneurship demands the deep participation and collaboration of numerous individuals: from technology development to marketing, from fundraising to daily operations. Every link in this chain is indispensable. Yet, if these key roles lack effective complementary balance, one side may easily overwhelm another, leading to dysfunction within the team—and even the risk of weaker groups being marginalized or eliminated.

In this chapter, we will explore the management wisdom embedded in ancient Greek maritime civilization—the philosophy of mutual complementarity and restraint—and apply it to the structure and management of modern entrepreneurial teams. Our goal is to provide entrepreneurs with a practical and resilient set of survival principles that ensure the healthy development and lasting success of their ventures.



S. Li, *Bridging the Innovation Gap*, Innovation, Technology, and Knowledge Management, https://doi.org/10.1007/978-3-032-22652-5_16

**Fig. 1** The ancient Aegean Sea—vast and glimmering, scattered with countless islands where the islanders engaged in fair and equal trade

## 2 Learning Management Wisdom from the Waves of Ancient Greece: How Geography Shapes Civilization

Geographical environment is often the decisive force that shapes the character of a civilization. When we look at ancient Greece, we find it fundamentally different from its contemporary land-based civilizations. For instance, in the vast plains of China or along the fertile banks of the Nile in ancient Egypt, the abundance of arable land made cultivation easy—but also made these regions easy to conquer and unify. Powerful central governments could thus arise, ruling over massive populations and resources through military might, administrative decrees, and rigid hierarchies. Under this "continental mindset," power tended to be highly centralized, and individuals, when facing the machinery of the state, often lacked bargaining power—let alone the right to refuse coercion (Fig. 2).

However, the picture of ancient Greece was entirely different. The Aegean Sea, scattered with countless islands, naturally dispersed its population into numerous relatively independent communities. The sea itself served both as a barrier and a bridge, separating yet connecting these societies. This geographic fragmentation made it nearly impossible for any single city-state to dominate the entire Greek world through sheer military force. Even a militarily superior polis could not easily march across the waters as one might across plains, to destroy or enslave other islands. The islands' defensible terrain granted each community strong autonomy and resilience—even when facing powerful forces, they retained both the courage and the right to say "no."

For this reason, when the inhabitants of different islands needed to exchange resources, they had to rely on principles of equality rather than coercion. Everyone

**Fig. 2** The geographical environment of ancient Greece shaped the unique characteristics of its civilization

had multiple choices: if one trader attempted deceit or offered unfair terms, another trader could simply turn to the next island or partner. This freedom to choose and the right to refuse became a natural force of balance, fostering the early growth of a market economy.

Politically, since power could not be easily centralized, each city-state tended to develop democratic and consultative mechanisms that allowed citizens to participate in decision-making—thus avoiding the tyranny of a few. In this sense, the maritime geography of ancient Greece, by granting individuals and communities a high degree of independence and freedom of choice, unknowingly created a primitive model of complementary balance, which laid the groundwork for its market economy and democratic ideals.

This voluntary exchange—rooted in equality and choice—stood in stark contrast to the top-down coercive systems common in continental civilizations. It also offers profound insights for understanding today's business world, particularly the operation of modern startup teams.

## 3 The "Island" Ecology of Startup Teams: Division of Roles and the Risk of Imbalance

Bringing the concept of the Greek "islands" into the context of modern startups reveals an astonishing parallel. A startup company is not a monolithic entity, but rather a collection of individuals and departments—each with distinct expertise and indispensable importance—functioning like islands of specialized purpose, together supporting the voyage of the company's ship.

Imagine a typical startup team:

Technical personnel: They are the core *builders* and *engineers* of the company, responsible for product development, iteration, and maintenance—the very hull and engine of the ship.
Managers: They are the *captains* and *navigators*, charged with strategic planning, resource allocation, and team coordination, ensuring the ship sails in the right direction.
Financiers: They are the *suppliers of fuel*, responsible for liaising with investors and providing the financial sustenance that keeps the voyage ongoing.
Operations personnel: They are the *sailors* and *deck officers*, handling daily maintenance, user experience optimization, and community management—ensuring smooth sailing and passenger comfort.
Marketing personnel: They are the *lighthouse keepers* and *harbor heralds*, driving brand promotion, user acquisition, and market analysis—guiding the ship toward the most prosperous ports.
Financial officers: They are the *accountants* and *risk guardians*, overseeing capital management, cost control, and compliance—ensuring the balance of accounts and the safety of the voyage (Fig. 3).

These roles, though independent, are also tightly interconnected—each indispensable to the company's overall function. Every role holds responsibility for a vital part of the organization's operations, like structural pillars supporting a shared edifice. Yet this "island-like" ecology of division also carries an inherent risk of imbalance. Without effective mechanisms of complementary balance, one "island" may dominate others—due to temporary strategic importance or positional power—forcing others into submission and creating a hierarchy where the weaker parties risk marginalization or elimination.

One of the most common forms of imbalance is finance-driven dominance. In the early stages of a startup, capital is the company's lifeline. Financing personnel, eager to secure investment, may overpromise product capabilities or submit to investors' short-term return expectations, placing enormous pressure on the technical team to deliver unrealistic results—sometimes even forcing them to adopt low-quality or unsustainable technical solutions. Once funding is obtained, financiers' voices may grow disproportionately loud, while the influence of the technical team diminishes, leaving them to compromise. Over time, this erodes the company's technological foundation and can trigger the loss of key engineering talent.

Another frequent issue is sales- or market-driven imbalance. When market teams, under pressure to hit sales targets or rapidly expand the user base, push for constant product adjustments or demand "customized" features that stray from the company's core vision, tension arises. If management sides excessively with the sales department—simply because it brings in visible revenue—while dismissing the technical team's concerns about long-term sustainability or technical debt, the result is burnout, creative stagnation, and eventual product dilution. In this "sellers over shipbuilders"

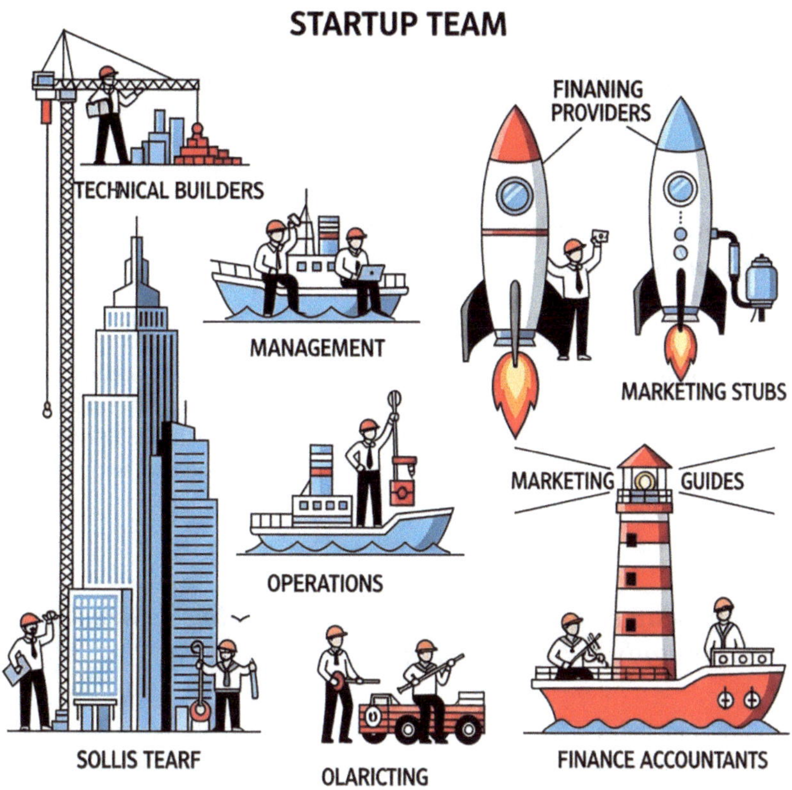


**Fig. 3** The division of roles and collaboration within a startup team

scenario, the ship may move faster temporarily, but it soon loses direction—and its identity.

A third pattern, management-centered imbalance, is also common. When leadership, especially the CEO, exercises excessive centralization—making decisions based solely on personal experience or preference, without adequately consulting domain experts—disaster often follows. For instance, a non-technical manager who dictates the system architecture, or a financial controller who excessively restricts R&D spending, can halt progress entirely. In such environments, departments lose autonomy and invention energy, professional expertise is undervalued, and the team's overall efficiency and morale deteriorate, leading to high turnover.

Ultimately, the victims of imbalance are often those in structurally weaker positions. The concern—*"Will the engineers be pushed out?"*—is a quintessential example of this risk. In many startups, especially those led by non-technical founders, the technical department is viewed as a "cost center" rather than a profit driver. When financial pressure mounts or market competition intensifies, engineers are often the first to face "optimization." Without mechanisms to voice their value or to counterbalance external demands, they become vulnerable—marginalized, replaced, or driven out. The stagnation of product invention and eventual company decline become inevitable consequences.

A team without complementary balance is like a ship where only the bow surges forward while the stern teeters on collapse—sooner or later, it will sink.

## 4 Building a "Maritime Order" for Startups: The Practice of Complementary Balance

Recognizing the risks of imbalance helps us understand how to construct within startups a form of "maritime order"—much like that of ancient Greek civilization—a system of effective complementary balance. This doesn't mean deliberately creating conflict, but rather designing structures, processes, and culture that enable the various "islands" of the organization to both restrain and reinforce one another, maintaining a healthy and dynamic equilibrium.

### *4.1 Clarifying Boundaries and Empowering Roles: Granting Sovereignty to Each "Island"*

To achieve complementary balance, one must first—much like how ancient Greece defined the boundaries of its islands—clearly delineate the responsibilities and decision-making powers of each functional module. Startups should invest early in crafting precise role descriptions, defining each position's core duties, key performance indicators (KPIs), and areas of final decision authority.

This is where the principle of ownership comes into play. Each department head—whether the CTO, marketing director, or finance manager—should act as the sovereign of their own "island," possessing full ownership and final decision rights within their domain of expertise. This ownership is not autocracy, but rather a recognition of professional authority: in specialized matters, their judgment should carry priority, and after sufficient consultation, they should hold the final say. For instance, technical architecture should be led by engineers, while market strategy should be defined by marketing experts.

This sovereignty implies trust and delegation. Leaders must avoid micromanagement and allow experts to do what they do best. Even in the face of disagreements, professional judgment should be respected first. A well-known example is Google's *"20% Time"* policy, which empowered engineers to pursue independent projects—giving rise to inventions like Gmail and Google Maps. Such empowerment not only improves efficiency but also gives each "island" the capacity to resist external overreach. Only when every island has genuine sovereignty can diverse voices coexist and prevent domination by any single faction.

## 4.2 Building Multidimensional Communication and Collaboration Mechanisms: Constructing "Bridges Between Islands"

Independent sovereignty is vital—but without connection, islands become isolated. Thus, establishing open, transparent, and efficient communication and collaboration mechanisms is akin to building bridges between islands, enabling information flow and mutual oversight.

First, regular cross-departmental meetings are essential. These should not merely be top-down reporting sessions, but spaces for open dialogue, challenge-sharing, and feedback. For example, the technical team should understand the sales obstacles faced by the marketing team, while the marketers should appreciate the engineering challenges behind complex features. Only when every team comprehends the others' pain points can the organization make holistic decisions instead of fragmented ones.

Second, project-based collaboration fosters integration. For each major initiative—product launch, marketing campaign, or user growth effort—form cross-functional teams combining technology, marketing, operations, and more. These collaborations naturally produce friction, but through continual communication and compromise, true complementarity emerges. For instance, when engineers explain the technical limitations of a feature, marketers can adjust expectations—and vice versa. Such collaboration minimizes information asymmetry and prevents teams from "building ships in isolation."

Informal communication is equally crucial. Encouraging casual conversations, social activities, or team-building events strengthens empathy and trust across departments. When colleagues develop personal rapport, they become more open to listening—even to critique—in a constructive spirit.

Finally, decision transparency is indispensable. Major decisions and their rationales should be visible to all relevant parties. Even if one team or individual has final authority, others must understand *why*. For example, if the finance department decides to reduce a project's budget, they should explain the data and reasoning behind it rather than simply issuing an order. This transparency curbs power abuse and encourages collective accountability. Spotify's "Squads" and "Tribes" model exemplifies this—combining small-team autonomy with large-scale coordination, achieving both flexibility and coherence through transparent collaboration (Fig. 4).

## 4.3 Equity and Incentive Design: Building a "Community of Interests"

If the complementary balance in ancient Greece was grounded in geographic independence and the freedom of choice, then in a modern startup, binding all core members tightly together on the same "ship"—making them a true community of shared interests—is the fundamental guarantee of complementary balance. When

**Fig. 4** In team role division, it is essential to clarify each role's responsibilities, rights, boundaries, and empowerment. Each role functions like an "island," and each island should be granted a certain degree of sovereignty. This sovereignty does not imply complete independence; by building "bridges between islands," we establish multidimensional communication and collaboration mechanisms to achieve coordination among different roles

each "island's" residents fully understand that their own fate is inseparable from the course of the entire ship, they naturally restrain one another and collectively maintain the ship's health.

At the heart of this is the art of founder equity allocation. In the early stages, equity among founders should reflect each individual's contribution, risk undertaken, and future value creation. Avoid letting any one founder dominate or disproportionately favor a single role. A fair equity structure, established from the outset, sets the tone for complementary balance, motivating each core founder to protect the company's long-term interests while restraining short-term opportunistic behavior.

Equally crucial is an Employee Stock Ownership Plan (ESOP). By granting core employees—and ideally all employees—a stake in the company, even technical staff holding significant equity become more than mere wage earners; they become

**Fig. 5** By designing equity and incentive mechanisms, a community of shared interests is built, aligning everyone's stakes on the same "ship" and thereby fostering cohesion

"minority shareholders." This ownership incentivizes them to drive technical invention, maintain product quality, and exercise influence to counteract short-term pressures that could harm the company's long-term prospects—for example, requests to sacrifice product integrity for immediate revenue. In this way, they gain enhanced voice and authority within the team (Fig. 5).

Moreover, performance evaluation and incentive mechanisms should be carefully designed. They should not focus solely on individual or departmental performance but also encourage cross-departmental collaboration and invention. For example, team collaboration rewards can be established, or a portion of performance metrics can be tied to the company's overall results, guiding all members to focus on the company's holistic development. Many technology companies in Silicon Valley have been able to attract and retain top talent largely because they provided substantial early-stage equity incentives to core employees. This not only generated wealth effects but, more importantly, turned employees into true owners of the company, endowing them with intrinsic balancing power.

## *4.4 The Role of Leaders: The Art of Balance*

In the "oceanic order" of a startup team, leaders—especially founders or CEOs—serve as the ultimate guardians and guides of the complementary balance mechanism. They are no longer commanding dictators but act as fair arbitrators and wise helmsmen, ensuring that all forces coexist harmoniously and operate effectively.

**Fig. 6** In a startup team, the founder or CEO serves as the ultimate guardian and guiding force of the complementary balance mechanism. They must coordinate and balance all parties, minimize internal friction, and optimize overall value

First, leaders must avoid bias and favoritism. They cannot listen exclusively to the opinions of a dominant department; instead, they must gain a comprehensive understanding of all perspectives and challenges. This requires actively listening to the voices of all "islands"—technology, marketing, operations, finance—and deeply understanding each one's position and concerns (Fig. 6).

Secondly, leaders need to establish fair decision-making processes. When conflicts or disagreements arise between departments that cannot be easily reconciled, leaders must intervene and make impartial judgments. These decisions should not be based on personal preferences or favoritism toward any department, but on facts, data, and the company's long-term best interests. Implementing clear dispute resolution mechanisms—such as regular executive coordination meetings or an independent arbitration panel—can effectively reduce internal friction.

Moreover, leaders should encourage constructive conflict. A healthy team is not one without disagreements, but one that treats conflict as an opportunity to identify problems and optimize solutions rather than as internal warfare. Leaders need to foster a culture where differing opinions can clash and be discussed openly, guiding team members to focus on problem-solving rather than blaming each other. For example, Elon Musk encourages engineers at SpaceX and Tesla to point out problems directly, even challenging his own decisions when necessary.

Finally, and most importantly, leaders must have—and consistently uphold—a clear long-term vision. This vision acts as the North Star, aligning short-term decisions and preventing any department from pursuing immediate gains at the expense of the company's long-term development. Steve Jobs' leadership at Apple exemplifies this principle: he skillfully balanced the complexity of technical implementation with urgent market demands, guiding product and engineering teams to ensure Apple's offerings were both innovative and market-aligned. A leader's fairness, wisdom, and foresight are the ballast that keeps the team's complementary balance mechanism stable and effective.

## 5 Beware of "Continental Thinking" in Startup Teams

While building a "marine order" is critical in startup teams, it is equally important to guard against the encroachment of "continental thinking." This mindset—overemphasizing individual heroism or centralized power—is the greatest threat to complementary balance and often pushes startups toward failure.

The most typical manifestation is founder dictatorship. Some founders, especially after achieving initial success, may become overly confident, believing they are infallible. They refuse to accept team input and may suppress dissent, thinking that everything must be decided solely by themselves. Such a "one-person autocracy" may barely sustain a small company with relatively simple problems, but as the company grows and faces more complex markets and technological challenges, decision-making inevitably suffers. In such a high-pressure environment, the team loses its innovative vitality, and top talent eventually leaves because they cannot thrive in a space where their expertise is ignored or suppressed.

Equally dangerous is the dominance of a single department. For example, in a technology-driven company, if the tech department becomes too powerful and disregards market and operational needs, clinging to a "technology above all" ideology, the product may drift from market realities, making it difficult to achieve a viable business model. Conversely, if the sales or marketing department dominates, prioritizing short-term revenue over product quality, they may compel the tech team to build unsustainable "castles in the air," ultimately damaging the company's reputation and causing user loss. These scenarios exemplify "continental thinking" at the departmental level—one department pursues its own interests and attempts to impose power over others rather than seeking the overall optimal solution. Numerous startup failures demonstrate that internal power struggles, fractured core teams, or the marginalization of a critical department are common reasons for decline.

Another severe consequence of continental thinking is the lack of exit mechanisms, leading to talent loss and a vicious cycle. Ancient Greek merchants maintained equality partly because they always had "many choices"—if one island's trade was unfair, they could move to another. In a startup team without complementary balance, if technical personnel feel undervalued, ignored, or unheard, and no internal mechanisms exist to address these issues, they perceive they have "nowhere to go" and may ultimately leave.

The loss of core talent further weakens that "island," putting it at a disadvantage in future checks and balances, creating a vicious cycle. For instance, if a core technical team departs, the company loses its most valuable invention engine. New product development stalls, and existing product maintenance may suffer. In the startup ecosystem, top talent has options—they will not tolerate an unhealthy team culture or remain in an environment where they cannot realize their potential. Talent attrition not only increases direct recruitment costs but also negatively impacts morale, culture, and long-term development. Recognizing and preventing this "continental thinking" is essential for successfully establishing a sustainable "marine order" in a startup.

## 6 Toward a "New Marine Civilization": Continuous Self-Evolution

In today's complex and rapidly changing market, startups are like ships navigating turbulent seas. The complementary balance of a "marine order" is not a static, one-time setup; it must continuously learn and adapt as the company evolves and the market environment shifts. Only through ongoing adjustment can the team maintain flexibility and vitality, evolving into a forward-looking "new marine civilization."

First is learning and adaptation (Fig. 7). At different stages of development, a startup's focus inevitably shifts. During the prototype phase, technology often takes priority, and the R&D team may wield more influence and resources. Once the product enters the market, marketing and operations gain prominence, requiring greater decision-making authority and resources. As the company grows and enters maturity, financial management, compliance, and organizational complexity increase, and the influence of management and finance naturally rises. Therefore, the balance of power and points of internal checks and balances must be dynamically adjusted according to the company's stage. Similarly, changes in the external environment—such as intensified market competition, technological invention, or evolving user needs—require continuous recalibration of internal balances. A successful startup team should be like a nimble sailboat, adjusting its sails according to the wind and currents rather than rigidly sticking to a fixed course.

Second is the importance of a continuous internal reflection mechanism. Teams should regularly conduct retrospectives to assess whether current collaboration patterns and power structures remain effective. For example, "health check" meetings can allow departments to anonymously provide feedback on cross-departmental challenges and imbalances. This mechanism helps identify and resolve issues before they escalate into major crises. When a department gains excessive influence or a bottleneck emerges, the team can collectively explore solutions, reallocate resources, or adjust workflows. This self-evolving capability is key to maintaining the long-term effectiveness of a complementary balance mechanism.

Ultimately, the success of a startup team lies in cultivating a "citizen of the ocean" spirit among all members. At its core, this spirit emphasizes recognizing one's own importance while respecting the independence and contributions of others, fostering shared governance and outcomes.

This entails:

**Fig. 7** The team must collaborate closely, exploring ways to continuously evolve and adapt in a dynamic market environment

Ownership mindset: Encourage each member to think and act as if they are the "owner" of the company, focusing not only on their own responsibilities but also on the long-term interests and overall success of the organization.

Empathy and perspective-taking: Team members from different departments should strive to understand each other's positions and challenges. Engineers need to appreciate the pressures faced by marketing staff in customer interactions, while marketers should grasp the technical debts and complexities engineers encounter. Such understanding forms the foundation for effective communication and collaboration.

Shared success and accountability: Foster a culture of shared risk and shared rewards. When the company succeeds, all team members should feel recognized and celebrate together; when setbacks occur, they face them collectively rather than blaming one another.

Long-term orientation: Guide team members to consider issues from the company's broader and long-term perspective, rather than focusing solely on short-term departmental gains. When everyone prioritizes the company's sustained success, constructive constraints and compromises naturally emerge for the collective good.

## 7 Conclusion

The journey of entrepreneurship is full of unknowns and storms. No fixed formula guarantees success, yet the "complementary checks and balances" wisdom from ancient Greek maritime civilization offers a solid management anchor. It reminds us that a healthy startup team is neither dominated by a single strong force nor ruled by one department over others. Instead, it is an ecosystem of independent yet interdependent "islands," each with unique, irreplaceable value. Through clear boundaries, open communication, fair mechanisms, and just leadership, forces can mutually restrain and promote one another, ultimately forming a strong and harmonious collective power.

Just as the ancient Greeks relied on mutual trust and choice to navigate prosperous trade routes across turbulent seas, modern entrepreneurs must respect the independence and value of every team member. By building a truly complementary and balanced internal environment, the startup ship can ride the winds and waves toward success. The future belongs to those who can master the wisdom of "maritime civilization" and establish this subtle yet powerful equilibrium within their teams. Do you also agree that, in today's fast-changing entrepreneurial environment, this ancient-inspired art of balance is more crucial than ever?

## Further Reading


1. J. Katzenbach and D. Smith, *The Wisdom of Teams: Creating the High-Performance Organization*, HarperBusiness, 2005.
2. H. Mintzberg, *Managing*, Berrett-Koehler, 2009.
3. X. Cao, *Strategic Management and Organizational Development*, Springer, 2025.
4. R. E. Freeman, *Strategic Management: A Stakeholder Approach*, Pitman, 1984.
5. M. Tushman and C. O'Reilly, *Lead and Disrupt: How to Solve the Innovator's Dilemma*, Stanford Business Books, 2016.
6. L. Gratton, *The Shift: The Future of Work is Already Here*, HarperCollins, 2011.
7. P. Kotler and K. L. Keller, *Marketing Management*, 16th ed., Pearson, 2022.
8. A. Edmondson, *Teaming: How Organizations Learn, Innovate, and Compete in the Knowledge Economy*, Jossey-Bass, 2012.
9. X. Cao, *Modern Business Management*, Palgrave Macmillan, 2025.
10. D. Ulrich, *HR from the Outside In: Six Competencies for the Future of Human Resources*, McGraw-Hill, 2012.

# Chapter 17
# The Death of the Neanderthals: Why Strength and Intelligence Could Not Save Them

## 1 Introduction

In the long evolutionary history of humanity, Neanderthals once dominated Europe and West Asia. With their robust physiques, extensive hunting experience, and relatively large brain capacities, this ancient human group survived tenaciously through harsh ice ages. In fact, compared to modern humans, Neanderthals possessed stronger bodies and even larger brains. Yet, around forty thousand years ago, they mysteriously vanished from the Earth. Why did such a seemingly formidable and highly adaptable population ultimately become extinct? This question has captivated both scientists and the general public alike.

In this chapter, we attempt to analyze the causes behind the extinction of the Neanderthals through a study of their lives, while also reflecting on what lessons modern society can draw about surviving and thriving in an era of rapid change and complex information environments.

## 2 The Strong and Intelligent Neanderthals

Around 400,000 years ago, Neanderthals, as a branch of ancient humans, gradually migrated from their African origins to Europe and West Asia. They thrived during prolonged glacial periods, adapting to extreme cold climates and harsh natural environments. Compared with contemporary Homo sapiens, Neanderthals were particularly notable for their size and strength. Archaeological research indicates that the average adult Neanderthal stood between 160 and 170 centimeters tall, with males potentially even taller. Their skeletons were thick, muscles well-developed, and body weight ranged from 70 to 90 kilograms—far exceeding that of contemporary modern humans. Such a physique gave them a clear advantage in hunting large game, with



S. Li, *Bridging the Innovation Gap*, Innovation, Technology, and Knowledge Management, https://doi.org/10.1007/978-3-032-22652-5_17

powerful musculature helping them dominate prey and effectively withstand attacks from predators and the icy conditions of their environment.

Neanderthals' skulls were also distinct: they had low foreheads, wide and pronounced brow ridges, and broad nasal cavities. These anatomical features are believed to be adaptations to cold climates, aiding in warming inhaled air. Notably, Neanderthals had an average brain volume of approximately 1500 milliliters, slightly larger than the modern human average of about 1350 milliliters. Traditionally, brain size has been considered an indicator of intelligence, leading some to speculate that Neanderthals' cognitive abilities might have even surpassed those of modern humans. However, brain volume alone is not the definitive measure—brain structure and functional complexity are far more critical. Even so, this evidence underscores that Neanderthals were far from "primitive" in terms of cognition.

Moreover, Neanderthals exhibited rich and diverse cultural behaviors. They were representatives of the Mousterian culture, known for its intricate and sophisticated stone tools. Neanderthals manufactured and used a wide variety of tools, including scrapers, drills, and hand axes. These implements were employed not only for hunting and butchering animals but also for skinning, woodworking, and other daily activities. Archaeological reconstructions and experimental studies have shown that creating these tools required considerable skill and planning, demonstrating their mastery of complex technical craftsmanship.

Beyond stone tools, Neanderthals also harnessed fire, using it for warmth, cooking, and even driving away predators—significantly improving their quality of life and survival odds. Archaeological evidence further indicates that they could construct simple shelters, using animal hides and wood to create temporary encampments that offered protection from the elements.(Fig. 17.1)

Even more surprisingly, some research suggests that Neanderthals may have possessed rudimentary language capabilities. While their linguistic systems were likely not as complex as those of modern humans, they appear to have had some capacity for symbolic communication. Simple symbols and recurring patterns found in cave art hint at the embryonic stages of cultural and informational transmission.

At some archaeological sites, researchers have also uncovered intentionally arranged bones and stone tools, which may represent ritual behaviors or symbolic cultural practices. Simple symbols and recurring patterns found on cave walls, though rudimentary, provide crucial clues to early human cultural transmission. These findings indicate that Neanderthals already had a certain foundation in social organization and cultural continuity, far from being completely "primitive."

In summary, Neanderthals possessed formidable survival capabilities in terms of physical strength, technological skill, and social life. In the cold and harsh conditions of the Ice Age, they were able to live and reproduce over long periods, continuously adapting to environmental changes, becoming top predators and highly adapted inhabitants of their regions. By all logic, they should have been able to sustain their population, and even grow stronger over evolutionary time, becoming a significant branch in human development.

However, in reality, Neanderthals mysteriously disappeared around 40,000 years ago, raising questions among scientists. Did this once-powerful ancient human group

**Fig. 17.1** Around 400,000 years ago, Neanderthals lived across Europe and West Asia. The harsh natural conditions shaped both their robust physiques and their intelligent minds

go extinct due to low intelligence or technological backwardness? The answer is clearly no. Modern research shows that Neanderthals were comparable to modern Homo sapiens in many respects; their extinction inevitably involved more complex social, cultural, and environmental factors. Understanding these factors is crucial not only for unraveling the mysteries of human evolutionary history but also for gaining insights into how modern society can navigate rapid change and thrive in a complex information and knowledge environment.

## 3 Homo Sapiens and Neanderthals: A Contest of Information Sharing

Modern Homo sapiens began leaving Africa around 50,000 years ago, entering Europe and West Asia, where they coexisted for a considerable period with Neanderthals, who had already been living there for hundreds of thousands of years. Archaeological evidence shows that in some regions, the two species even shared habitation to some degree. More importantly, advances in modern genetic sequencing have allowed us to glimpse the relationship between these two ancient humans. Scientists analyzing the genomes of contemporary non-African populations have been surprised to find that approximately 1% to 4% of their genetic material derives from Neanderthals. This discovery indicates that interactions between Homo sapiens and Neanderthals were not merely superficial—they exchanged genes, reflecting a degree of biological mixing. This genetic exchange highlights a certain level of interaction between the species and marks an indelible imprint of Neanderthals in the gene pool.

However, despite genetic overlap, Homo sapiens and Neanderthals exhibited strikingly different cultural and technological patterns. Archaeological evidence clearly demonstrates this contrast. Neanderthal toolkits remained relatively static over long periods, with little significant invention. In contrast, modern humans exhibited remarkable cultural and technological diversity and creativity. Homo sapiens invented finer and more varied stone tools, such as sewing needles, fishhooks, and complex hunting weapons; they also created ornaments, beads, and items symbolizing status and belief, and even painted elaborate cave art expressing their understanding of nature, society, and the spiritual world. These cultural and technological leaps were more than mere inventions in tools—they reflected profound changes in human cognition and social structures.

What, then, allowed modern humans to ultimately prevail in this evolutionary contest? Why did seemingly stronger and more experienced Neanderthals gradually disappear, while the apparently "weaker" Homo sapiens thrived?

Among the many factors, one core answer stands out—the capacity for information sharing and cultural transmission.

In archaeology, scholars increasingly recognize that the long-term stagnation of Neanderthal culture and technology was not due to a lack of intelligence but rather a lack of efficient knowledge exchange and invention mechanisms. Over hundreds of thousands of years, Neanderthal cultural forms and tool technologies changed very little. Invention stagnated, and breakthrough technological progress was rare. This suggests that they struggled to effectively transmit existing skills and knowledge to larger groups and had difficulty accumulating and passing down techniques to subsequent generations, limiting the ongoing development and advancement of their technology.

In contrast, modern humans possessed highly developed language systems, symbolic expression abilities, and complex social structures. Through verbal communication, they could effectively convey information—not just through direct imitation, but also through abstract concepts and planning. Social networks among Homo sapiens were far more developed than those of Neanderthals, with frequent and diverse interactions between different groups. Knowledge could spread rapidly and be continually improved across communities. Information transfer extended beyond one-on-one interactions, encompassing group cooperation, cultural rituals, and educational transmission.(Fig. 17.2)

From a more abstract perspective, information and skills are essentially nonrivalrous resources. Unlike material resources, sharing information does not deplete it; in fact, it may increase in value through communication and feedback. To illustrate, consider a simple example (from a story told by my physics professor during a university course at Hefei University of Technology in 2002): If you and I each have an apple, giving your apple to me means you lose it. But if you and I each possess a skill or knowledge, exchanging them does not diminish either of our abilities; I still retain my skill, you retain yours, and we both gain the other's skill. Through sharing and interaction, the total amount of skills increases, collective intelligence accumulates, and overall societal capability is enhanced.

**Fig. 17.2** Compared to Neanderthals, Homo sapiens had no clear advantage in intelligence or physical strength. However, one crucial difference was that Homo sapiens were far more adept at communication than Neanderthals. This seemingly minor distinction provided a tremendous advantage, allowing knowledge and information to be widely replicated and transmitted

Neanderthals lacked such efficient mechanisms for communication and knowledge transmission, which led to technological stagnation. Although they possessed robust physiques and a certain degree of social cooperation, their inability to effectively share and accumulate information meant that each generation often had to "reinvent the wheel," unable to rapidly build upon the experiences of their predecessors. This lack of sustained invention limited their competitiveness and adaptability in terms of technology.

In contrast, modern Homo sapiens leveraged language and complex social structures to construct extensive information networks. The rapid accumulation and transmission of knowledge enabled continuous technological invention and cultural enrichment. This not only accelerated the optimization of survival skills but also enhanced Homo sapiens' ability to adapt to environmental changes and societal challenges. It was precisely this efficient information sharing and cultural transmission that proved to be the decisive factor in their evolutionary success.

The contest between Neanderthals and modern humans was thus not merely a battle of strength and intelligence but a competition of information and cultural transmission capabilities. The advantage of Homo sapiens lay in their superior mechanisms for sharing knowledge, allowing them to accumulate and innovate rapidly, while the extinction of Neanderthals directly reflected their insufficient communication and transmission systems. This historical lesson remains profoundly relevant to contemporary society.

## 4 Archaeological Evidence: Differences in Cultural Transmission and Technological Invention

Across numerous archaeological sites in Europe and West Asia, scientists can clearly distinguish two distinctly different sets of human cultural artifacts, representing the lifestyles and cognitive levels of Neanderthals and modern humans. These differences are evident not only in their tools but also in cultural expressions, artistic creations, social structures, and the methods of technological transmission, serving as key clues to understanding the divergent fates of the two groups.

Firstly, Neanderthal stone tool assemblages exhibit marked technological conservatism and stagnation. This toolkit, known as the Mousterian culture, is characterized by relatively fixed tool shapes, limited types, and minimal change over hundreds of thousands of years. Across multiple Neanderthal sites in France, Germany, and Spain, one finds these typical forms: scrapers, hand axes, and points. While practical, these tools show no fundamental invention. Archaeologists note that this long-term technical stability indicates that Neanderthal technological transmission relied largely on imitation and repetition, with few breakthroughs, meaning their cultural knowledge could not accumulate and advance like that of modern humans.

In contrast, the cultural remains of modern humans display significant leaps in both technology and art. The most representative example is the famous Lascaux Cave paintings in southern France. Created around 17,000 years ago, these murals depict vividly rendered animals such as bison, horses, and deer, with flowing lines and rich colors, demonstrating highly developed visual artistic skills and complex symbolic expression. These works are not merely artistic creations but a use of symbolic systems, indicating sophisticated cognitive and communicative abilities.(Fig. 17.3)

Furthermore, modern human sites reveal a diversity of ornamental items and innovative tools, such as bone sewing needles, fishing hooks, traps, and necklaces or decorations made from shells and bird feathers. These artifacts reflect a deep understanding of aesthetics, identity, and social relationships. In contrast, such complex symbolic objects are rarely found at Neanderthal sites, indicating that their cultural expression was comparatively primitive.

**Fig. 17.3** Archaeological findings reveal a significant disparity between Neanderthals and modern humans in cultural transmission and technological invention. Neanderthals' cultural expression tended toward stability and conservatism, whereas modern humans demonstrated remarkable invention and cumulative cultural development

More importantly, the burial rituals of modern humans were far more elaborate and symbolically meaningful. For example, at the Kamenja Cave in Croatia and the Saint-Céspulcre site in France, archaeologists discovered that modern humans decorated bodies with colored pigments and buried grave goods alongside the deceased. This indicates not only a concept of life and death but also an awareness of social identity and spiritual beliefs. Such rituals fostered cultural recognition and social cohesion among group members, providing a solid foundation for the intergenerational transmission and accumulation of cultural knowledge.

From this archaeological evidence, we can observe the substantial differences between Neanderthals and modern humans in cultural transmission and technological invention. Neanderthals' cultural expression leaned toward stability and conservatism, whereas modern humans demonstrated remarkable invention and cumulative cultural development. These technological and cultural differences were fundamental to the divergence in their respective fates.

## 5 The Pitfall of "Reinventing the Wheel": The Neanderthals' "Island Effect"

A deeper reason for the stagnation and eventual decline of Neanderthal culture lies in the limitations of their group structure and social connections. Archaeologists and anthropologists note that Neanderthal groups were typically small, widely dispersed, and lacked effective, widespread networks for communication and information flow.

This "island effect" meant that knowledge and skills circulated only within a limited circle, making cross-regional or inter-group transmission and accumulation difficult.

This situation has a modern parallel, commonly referred to as "reinventing the wheel." When a team or individual refuses external information and resources, relying solely on their own trial-and-error efforts, efficiency is extremely low, invention is constrained, and development inevitably suffers. Neanderthals, similarly, were confined to their small circles, and each generation had to relearn and reinvent many fundamental techniques. Without a system for continuous cultural transmission and improvement, they could not accumulate true cultural wealth, and technological development stagnated.

For instance, the tools and methods Neanderthals used for hunting remained nearly unchanged over tens of thousands of years, as confirmed by repeatedly discovered stone implements with almost identical forms in archaeological sites. In contrast, modern human tools evolved rapidly, with frequent inventions in design and manufacturing. This stark contrast vividly illustrates the importance of cultural transmission mechanisms. Neanderthals' lack of effective information channels hindered the accumulation and optimization of experience and technology.

Isolation and limited communication also meant Neanderthals struggled to form broader cooperative networks. Large-scale group collaboration and knowledge sharing are essential drivers of technological breakthroughs. Small, dispersed groups find it difficult to pool resources for complex collaboration or to develop sophisticated tools, further restricting their adaptability and competitive survival.

Overall, the Neanderthals' "island effect" was a key social factor that impeded cultural invention and ultimately contributed to their extinction. This historical lesson also reminds modern society that in the face of rapid change and challenges, it is crucial to avoid the trap of "reinventing the wheel," actively absorbing external information and experience, and promoting cross-boundary collaboration and resource sharing.

## 6 Modern Lessons: How Can we Avoid Becoming "Information Islands"?

Although the extinction of Neanderthals occurred hundreds of thousands of years ago, the lessons it offers remain profoundly relevant today. History serves as a mirror: by examining this trajectory of human evolution, we can better recognize the importance of information sharing, knowledge transmission, and cultural invention in modern society. Especially in today's rapidly advancing technological and globalized era, avoiding "information islands" is essential for the sustained development of individuals, teams, and entire societies.

## 6.1 Rejecting Closed-Door Reinvention: Leveraging Existing Knowledge—Learning and Transmission as the Foundation of Invention

Part of the Neanderthals' failure stemmed from cultural and technological stagnation: they could not transform existing experience and knowledge into new inventions. Each generation had to "reinvent the wheel," lacking effective inheritance and accumulation of prior achievements, which placed them at a disadvantage in competition with modern humans. The same principle applies to modern society: refusing to absorb and utilize historical and contemporary knowledge, remaining insular, inevitably hinders progress.

From a business perspective, many failing companies succumb precisely because they operate behind closed doors, failing to learn from advanced industry technologies and management practices, ultimately being eliminated by the market. Conversely, successful companies like Apple and Google maintain leadership in technological invention through open collaboration, attracting top talent worldwide, and leveraging advanced technologies. Open learning and knowledge transmission not only save the cost of repetitive trial and error but also lay a solid foundation for invention.(Fig. 17.4)

Academic research follows the same logic. Scientific discoveries are typically built upon previous work; any research team that refuses to share data or collaborate risks falling behind rapidly. The rise of Open Access initiatives and interdisciplinary cooperation aims to promote the widespread dissemination and sharing of knowledge, driving continuous scientific advancement.

## 6.2 Actively Socialize: Proactively Share and Learn

In the age of information explosion, the production of data and knowledge far outpaces previous eras. Individuals and organizations must actively participate in information exchange and sharing to avoid becoming "information islands." This is not only about accumulating resources but also a reflection of competitiveness.

There are countless success stories in modern society. Take open-source software as an example: the Linux operating system, the Python programming language, and the TensorFlow framework all rely on global collaboration and sharing among programmers, forming robust ecosystems. Participants contribute code, experience, and feedback, enabling collective progress. In contrast, projects that isolate themselves and refuse openness often develop slowly or even become marginalized.(Fig. 17.5)

The same principle applies within companies. Encouraging employees to communicate across departments, share knowledge, and collaborate in teams can spark greater invention and improve efficiency. Many leading technology firms have established internal knowledge repositories, invention labs, and regular communication

**Fig. 17.4** Learning and knowledge transmission are the foundation of invention

mechanisms to promote information flow, preventing the waste and inefficiency caused by "information islands."

On a societal level, social media and online communities have further accelerated the rapid dissemination of knowledge and information. Whether through specialized academic forums or broad technical discussion groups, these platforms provide members with opportunities to learn and share. Actively participating in these networks allows individuals and organizations to quickly access cutting-edge information, adjust strategies in time, and enhance competitiveness.

Such proactive social engagement and information exchange not only drive technological progress but also foster cultural diversity and the collision of innovative ideas, keeping society vibrant and creative.

Fig. 17.5 Active social interaction and sharing are a key driving force behind social progress

## *6.3 Ensuring Information Flow and an Inclusive Culture*

One crucial factor in the success of modern Homo sapiens is their open and complex social structure, which facilitates communication and integration across groups and cultures. For contemporary society, building an open social structure is likewise fundamental to avoiding "information silos" and promoting invention.

First, open communication channels form the foundation for free information flow. Whether in corporations, government agencies, academic institutions, or community networks, smooth information pathways allow problems to surface quickly and innovative solutions to spread rapidly, preventing the limitations and disadvantages of isolated knowledge. Many companies adopt flat organizational structures to encourage open dialogue across hierarchical and departmental boundaries, reflecting this principle.

Second, an inclusive cultural environment provides fertile ground for diverse information and innovative ideas. Modern society increasingly values diversity and inclusivity—not just in ethnicity and culture but also in thought and work styles. The collision of different perspectives often sparks original breakthroughs. Conversely, environments that reject diversity and inclusiveness tend to produce rigid thinking, stifling invention.

Open social structures are also evident at the international cooperation level. Globalization promotes exchanges in technology, culture, and economics across countries and regions. Large international research projects, such as the International Space Station, the Human Genome Project, and current climate change studies, all rely on open collaboration and information sharing. Any country or organization that remains closed off will inevitably face difficulties in addressing global challenges.

Moreover, emerging digital technologies such as the internet, big data, and artificial intelligence have greatly facilitated information flow and open invention. Governments and enterprises increasingly adopt data-sharing policies, encouraging invention and optimization based on shared resources. In contrast, information silos and data isolation lead to wasted resources and reduced competitiveness.

## *6.4 Coordination of Supply Chains and R&D: Leveraging Existing Resources for Invention*

In today's highly complex and globalized economy, supply chains play a crucial role. Modern supply chains are not merely channels for the flow of goods and products but also networks for transferring technology, knowledge, and experience. They efficiently integrate resources from around the world, bringing together diverse technical and professional expertise throughout the manufacturing and service delivery process. This integration allows many technical challenges to be explored and validated by predecessors, eliminating the need to start from scratch.

Consider the historically significant example of fire-making. Early humans invested tremendous time and effort in experimenting with friction-based fire-starting methods. This breakthrough was a cornerstone of civilization at the time. Today, we no longer need to spend years reinventing fire-making, because this knowledge has been widely disseminated as public knowledge. Modern tools like lighters and electric igniters allow us to generate fire instantly. This example vividly illustrates the importance of knowledge accumulation and the value of leveraging existing resources.

Similarly, modern entrepreneurs and R&D teams face challenges very different from those of the past. Today, many basic technical components, raw materials, and even complete modules are already supplied through established supply chains. This means entrepreneurs no longer need to "reinvent the wheel" as the Neanderthals might have, painstakingly producing every part themselves. A more effective strategy is to leverage existing supply chains, identify reliable partners and suppliers, and use mature technologies and products to rapidly build solutions and services. Supply chains serve as bridges carrying the wisdom and experience of predecessors, encapsulating complex technical details within standardized and modular products, thus enabling innovators to focus on solving core challenges at a higher level.(Fig. 17.6)

For example, manufacturing a modern smartphone involves thousands of components and technologies, from chip design to displays, from battery management to camera modules, most of which are produced by different suppliers worldwide. A startup attempting to develop all of these technologies independently would face high costs, long timelines, and a high risk of failure due to lack of expertise. By contrast, utilizing mature modules via the supply chain allows entrepreneurs to concentrate on software development, user experience, and innovative applications, significantly improving R&D efficiency and market responsiveness.

In addition, the supply chain is not merely a channel for product components; it also serves as a platform for exchanging innovative ideas and market intelligence. Partners within the supply chain frequently share industry trends, technological advances, and user feedback, facilitating continuous optimization across the ecosystem. This flow of information and integration of resources greatly reduces redundant effort and resource wastage while driving industrial upgrading and technological invention. In this sense, the supply chain itself becomes a catalyst for enterprise invention rather than a simple logistics conduit.

Of course, this does not imply that all R&D work can rely entirely on the supply chain. For truly cutting-edge technological breakthroughs and problems lacking existing solutions, companies and research institutions must invest significant resources in original R&D. These efforts typically involve fundamental scientific research, experimental design, and technical validation, all of which carry high risks

**Fig. 17.6** Fully leveraging existing supply chains essentially means sharing the achievements and knowledge of predecessors. Resources that can be accessed through the supply chain should not be redundantly redeveloped as R&D. The problem should be broken down into parts that can be addressed through the supply chain and parts that cannot; investing R&D efforts only in the latter represents a practical and efficient path to invention

and costs. Yet, it is precisely these breakthroughs that expand technological frontiers and give rise to new industries.

The key lies in discerning and selecting which technological challenges can be solved using existing supply chain resources and which require independent invention. Mistakenly treating all problems as entirely new and attempting to "reinvent the wheel" not only wastes valuable resources but can also result in project failure and loss of market competitiveness. Conversely, companies adept at leveraging supply chain advantages can focus on core invention, respond rapidly to market demands, and achieve differentiated competitive advantage.

On a broader scale, an efficient supply chain and standardized technologies enhance the overall effectiveness and sustainability of the economic system. They allow parties to capitalize on each other's strengths through trust and collaboration, avoiding redundant construction and inefficient competition. This not only lowers the barriers to technological invention but also significantly promotes global knowledge and resource sharing, advancing societal progress as a whole.

In summary, the coordination between supply chains and R&D represents a wise strategy for resource integration. By borrowing existing technological resources and experience and avoiding redundant reinvention, invention efficiency and market responsiveness are greatly enhanced. Only when truly unsolved technological challenges are identified should full-scale original R&D be pursued. In this way, enterprises and society can avoid the "Neanderthal-like" information isolation trap and achieve sustainable development and continuous invention.

## 7 Conclusion

Neanderthals, once the strongest humans adapted to harsh environments, had robust physiques, even larger brain capacities than modern Homo sapiens, rich hunting skills, and certain social organizational abilities. Yet, despite these survival advantages, they ultimately failed to persist through the long currents of evolution. Scientific research reveals that the key reason was neither physical weakness nor intellectual inferiority, but the lack of a more crucial capability—effective information transmission and sharing. Unable to accumulate and pass on knowledge, skills, and culture, Neanderthals had to "reinvent the wheel" in every generation, preventing the formation of a continuously advancing civilization and leading to their gradual disappearance in competition with modern humans.

In contrast, modern humans built vast and efficient information networks through highly developed social cooperation. These networks enabled rapid knowledge accumulation and invention, driving continuous technological advancement and societal progress. Every leap in human civilization—from the advent of agriculture and the invention of writing to the Industrial Revolution and the Information Age—ultimately relies on open and shared information. We advance further and grow stronger through mutual exchange, learning, and collaborative creation.

This epic evolutionary journey offers profound lessons for contemporary society. Individual intelligence and physical prowess alone are no longer sufficient to navigate a rapidly changing and complex world. Individual capability is limited, while collective wisdom holds virtually limitless potential. The extinction of Neanderthals warns us that closed-off, non-collaborative strategies will inevitably fail, whereas the success of modern humans highlights the immense value of openness, sharing, and cooperative synergy.(Fig. 17.7)

In facing the fast-changing societal landscape and increasingly complex global challenges of the twenty-first century, we need this tradition of sharing and cooperation more than ever. Whether in technological invention, economic development, cultural heritage, or social governance, active communication, and open collaboration are indispensable. Enterprises must engage in cross-sector partnerships, scientists must share data, social members must embrace inclusivity and understanding, and nations must strengthen collaboration to collectively tackle global issues such as climate change, public health, and resource allocation.

Only by embracing the open flow of information and actively promoting the dissemination and integration of knowledge can we continuously adapt to environmental changes and drive the sustained progress of society. Just as the language and cooperation of ancient modern humans allowed them to secure an enduring advantage, we today must uphold the principles of openness and sharing to build a more prosperous and flourishing civilization.

The story of the Neanderthals, though an echo from ancient times, resonates ever more strongly in the modern world. It serves as a reminder that any individual, team, or society that isolates itself and refuses to share will ultimately face elimination. Only through collaboration and the sharing of wisdom can we stand out in the fierce competition of our era and create new glories for human civilization. Therefore, let us remember the lessons of history, embrace an open mindset, and take proactive actions to foster information exchange and cultural invention, allowing the spark of wisdom to burn brightly in every heart.

**Fig. 17.7** Neanderthals and modern humans experienced dramatically divergent fates in the course of evolutionary history due to differences in social behaviors. This is the key insight this chapter seeks to convey by analyzing the underlying reasons

## Further Reading

[1]. R. Boyd and P. J. Richerson, *Culture and the Evolutionary Process*, University of Chicago Press, 1985.
[2]. X. Cao, *Strategic Management and Organizational Development*, Springer, 2025.
[3]. X. Cao, *Modern Business Management*, Palgrave Macmillan, 2025.
[4]. E. G. Carayannis, Ed., *Encyclopedia of Creativity, Invention, Innovation and Entrepreneurship*. New York, NY: Springer, 2013. doi:https://doi.org/10.1007/978-1-4614-6616-1.
[5]. F. L. Coolidge and T. Wynn, *The Rise of Homo sapiens: The Evolution of Modern Thinking*, Wiley-Blackwell, 2009.
[6]. J. Hawks, *Human Evolution: A Very Short Introduction*, Oxford University Press, 2020.
[7]. D. Henrich, *The Secret of Our Success: How Culture is Driving Human Evolution, Domesticating Our Species, and Making Us Smarter*, Princeton University Press, 2015.
[8]. S. Mithen, *The Prehistory of the Mind: A Search for the Origins of Art, Religion and Science*, Thames & Hudson, 1996.
[9]. C. Stringer, *The Origin of Our Species*, Allen Lane, 2011.

[10]. H. Tomasello, *The Cultural Origins of Human Cognition*, Harvard University Press, 1999.
[11]. E. O. Wilson, *The Social Conquest of Earth*, Liveright, 2012.

# Chapter 18
# The First Principles of Success: Imitate those Who Have Achieved Results

## 1 Introduction

Have you ever felt puzzled? Some people around you seem not to work particularly hard, yet they effortlessly reap high rewards; meanwhile, despite your diligence, you remain stuck in place. This phenomenon is not coincidental—it reveals a core aspect of success that most people overlook: direction and path. Intelligence and hard work are indeed accelerators of success, but they alone cannot determine it. In fact, the first principle of success is: imitate those who have already achieved results.

## 2 The Paradox of Success: The Limits of Diligence and Intelligence

We all desire success and hope to achieve our goals through our own efforts. In mainstream values, "diligence" and "intelligence" are held as the pillars of success. From a young age, we are taught that "the early bird catches the worm," that "diligence can make up for shortcomings," and that we must "think more." We are inspired by countless success stories, believing that as long as we invest more time and energy, we will obtain ideal returns.

However, reality often proves frustrating. If we define success merely as a linear relationship between "input" and "output," a perplexing paradox emerges: why do some people invest enormously yet yield very little?

Let us analyze this issue through a hypothetical example:

> In a small village in Gansu, China, there is a young man named Li Ming, who may be smarter and more diligent than his peers. Every day he rises before dawn to work in the fields, and after sunset, he takes a second job at a town restaurant. On weekends, he studies computer programming on his own. He firmly believes that



S. Li, *Bridging the Innovation Gap*, Innovation, Technology, and Knowledge Management, https://doi.org/10.1007/978-3-032-22652-5_18

as long as he works harder than others, he can change his destiny. Yet, after a year of relentless effort, his annual income may still fall far below that of an ordinary worker in Shenzhen. This story is not unique—it plays out across China's vast landscape every day.

Li Ming's predicament highlights the limitations of personal effort. The reason his hard work does not yield high returns is that the direction of his effort is constrained by his environment, the information he can access, and his inherent social circle cognition. His "intelligence" allows him to learn farming or computer repair faster than others; his "diligence" gives him more hours to invest. Yet none of this fundamentally changes the ceiling of the track he is on. He is trapped in a "local optimum" dilemma. Through his intelligence and hard work, he achieves the best possible result within his current environment, but this result is far from the greater "global optimum."

It is like a game: Li Ming has perfected every task in his small Gansu village, becoming the strongest villager, yet due to regional limitations, he has no idea how to elevate himself further. His so-called diligence is merely repeated labor on low-value land; his so-called intelligence is only marginal efficiency gains within limited informational boundaries.

Therefore, success is not simply a matter of input versus output—it is a matter of choosing the correct path. In the right direction, one unit of effort yields a unit of return; in the wrong direction, even a hundredfold effort may vanish into thin air. (Fig. 18.1).

**Fig. 18.1** The Path to Success of Li Ming, a Young Villager

## 3 Imitating those Who Have Achieved Results: The Shortcut to Success

Since intelligence and diligence have their limitations, is there a method that allows us to advance efficiently in the right direction, even achieving exponential growth? The answer is: imitate those who have already succeeded. This is not opportunism or cutting corners; it is a strategic and wise choice. This approach can significantly reduce trial-and-error costs and directly transform others' successful experiences into your own knowledge and abilities.

Let's return to Li Ming, the young villager from Gansu mentioned earlier. He does not need to rely on extraordinary intelligence or extreme diligence. He can make a more important choice—move to Shenzhen and integrate into the lifestyle and work circles of Shenzhen's youth. This is not merely a change of city; it is an upgrade of his underlying operating system. Instead of continuing to toil on his own land, he could choose to work in Shenzhen, following the paths already validated by countless Shenzhen workers. Through observation, imitation, and practice, he can subtly acquire the cognitive patterns and behavioral habits of Shenzhen people. Once he adapts to Shenzhen's work environment, he does not need to be significantly smarter or more diligent than others to easily reach an income far exceeding the highest earnings in his Gansu village, thereby achieving a leap in income.

This method of imitating successful people involves two core principles:

First, have a clear goal and choose the right target. The person you imitate must be someone with a background similar to yours who has already achieved success in a specific field. Blindly imitating someone whose conditions are vastly different from yours can easily fail due to "mismatched context." For example, a completely inexperienced startup founder who tries to replicate Elon Musk's Starlink project from the outset will only waste enormous resources. A wiser approach is to first imitate the founder of a successful small tech company, learning their product iteration, team management, and marketing strategies. This is like being on a vast map: you first need to find a traveler who has already reached the destination and request a detailed route from them.

Second, engage in full-spectrum, immersive imitation. Mere observation is not enough. True learning requires immersive, comprehensive engagement. This is similar to learning a language: watching American TV shows or listening to broadcasts cannot replace living fully in the U.S. Real imitation must cover multiple dimensions, including language, behavior, thought patterns, and environmental adaptation. You must not only learn what they say and do, but also understand why they say and do it, and under what circumstances (Fig. 18.2).

However, there is a trap to be wary of: the "Dong Shi mimicking Xi Shi's frown" phenomenon. If we imitate only a single successful individual, it is easy to blindly copy unnecessary or even detrimental traits, mistaking them for the keys to success. For example, a successful entrepreneur may have a short temper due to personal traits, but their success does not stem from this; it comes from their exceptional

**Fig. 18.2** Imitating a single successful individual can easily lead you to mistake their flaws for the keys to success. However, imitating a group of successful people allows us to discern what truly lies at the core of success, much like the lesson from the story of Dong Shi mimicking Xi Shi's frown

business insight. If the imitator only learns the temper but overlooks the insight, the result is completely misguided. Therefore, the depth of imitation lies in identifying commonalities from individuals and extracting the essence from a group.

When the young man Li Ming from Gansu goes to Shenzhen, his role models are not just a single "Li Hua," but the collection of people around him—"Li Hua, Zhang San, Wang Wu…"—a group of individuals who have all achieved results. This group provides him with a valuable "sample library." He will discover that although these Shenzhen youths may have different personalities, what they share—sensitivity to opportunities, pursuit of work efficiency, openness to new things, and effective communication—constitutes the universal "first-principle qualities of success" that lead to high income. Through comparison and observation, he can easily filter out individual flaws and focus only on the principles that truly produce results.

This method is called a "shortcut" because it maximizes efficiency by avoiding "reinventing the wheel," directly leveraging the success experiences of predecessors to achieve the greatest returns with minimal effort.

## 4 Observation and Immersion: From Information Acquisition to Cognitive Upgrade

Many people mistakenly believe that "reading books, attending lectures, or watching videos" constitutes learning from successful individuals. In reality, this is merely observation. Observation allows you to understand success from one angle but cannot

**Fig. 18.3** Only through firsthand immersion, rather than mere observation, can one fully understand the core processes and key elements of cooking, and truly learn to become a master chef

form a complete cognition. It is like a flat map—you can see the surface but cannot perceive the depth of three-dimensional space.

Take learning culinary skills as an example: you can watch countless videos of Michelin-star chefs, familiarizing yourself with every step, yet when you stand in front of the stove yourself, you still cannot produce dishes of the same quality. This is because you lack immersion (Fig. 18.3).

To achieve true "immersion," we need to engage in deep learning across four dimensions:

First, the behavioral dimension. This is not merely about mimicking the observable actions of successful individuals, but about capturing the subtle, non-verbal habits. For example, an outstanding salesperson not only communicates the advantages of a product to clients but also builds trust through body language, speech pace, and tone. A learner should observe closely, even engage in shadowing, to capture these details.

Second, the cognitive dimension. This is the core aspect, requiring you to interact deeply with successful individuals and even observe their thought processes during real decision-making. For instance, a successful investor bases decisions not solely on financial statements but on profound insights into industry trends, management teams, and macroeconomic conditions. You need to ask questions, participate in reviews, and engage in discussions to understand their decision-making framework.

Third, the social network dimension. Integrate into the social circles of successful people to absorb collective intelligence. No one succeeds alone; success is often the result of collaborative effort within a network. These circles may include industry associations, executive clubs, or private interest groups. Within these networks, you gain access to non-public information, deeper collaboration models, and an intangible energy field—a knowledge spillover effect that subtly elevates your cognitive level.

Finally, the environmental dimension. Immerse yourself in the working and living environments of successful people to experience implicit rules and ecosystem logic. Just like an entrepreneur in Silicon Valley, you not only gain exposure to cutting-edge technology but also experience the local invention culture, tolerance for failure, and fast-paced work ethos. These environmental factors are often decisive in determining success.

## 5 Imitation and Invention: First Imitate, Then Surpass

Some may worry: "If I keep imitating, will I ever surpass others?" The truth is no. Imitation is the starting point for accumulating knowledge and resources, not the endpoint. Just as an architect must first study and master existing structural and mechanical principles before designing a new building, one must grasp foundational rules before innovating. Many outstanding companies and individuals began with imitation and eventually surpassed their predecessors.

Take Apple as an example. Early in his career, Steve Jobs visited Xerox PARC in Palo Alto and was captivated by the graphical user interface (GUI). He did not stop at superficial imitation but brought the concept back to Apple, integrating it with his deep understanding of aesthetics and user experience. Ultimately, Apple innovated in design, ecosystem integration, and marketing, creating a unique Apple ecosystem that surpassed Microsoft.

A similar story occurred with Huawei. In its early years, Ren Zhengfei admitted that Huawei "copied" technologies and management models from foreign telecom giants and even hired IBM as a consultant. Yet, they did not simply replicate; they adapted to China's context and corporate culture, invested heavily in R&D, optimized their supply chain, and pursued a global strategy, ultimately becoming a leader in the global telecommunications industry.

It is important to emphasize that imitating successful individuals is a continuous, dynamic, and long-term process. It is not a one-time task but a core strategy spanning one's career and even life. When you imitate a successful person and achieve similar results, your journey does not end—it advances to a higher level.

It is like climbing a mountain. You first follow the route of a successful climber, learning their techniques and equipment, eventually reaching the summit. Once at the top, you see higher, more majestic peaks. You do not settle but instead seek a more experienced climber to learn how to conquer these greater challenges.

This principle also applies to personal growth and business development. For example, a new salesperson who imitates the "sales champion" in their team masters communication and client management skills, eventually becoming a top performer. At this point, new challenges arise: how to manage a team? How to develop strategy?

Their next role model may no longer be a sales champion but a senior executive or a successful entrepreneur. They begin to imitate higher-level thinking patterns, decision-making logic, and resource integration skills.

Thus, this process can be summarized as a cycle of imitation–immersion–surpassing, continuously driving stepwise growth:

- Stage One: Entry-level Imitation. Choose successful individuals with a similar background and fully immerse yourself to replicate their experience, achieving a leap from "nothing" to "something."
- Stage Two: Surpassing through Imitation. As your abilities reach a new level, your goals upgrade. Seek a more successful role model to learn higher-dimensional skills, evolving from "something" to "excellence."
- Stage Three: Innovative Imitation. Once you have mastered advanced abilities in multiple domains, cross-integrate these experiences to innovate in unexplored fields.

This continuous, evolving process ensures you do not stagnate in your comfort zone and enables long-term growth.

## 6 Implications for Entrepreneurs

For entrepreneurs, the principle of "imitating those who have achieved results" is particularly crucial, helping them navigate uncertain business environments steadily.

In the early stages of a venture, the most valuable resources are time and energy. Instead of squandering them on the highly uncertain task of "starting from zero," it is wiser to follow these strategies:

First, choose replicable success models. Early-stage entrepreneurs need not pursue disruptive invention immediately. Start by imitating verified successful cases in the market, copying their business model, team operations, and resource integration. For example, if you want to open a café, rather than inventing an entirely new business model, first imitate a successful chain brand—learn their location selection, décor, menu, and operational processes. This allows rapid market entry, initial cash flow, and validation of your operational capability.

Second, immerse in high-quality networks. Actively engage with successful individuals in your industry and participate in their ecosystem. You can do this through industry forums, online communities, or by seeking a successful entrepreneur as a mentor. Each interaction allows you to learn their thinking patterns, decision-making logic, and behavioral models—your most valuable intangible assets.

Third, innovate on the foundation of imitation. Once you accumulate sufficient knowledge and resources, channel your insight and energy into untapped markets or technological breakthroughs. At this stage, invention becomes more insightful and likely to succeed. For example, after mastering café operations, you might

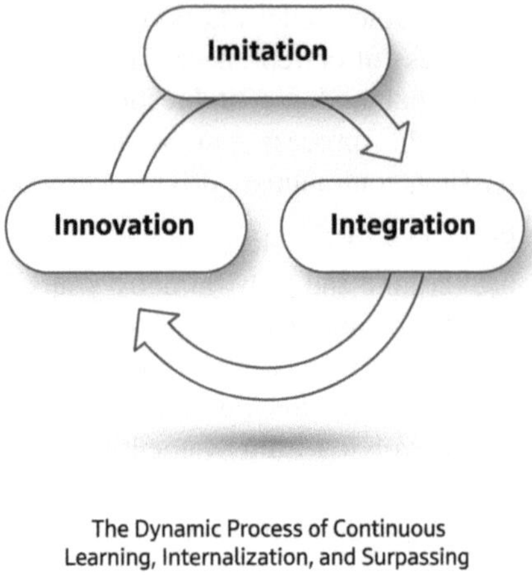


**Fig. 18.4** Success is a dynamic process of continuous learning, internalization, and surpassing, forming a closed loop of imitation–immersion–invention

consider integrating technology, community engagement, or cultural elements to create a unique brand. Such "incremental inventions" often have a higher chance of success than starting entirely from scratch (Fig. 18.4).

## 7 Conclusion

Diligence and intelligence are certainly important, but they are not the core of success. The first principle of success is to imitate those who have already achieved results. First, choose the right role models to imitate and use their path to success as your blueprint. Next, fully immerse yourself in their environment, transforming superficial observation into deep cognitive upgrade. This process is a continuous cycle: whenever you reach a stage of success, actively seek higher-level role models and keep evolving. Finally, on the foundation of accumulated knowledge and experience, focus your wisdom and effort on unexplored areas to achieve true invention. For entrepreneurs, this means: first imitate, then innovate; first immerse, then create; first understand the rules, then break them. Following this principle not only drastically reduces trial-and-error costs but also enables steady progress in complex business environments, achieving a leap from ordinary to extraordinary.

## Further Reading

[1]. R. MacArthur and E. Wilson, *The Theory of Island Biogeography*, Princeton University Press, 1967.
[2]. X. Cao, *Modern Business Management*, Palgrave Macmillan, 2025.
[3]. E. O. Wilson, *Sociobiology: The New Synthesis*, Harvard University Press, 1975.

[5]. X. Cao, *Strategic Management and Organizational Development*, Springer, 2025.
[8]. C. W. Clark, *Mathematical Bioeconomics: The Optimal Management of Renewable Resources*, 3rd ed., Wiley, 2010.
[7]. F. L. Coolidge and T. Wynn, *Cognitive Archaeology and Human Evolution*, Cambridge University Press, 2009.
[6]. R. Boyd and P. J. Richerson, *Not By Genes Alone: How Culture Transformed Human Evolution*, University of Chicago Press, 2005.
[10]. D. Kahneman, *Thinking, Fast and Slow*, Farrar, Straus and Giroux, 2011.
[9]. P. J. Richerson and R. Boyd, *Culture and Evolution*, University of Chicago Press, 2005.
[4]. M. Ridley, *The Origins of Virtue: Human Instincts and the Evolution of Cooperation*, Penguin, 1996.

# Chapter 19
# From Evolutionary Strategies to Business Wisdom: Navigating the Survival Rules of an Uncertain Era

## 1 Introduction

The history of human evolution is a grand epic of survival, competition, and adaptation. It was not the result of a single species' accidental triumph, but the outcome of the alternating application of two profound strategies: r-selection and K-selection.

r-selection refers to a "produce many, nurture few" reproductive strategy. Under this model, a species tends to generate a vast number of offspring rapidly in uncertain or turbulent environments, while investing minimally in each individual. The advantage of this strategy lies in its sheer numbers and the genetic variation it produces; even if the majority of offspring fail to survive, some will inevitably adapt to environmental changes and survive, ensuring the continuity of the species.

In contrast, K-selection is a "quality over quantity" strategy. It typically occurs in relatively stable environments with limited or even harsh resources. Here, species produce fewer offspring but invest significant energy and resources in nurturing each one, ensuring a higher survival rate and competitive capability. The key to this strategy is the precise transmission of survival advantages from one generation to the next through accumulated experience and skills.

These two seemingly opposing survival philosophies not only chart the trajectory from life's emergence to its flourishing but also act like two sharp scalpels, dissecting the underlying logic of corporate management and personal growth, offering invaluable insights. This chapter aims to liberate the wisdom of r- and K-selection from the confines of biology and present it as a universal strategic thinking framework. We will first review how humans employed these two strategies to achieve evolutionary success and build civilization; next, we will apply this framework to business strategy, exploring how to make optimal choices in different market environments; finally, we will reflect on personal growth paths, providing a fresh perspective for planning careers and life.



S. Li, *Bridging the Innovation Gap*, Innovation, Technology, and Knowledge Management, https://doi.org/10.1007/978-3-032-22652-5_19

# 2 The Echo of Evolution—Human Origins and Strategic Choices of Civilization

The course of human evolution exemplifies the dynamic switching between r- and K-selection. Though each phase lasted tens of thousands or even hundreds of thousands of years, they clearly illustrate which survival philosophy leads a species to success under different environmental conditions.

## *2.1 Africa: The r-Selection Cradle—Exploring Genetic Breadth*

All modern humans originated in Africa, not by geographical accident, but as a profound implementation of r-selection strategies. Ancient Africa was a land of rapid environmental changes. The dramatic tectonic activity of the Great Rift Valley, coupled with repeated ice ages and interglacial periods, created extremely unstable resource distribution, making survival a constant challenge.

In such a turbulent ecosystem, early humans who could reproduce quickly and generate greater variation among offspring held an overwhelming survival advantage. They had neither the time to meticulously nurture each child nor the opportunity to settle long-term and develop complex technologies. Instead, they needed to migrate continuously and adapt, with survival relying on sheer numbers and adaptability. (Fig. 19.1).

Fossil and genetic evidence strongly support this assertion. Studies indicate that Homo sapiens first appeared in Africa approximately 300,000 years ago. As the "species factory" of early humans, Africa possessed the highest population density and the oldest genetic lineages. Around 70,000 years ago, a group of Homo sapiens migrated out of Africa, embarking on their epic global journey. Compared to any other region in the world, African populations exhibit the greatest genetic diversity, precisely illustrating the core principle of r-strategy: a vast gene pool and numerous variants serve as the optimal tools for coping with uncertain environments. In this "broad-net" approach, each new individual potentially carries unique genetic traits suited to novel environments.

It was this rapid genetic variation and extensive adaptability that ultimately allowed Homo sapiens to outcompete other archaic humans, such as Neanderthals, becoming the dominant species on Earth. For instance, bipedalism, a crucial trait, is considered an adaptive evolution to the changing savanna environment, enabling humans to travel long distances more efficiently in search of food and water while maintaining body temperature in high heat. Meanwhile, a smaller gut and larger brain capacity indicate that humans learned to obtain high-energy foods through cooking and cooperation, supporting rapid brain development. Africa, with its ever-changing landscapes, was precisely the cradle where humans applied the r-strategy to advance species evolution. (Fig. 19.2).

**Fig. 19.1** Africa's unique geography and climatic factors collectively determined that all human races originated in Africa, rather than in Asia or Europe

## 2.2 *The K-Selection Stage of Eurasia: Deep Accumulation of Civilization*

However, as humans spread across the globe, the dawn of civilization first illuminated specific regions of Eurasia. This was not due to differences in intelligence, but rather a strategic shift in survival approaches. Regions such as the "Fertile Crescent" in the Middle East and the Yellow River basin featured relatively stable climates and abundant land. This environmental stability allowed humans to break free from the nomadic, hunter-gatherer mode of existence and enter a new era of settlement and agriculture. This marked a strategic transition from r-selection to k-selection. The advent of agriculture was a milestone of this shift. In the Fertile Crescent, wild cereals like wheat and barley were easy to domesticate, and docile animals such as sheep and goats provided a stable source of meat and labor. This contrasted sharply with Africa, where species like zebras and African buffalo were difficult to domesticate.

**Fig. 19.2** In the fertile lands of Eurasia, humans transitioned from hunting and gathering to agriculture, thereby giving rise to early civilizations

Humans no longer relied on sheer numbers but focused their energy on intensive cultivation of land and deep domestication of a few key species. This was a k-selection model of "quality over quantity," investing substantial resources in the nurturing of a limited number of crops and technologies to ensure their sustainable development and inheritance.

This transition had profound consequences: humans began to achieve stable food surpluses, population densities increased, and villages and cities emerged. Complex irrigation systems, the invention of writing, and bronze smelting were all products of deep intergenerational knowledge accumulation. In a stable environment, humans could focus on solving concrete problems, and through social division of labor and precise collaboration, individual intelligence was transformed into the vast collective energy of civilization. It was this k-selection strategy, rather than mere population size, that forged the brilliance of civilization.

## 3 The Commercial Jungle—The Evolutionary Laws of Business Strategy

Applying the wisdom of evolution to the business world reveals that the macro environment of a company determines its optimal survival strategy.

## *3.1 R-Selection: Explosive Growth in Chaos*

In today's rapidly changing commercial jungle, emerging technology markets and disruptive startup sectors resemble an "African continent" full of both opportunities and challenges. Here, traditional business rules are broken, competitive patterns are not yet fully established, and uncertainty is the only certainty. For companies operating in this environment, blindly pursuing perfection and long-term planning is dangerous. The most effective strategy is r-selection.

Companies must adopt a "run and fix" approach like early Homo sapiens: rapidly launch minimum viable products (MVPs) and iterate quickly based on market feedback. This strategy does not aim for perfection in each product but seeks overall rapid response and broad coverage to seize opportunities before competitors. Early Google and Amazon are prime examples of r-selection. Google's search algorithm at its founding was far from perfect, but through rapid iteration and massive search data, it quickly outpaced competitors. Amazon expanded its product lines continuously—from books to retail to cloud computing—growing like a snowball; its strategic core was simply "produce more."

## *3.2 K-Selection: Forging Excellence in Stability*

However, once a company enters a relatively mature and competitive market, the rules of survival change completely. Market shares are divided, and consumers have higher expectations for products and services. At this stage, the most effective strategy shifts to k-selection. Companies must concentrate resources on high-quality products and services, establishing competitive barriers through technological invention and brand building. This strategy prioritizes depth and quality over speed and quantity, requiring long-term R&D investment, meticulous management, and deep customer insight to build an impenetrable moat.

Apple, Toyota, and Hermès are exemplary cases of k-selection. Apple invests heavily in R&D each year to ensure its products lead in design and performance; Toyota excels in quality control through lean production; Hermès secures its brand value with nearly obsessive craftsmanship. These companies understand that in stable, mature markets, only a relentless focus on quality and sustained investment in core technology can maintain competitiveness.

## *3.3 Strategic Evolution and Switching*

Truly great companies not only choose the right strategy but also know when to switch strategies. Amazon exemplifies this: in its early stage, it expanded aggressively using r-selection, but once it gained market dominance, it shifted to k-selection, building a robust logistics network, launching Prime membership, and developing AWS, establishing an almost insurmountable competitive barrier. Likewise, many startups transition from "wild growth" in early funding rounds to more refined operations emphasizing product quality and user experience. This strategic flexibility is key to success at different stages of business development.

## 4 Personal Growth: The Dynamic Balance of Breadth and Depth

The wisdom of r- and k-selection also applies to individual development. Many emphasize the importance of "focus," but it is crucial to recognize that focus is conditional. One's growth path should adjust according to different stages and environmental contexts.

### *4.1 Exploration Phase: The r-Selection Model*

In the early stages of a career, or when facing a transition, one often lacks a clear understanding of personal interests, strengths, and market demands. At this point, the wisest choice is to adopt an r-selection strategy. This means boldly trying different roles, learning various skills, and exploring multiple industries. This "multi-point experimentation" approach helps broaden one's horizons, rapidly accumulate experience, and ultimately discover the career path that truly fits. Locking oneself prematurely into a single direction may result in missed opportunities due to insufficient overall awareness.

### *4.2 Advancement Phase: The K-Selection Model*

Once an individual has accumulated sufficient experience and knowledge in a particular field, they enter the "maturity phase" of their career. At this stage, environmental uncertainty diminishes, yet competition intensifies. This is when it is crucial to decisively switch to a k-selection strategy. It entails concentrating efforts on a specialized area, and through continuous learning and practice, establishing professional barriers that are difficult to replicate. This is the true meaning of "focus." By delving deeply into a specific domain and producing high-quality output, one can build a personal brand, become an expert and leader in the field, and stand out in competition.

### *4.3 The Dynamic Balance of Personal Development*

A successful personal growth path does not follow a single strategy rigidly; rather, it dynamically alternates between r-selection's "broad exploration" and k-selection's "deep specialization." For example, an engineer might spend the first five years of their career working in different teams or projects, gaining exposure to diverse technology stacks to identify their interest points (r-selection). Five years later, upon discovering a passion for a particular domain—such as artificial intelligence algorithms—they can devote full energy to intensive study and research, becoming a top expert in that field (k-selection). This dynamic balance is key to maintaining competitiveness in a rapidly changing environment.

## 5 Conclusion: The Wisdom of Timing and Judgment

r-selection and k-selection, though seemingly opposite survival strategies, form the underlying code of many success stories. They are not merely binary opposites but are complementary and mutually reinforcing.

In today's world of uncertainty and disruptive technologies, what we need is not only the courage to experiment and the perseverance for deep mastery, but also the wisdom to act according to circumstances. In the chaotic initial stage, one must act like r-selected Homo sapiens, seizing opportunities with speed and breadth; in stability, one must act like k-selected civilizations, forging excellence through depth and quality. Only by following this dual strategy can we navigate the currents of evolution and find a path to survival and success—for ourselves, for our enterprises, and for humanity.

# Chapter 20
# From "Paper Publication" to "Product Endorsement": How to Win Public Trust

## 1 Introduction

In today's era of information overload, both cutting-edge scientific discoveries and the most disruptive commercial products face a common challenge: how to win public trust. An inspiring set of experimental data or a powerful prototype does not automatically translate into widespread recognition or credibility. Yet, gaining public trust is the prerequisite for securing investment from institutions and driving consumer adoption.

From peer review in prestigious academic journals to reputation building on mass digital platforms, the mechanism through which trust is constructed is undergoing a profound transformation. This shift concerns not only the evolution of marketing strategies but also the very foundation of how society forms value judgments.

This chapter delves into how trust is produced, verified, and transmitted across two seemingly distinct domains—science and business—and reveals why, in the digital age, traffic and word of mouth have become the key elements in building the next-generation trust system.

## 2 Paper Publication in the Scientific Community

In the world of scientific research, a groundbreaking discovery is only the first step of a long march. Every researcher knows that success in the laboratory does not equate to recognition in academia. You may observe astonishing data at the lab bench, even challenge long-standing theories, but if your findings remain confined to handwritten notes or spoken anecdotes, they will soon be forgotten—swept away by the tide of newer discoveries. (Fig. 20.1).



S. Li, *Bridging the Innovation Gap*, Innovation, Technology, and Knowledge Management, https://doi.org/10.1007/978-3-032-22652-5_20

**Fig. 20.1** In the scientific community, whether a research achievement gains recognition depends on its acceptance by experts and publication in reputable, high-impact journals. Once endorsed by such credibility, it can then earn broader public recognition

Therefore, the scientific community has long established a process for entering the "canon"—one must turn their findings into a paper and publish it in an authoritative journal. This is not merely a formality; it is, in essence, an act of credibility endorsement.

Why is it called an endorsement? Because the publication process is, at its core, a collective ritual of review and validation. A paper must undergo rigorous peer review, meaning that your research methods, experimental design, data results, and conclusions will all be subjected to sharp scrutiny from top experts. They will question details, probe for flaws, and even overturn parts of your assumptions—until your work is finally confirmed to be reliable, reproducible, and worthy of entering the annals of science.

Only when you survive round after round of such "academic interrogation" and eventually succeed in publishing your paper does your research truly become part of the disciplinary knowledge system. It is not merely a personal victory but a collective acknowledgment from the scientific community. And this acknowledgment becomes the foundation for future citations, dissemination, and even the acquisition of research funding and resources.

In other words, a paper is not the end of knowledge but the beginning of its socialization. It transforms your personal discovery into a shared intellectual asset for all humanity, while granting it an official label of trustworthiness. Within academia, this trust mechanism ensures the rigor and reliability of knowledge, forming the very architecture of modern science. Every citation, every new study that builds upon your work, is a silent validation of its credibility.

## 3 From "Lab Prototype" to "Market Success": Crossing the Trust Gap

The process of academic publication we just discussed mirrors, in many ways, the journey of turning an industrial prototype into a successful product.

Imagine you are an entrepreneur. After countless sleepless nights, your team finally builds a working prototype. It might be years ahead of its time or capable of disrupting an entire industry. Yet soon you realize—a prototype is not a product, just as research is not business.

Just as raw experimental data is only the material for a paper, a working prototype is far from being a market-validated product. In academia, you need the endorsement of peer review; in business, you need the endorsement of public trust.

The problem is that most consumers and investors are not technical experts. They can't read your code or algorithms, nor do they care about motor torque or chip computing power. Unlike peer reviewers, they won't deconstruct your logic from first principles—instead, they judge your product's reliability based on intuition and social signals.

This creates the real challenge of commercialization: how to build trust among non-experts.

In the past, this trust often came from institutional endorsements—an industry award, a feature in a major news outlet, or a documentary on national television. These served as the commercial equivalent of academic journals, offering an "official seal of approval." People assumed that if such authorities recognized your work, it must be trustworthy.

However, in the era of mobile internet and short video, this entire system has been radically reconstructed. Today, endorsements come not from elite institutions but from the compounding effect of traffic and reputation—the collective sentiment of the crowd. Trust is no longer conferred from the top down but generated bottom-up, through shared experience and emotional resonance. This shift has not only overturned traditional marketing logic but has fundamentally reshaped the way trust is produced and transmitted.

## 4 The New "Journals" of Public Trust: Traffic and Word-of-Mouth as Social Consensus

If *Nature* and *Science* were once the temples of scientists, then platforms like Douyin (TikTok), WeChat Video Accounts, Xiaohongshu, and Zhihu have become the new journals for entrepreneurs and products.

To gain public recognition, a product must constantly "publish content"—to be seen, discussed, and verified by a broad audience. A demo in a short video, a long-form analysis on Zhihu, or a detailed product experience post on Xiaohongshu all serve as the product's "papers." These forms of communication bypass traditional

**Fig. 20.2** Social consensus formed through traffic and word-of-mouth is a crucial factor in a product’s success

editorial processes and go straight into the arena of real-time peer review by the masses. (Fig. 20.2).

And the “peer review” mechanism for these new kinds of “papers” has shifted from a handful of experts to the general public: likes, comments, and shares have become the most direct “impact factors.”

- The number of likes functions like citation counts—it reflects how many people are willing to endorse the product and recognize its value.
- The number of comments serves as a form of peer review—users raise doubts, offer praise, or suggest improvements, collectively discussing the product’s strengths and weaknesses.
- The number of shares represents diffusion power—it shows that the product’s “academic value” is crossing boundaries, reaching and influencing wider audiences.

As these metrics climb, your product ceases to be a “personal discovery” and becomes a “collective consensus.” This kind of social consensus is far more powerful than any set of technical specifications. It helps you quickly attract potential customers, gives investors the sense that “the market is ready,” and even draws partners to your door.

In this sense, traffic platforms are no longer just publicity arenas—they have become the new factories of trust. What they produce is not merely exposure, but credibility and recognition. Every like and share is a “vote of confidence” cast by users. The accumulation of these trust signals ultimately transforms into immense brand momentum—something traditional advertising could never match. This creates a form of *co-created trust*, where users are no longer passive recipients of information but active participants in the process of building credibility.

## 5 Case Study: When the "Influencer Strategy" Becomes the New Product Launch

Looking across the emerging tech stars of recent years, a common pattern stands out: they not only invest deeply in R&D but also skillfully harness traffic to turn technology into a social phenomenon. This is very much like completing a major scientific project—not only focusing on the research itself but also dedicating great effort to writing and refining the paper so that it gains public recognition.(Fig. 20.3)

Take China's humanoid robotics field as an example:

- Unitree Robotics first gained recognition in the "academic circle" when its quadruped robot was featured by the prestigious *IEEE Spectrum*. Later, it appeared twice on the CCTV Spring Festival Gala—a "live-broadcast journal" watched by hundreds of millions. The exposure catapulted Unitree from a niche robotics company to a household name. The trust generated by such top-tier traffic far exceeded what any advertising budget could buy. Audiences saw a robot dancing gracefully on stage—an image far more convincing than any list of codes or technical parameters.
- Zhiyuan Robotics: its CEO, Zhihuijun, is himself a tech influencer with a massive fan base. His personal influence functions like a "high-impact journal," earning the company millions of followers and hundreds of millions in funding even before mass production. For investors, a "traffic-equipped" CEO is the ultimate risk mitigator—he has already laid a solid foundation of *social trust* for future products. Every technical post and prototype demonstration he shares is like publishing a "preprint paper," continually building public anticipation and confidence.
- Fourier Intelligence (a.k.a. "Zhuji Power"): when it entered the market, competitors were already well-known. So it chose to win through visual impact: a short video of a robot walking steadily on a rugged mountain trail—remaining upright even when pushed went viral on short-video platforms. This single clip resonated with audiences far more than any lengthy technical paper could. The viral spread not only brought massive exposure but directly accelerated fundraising, allowing Fourier to carve out a space in an intensely competitive field. This is the power of a *visual paper*: the most direct, empirical proof of reliability. In today's era, such evidence-based short videos are the most potent catalysts for building trust.

These cases all illustrate a clear point: in today's market, technological performance is a "required course," but whether the technology can be seen, understood, and trusted by the public is the "extra credit"—and often the decisive factor in success or failure. Successful companies without exception make "trust marketing" their core

**Fig. 20.3** In today's market, technology is only one aspect of a product's success. The true differentiator—and often the deciding factor between success and failure—lies in whether the technology can be *seen*, *understood*, and *trusted* by the public

strategy. They understand that in an age of information overload, only brands that can effectively build trust will stand out.

## 6 From Lab to Market: Marketing as the Reproduction of Trust

Marketing is by no means the traditional notion of mere selling. Truly effective marketing is a precise transmission of value. It makes complex technology easy to understand, turns cold data into intuitive experiences, and encourages potential users and investors to say in their hearts: "I believe in this."

Therefore, for entrepreneurs, marketing is no longer an "afterthought" following R&D; it is an equally important pillar of the "iron triangle" alongside R&D and production. It must be integrated into every stage of product development, from initial proof-of-concept to final market launch, always considering how to build and convey trust. This includes but is not limited to:

1. Transparency: Use short videos to showcase the challenges and breakthroughs during development, letting users witness the "birth story" of the product.
2. Personification: Make the founder or technical expert the brand ambassador, leveraging personal credibility to endorse the product.
3. Interactivity: Actively respond to user comments and questions, treating every piece of feedback as a valuable "peer review."

This consensus is not written in journals; it is written in users' likes, comments, shares, and purchases. It is an invisible "paper" composed of countless clicks and interactions, yet more powerful than any printed publication.

When your product is widely recognized by society, that is the true "proof of publication." It signifies that your invention has successfully transformed from a personal discovery into a societal consensus, beginning to have a tangible impact on the world. Only after gaining broad social recognition does fundraising and sales become significantly easier.

## Further Reading

[1]. D. A. Aaker, *Building Strong Brands*, Free Press, 1996.
[2]. X. Cao, *Strategic Management and Organizational Development*, Springer, 2025.
[3]. X. Cao, *Modern Business Management*, Palgrave Macmillan, 2025.
[4]. R. Cialdini, *Influence: Science and Practice*, 5th ed., Pearson, 2009.
[5]. S. J. DeVito, *The Interpersonal Communication Book*, 15th ed., Pearson, 2019.
[6]. E. Katz and P. F. Lazarsfeld, *Personal Influence: The Part Played by People in the Flow of Mass Communications*, Free Press, 1955.
[7]. P. Kotler, K. L. Keller, *Marketing Management*, 16th ed., Pearson, 2022.
[8]. S. Li, *Haircutting Robots*, Switzerland: Springer, 2025.
[9]. E. Rogers, *Diffusion of Inventions*, 5th ed., Free Press, 2003.
[10]. M. Solomon, *Consumer Behavior: Buying, Having, and Being*, 13th ed., Pearson, 2020.
[11]. N. Tufekci, *Twitter and Tear Gas: The Power and Fragility of Networked Protest*, Yale University Press, 2017.

# Chapter 21
# From Tulips to Bitcoin: How to Give a Product Lasting Monetary Value

## 1 Introduction

On the stage of the business world, there is a magic spell—scarcity. It acts like a halo, convincing countless people that as long as a product is "rare," its value will be eternal. Yet history and reality both tell us that this is merely a "paradox" of scarcity: mere rarity does not guarantee lasting value. What truly enables a product to transcend the category of consumables and become a vehicle of wealth is the interplay of scarcity, the hierarchy of human needs, strong monetary attributes, and social consensus.

This chapter will traverse history—from the frenzied Dutch tulip market, to the enduring brilliance of gold and diamonds, and onward to the modern digital realm of Bitcoin and luxury goods—delving into the truth about scarcity: what constitutes real versus pseudo-scarcity? How can monetary attributes fundamentally alter a product's fate? And, in today's commercial world, how can we consciously embed "monetary functions" into products to create brands that endure across cycles?

## 2 The Feast of the Bubble: The "Pseudo-Scarcity" of Tulips

In seventeenth-century Netherlands, tulips—exotic flowers imported from Turkey—became the object of a nationwide speculative frenzy. At the height of the craze, a rare bulb called "Semper Augustus" could fetch the price of a mansion in Amsterdam. People believed that this beautiful and uncommon flower possessed a magic that ensured it would never lose value.

However, in the spring of 1637, the feast ended overnight. Prices plummeted, countless speculators were instantly ruined, and market confidence collapsed faster than any plague. The tulip bubble remains one of history's most famous speculative cases, delivering a painful lesson: the scarcity of tulips was pseudo-scarcity.

 
S. Li, *Bridging the Innovation Gap*, Innovation, Technology, and Knowledge Management, https://doi.org/10.1007/978-3-032-22652-5_21

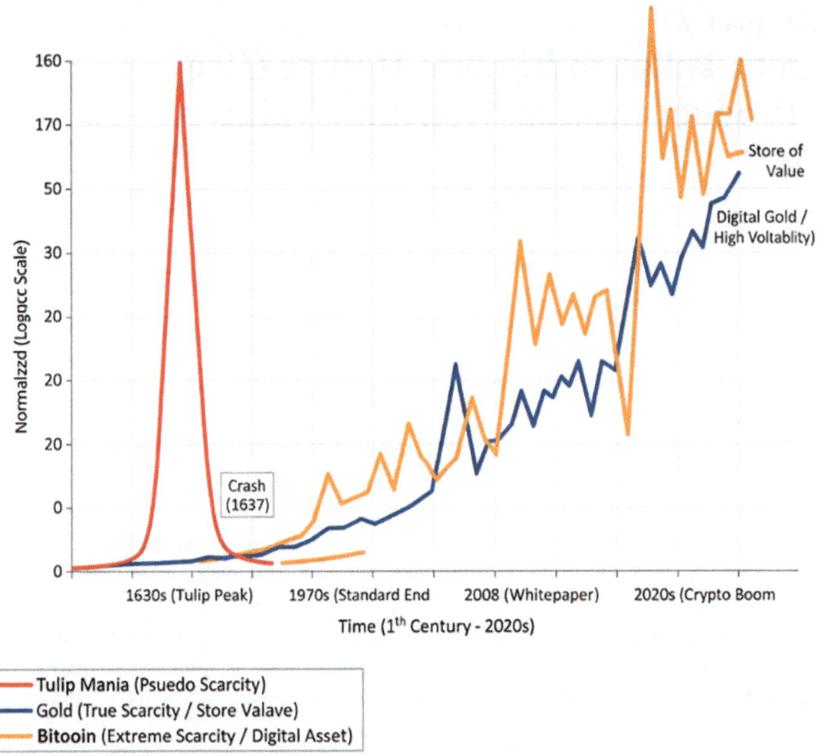


**Fig. 21.1** Comparative price curves of tulips, gold, and bitcoin

Why? Because the rarity of tulips was based on an illusion of reproducibility. In essence, tulips are a plant that can propagate rapidly. Once people perceived enormous profit potential, the expansion of supply was inevitable. When supply increased, the initial scarcity vanished. Speculators had purchased a "seed" that could be infinitely reproduced at the price of a mansion—its fate of collapse was already sealed. (Fig. 21.1).

## 3 The Eternal Moat: Gold, Art, and the Secret of "True Scarcity"

If tulips could not be replicated, their fate would have been entirely different. They would likely have become collectible items for the upper class—like gold, diamonds, or top-tier artworks—maintaining high value over the long term.

Gold and diamonds are typical examples of true scarcity, characterized by the following features:

- Extremely limited supply: Their reserves are finite, extraction is extremely difficult, and large-scale expansion in the short term is impossible.
- Chemical and physical properties: Gold does not corrode or rust and can be melted and reused indefinitely. These properties confer durability.
- Social consensus: After thousands of years of historical accumulation, human society has implicitly recognized gold as a legitimate "store of value."

Similarly, every top-tier artwork in the world is unique and cannot be replicated. Even the *Mona Lisa* exists in only one version. This "true scarcity" grants artworks the ability to endure across cycles. Although during economic crises, owners might sell for liquidity, causing temporary price drops, the value never truly "drops to zero overnight." True scarcity ensures a baseline value for a product, preventing complete collapse, though it still cannot entirely escape speculation or macroeconomic cycles.

## 4 The Value Amplifier: How Monetary Attributes Transform Product Destiny

In the logic of business, scarcity is only the entry ticket. To give a product lasting vitality and turn it into an "asset," it must be endowed with monetary attributes.

Monetary attributes mean a product can not only be consumed but also widely accepted by society as a "store of value" or "medium of exchange." As textbooks teach, for a product to qualify as money, it generally must meet these key criteria:

- Scarcity with low supply elasticity: Cannot be massively replicated or rapidly issued.
- Durability: Can be preserved over the long term without significant degradation.
- Divisibility: Can be easily divided or combined, facilitating small transactions.
- Portability: Easy to carry and transfer, reducing transaction costs.
- Broad social consensus: Widely trusted and recognized by the user community.

When a product meets all these conditions, it transcends mere "use value" and is granted "store-of-value" status by the market. This explains why products like Moutai, LV, and Bitcoin can command prices far above their manufacturing costs.

## 5 Modern Case Studies: Who Plays with Scarcity and Monetary Attributes

Luxury Goods: LV Bags and the Precision of "Controlled Scarcity".

The biggest difference between LV bags and tulips is that LV knows how to "control scarcity." Through strict limited editions, annual new collections, and carefully woven brand stories, it creates a sense of "controlled scarcity." Consumers purchase not just a handbag, but the identity, taste, and respect that LV represents.

By doing so, LV binds its products deeply to Maslow's higher-level needs (esteem and self-actualization). This strong cultural consensus allows LV bags to maintain high prices in the secondary market, giving them a "quasi-monetary" function—acting as a wealth carrier that can be liquidated at any time.

Collectibles: Pop Mart and the Risk of "Pseudo-Scarcity".

Pop Mart, through blind boxes, attempts to replicate the magic of scarcity in the collectible toy market. Its risk lies in "excessive supply elasticity." If a hidden figure can be endlessly replicated, its scarcity is doomed to vanish. Therefore, Pop Mart must continuously shift from "scarcity of a single figure" to "scarcity of brand culture," maintaining value through ongoing IP updates and emotional connections.

Bitcoin: Digital Gold and the Ultimate Scarcity Experiment.

Bitcoin's rise is based on the logic of extreme scarcity—the total supply is hard-coded at 21 million coins, with no inflation. At the same time, it possesses perfect monetary attributes: divisible, portable, durable, and difficult to counterfeit. It is thus called "digital gold," serving as a store of value without central authority endorsement.

However, Bitcoin is not invincible. Just as gold can lose purchasing power during social unrest or famine, when human needs sink to the most basic physiological level, the desire for food and water will surpass trust in digital assets. At that point, Bitcoin, like gold, faces a liquidity crisis. In other words, a product's value ultimately depends on the level of human needs it satisfies. (Fig. 21.2).

## 6 The Complete Logic of Value and Insights for Entrepreneurs

Whether a product can truly become an "asset that appreciates" depends on the convergence of three key factors:

Authenticity of Scarcity: True scarcity prevents value from dropping to zero, while false scarcity is ultimately destined to collapse.

Level of Human Needs Satisfied: The more a product caters to higher-level needs, the more vulnerable its value is during economic downturns.

Possession of Monetary Attributes: Scarcity, durability, divisibility, liquidity, and broad social consensus.

Only when these three elements are perfectly combined can a product genuinely possess long-term value that withstands market cycles.(Table 21.1)

## 7 Insights for Entrepreneurs

If you want to create a product with long-term value, you can consciously embed "monetary functions" into it by considering the following approaches:

**Fig. 21.2** Whether it's an LV bag, Pop Mart collectibles, or Bitcoin, all possess monetary attributes

**Table 21.1** Comparison of scarcity types and product value

| Category | Tulips (Pseudo-scarcity) | Gold/Artworks (True scarcity) | Bitcoin (Extreme scarcity) |
|---|---|---|---|
| Supply elasticity | Extremely high, can be mass-propagated | Extremely low, difficult to mine/create | Zero elasticity, programmed limit |
| Durability | Perishable, cannot be preserved long-term | Excellent, resistant to corrosion/physical wear | Perfect, digitally permanent |
| Social consensus | Short-term speculative craze | Long-term historical accumulation | Geek/fan community |
| Secondary market | Bubble burst, almost zero | Active, with liquidity risks | Active, highly volatile |

1. Artificially set supply boundaries: Reduce supply elasticity through limited editions, versioning, or numbering.
2. Enhance durability: Ensure the product can withstand the test of time and minimize wear and tear.
3. Build trust mechanisms: Use blockchain, traceability, and anti-counterfeiting technologies to reinforce the credibility of its scarcity.
4. Cultivate social consensus: Create unique cultural symbols and status markers that deeply bind the product to users' emotions.
5. Open secondary markets: Promote product liquidity, encouraging users to hold and accumulate it.
6. Preserve intrinsic utility: Avoid pure speculation, ensuring the product retains value even if its "monetary" function diminishes.

## 8 Conclusion

The collapse of the tulip market serves as a warning of human greed and speculation, showing that false scarcity only brings short-lived euphoria. The fates of gold and Bitcoin demonstrate that true scarcity can generate long-term value, but it still fluctuates with human needs and social trust. In today's business world, the most successful products are often not merely "consumables," but wealth carriers endowed with "monetary functions." Entrepreneurs who grasp this complete logic can evolve a product from a "one-time purchase" into a "long-term holding asset." Scarcity makes a product worthy of attention, monetary attributes make it worthy of trust, and fulfilling needs makes it genuinely valuable. This is the deepest truth in the commercial world—from tulips to Bitcoin.

## Further Reading

[1]. D. Ariely, *Predictably Irrational*, HarperCollins, 2008.
[2]. X. Cao, *Modern Business Management*, Palgrave Macmillan, 2025.
[3]. X. Cao, *Strategic Management and Organizational Development*, Springer, 2025.
[4]. E. H. Gombrich, *The Story of Art*, 16th ed., Phaidon Press, 1995.
[5]. P. Kotler, K. L. Keller, *Marketing Management*, 16th ed., Pearson, 2022.
[6]. K. Nakamoto, "Bitcoin: A Peer-to-Peer Electronic Cash System," 2008.
[7]. T. R. Nicholas, *Tulipmania: Money, Honor, and Knowledge in the Dutch Golden Age*, University of Chicago Press, 2005.
[8]. R. Shiller, *Irrational Exuberance*, 3rd ed., Princeton University Press, 2015.
[9]. A. D. Smith, *The Value of Things: Scarcity and Social Consensus*, Oxford University Press, 2018.
[10]. N. N. Taleb, *Antifragile: Things That Gain from Disorder*, Random House, 2012.

# Chapter 22 Perseverance and Adaptability—Understanding the Choices of Modern Youth through Agrarian and Nomadic Civilizations

## 1 Introduction: An Ancient Paradox

Throughout the vast course of human history, two distinct forms of civilization have stood in stark contrast to one another: the agrarian civilization and the nomadic civilization. The former is founded upon settlement, land, cultivation, and stability; the latter upon migration, herding, hunting, and adventure. These are not merely two different modes of production—they represent two fundamentally different ways of thinking and two divergent systems of values.

If we pull the lens back several millennia and imagine a scene: a community of agrarian peoples laboring diligently along a river valley—sowing, irrigating, and awaiting the harvest. Their world is built upon the stability of land and the cyclical rhythm of the seasons. Meanwhile, across a vast expanse of grassland, a nomadic tribe drives its herds of cattle and sheep, migrating continually with the changing water and pastures. Their world is founded upon uncertainty—on movement and spontaneous pursuit.

At first glance, these two ways of life appear to be merely environmental adaptations. Yet when crisis strikes, their fundamental differences are laid bare. When food suddenly becomes scarce, the nomadic tribe will not hesitate to depart, seeking new grazing grounds and fresh water sources; whereas thc agrarian community will grit its teeth and hold fast, trusting that when the winds and rains return in due season, the land will once again yield abundance (Fig. 1).

## 2 The Same Predicament, Yet Opposite Optimal Solutions

This divergence is not accidental—it is the product of environmental logic accumulated through long-term selection. Nature itself is a cold and impartial judge: it punishes those who make the wrong decisions and rewards those who make the right

 
S. Li, *Bridging the Innovation Gap*, Innovation, Technology, and Knowledge Management, https://doi.org/10.1007/978-3-032-22652-5_22

**Fig. 1** The differences between agrarian and nomadic civilizations

ones. Thus, nomadic peoples gradually developed cultures that celebrate risk-taking and embrace change, while agrarian societies internalized values that emphasize perseverance, continuity, and reverence for tradition.

The consequences of this difference have been profound throughout history. The Mongol cavalry's ability to sweep across Eurasia in an astonishingly short time stemmed from the nomadic culture's inherent flexibility, mobility, and adventurous spirit. In contrast, the enduring continuity of Chinese agrarian civilization—lasting thousands of years—rested upon its steadfastness and long-term commitment to "holding on to the land."

The question is, this divergence has not vanished with the passage of time. It continues to shape human behavior today—especially among entrepreneurs and young people. When confronted with an uncertain future, should one be like the nomads, daring to migrate and explore? Or should one be like the farmers, patient and steadfast, waiting for the land to bear fruit once more?

## 3 The Logic of Environment: The Distinct Survival Genes of Agrarian and Nomadic Civilizations

### *3.1 Nomadic Civilization: The Spirit of Adventure in Migration (Fig. 2)*

The defining characteristic of nomadic peoples is **mobility**. For those primarily engaged in pastoral nomadism, their wealth lies not in land but in livestock. Cattle and sheep depend on pastures—dynamic resources that shift with the seasons, climate, and rainfall. Once the grasslands are exhausted, staying put means starvation for the herds and collapse for the tribe. Only by continual migration can life be sustained.

For nomadic peoples who rely on hunting and fishing, the same logic applies. When game or fish in one region becomes scarce due to overhunting or environmental

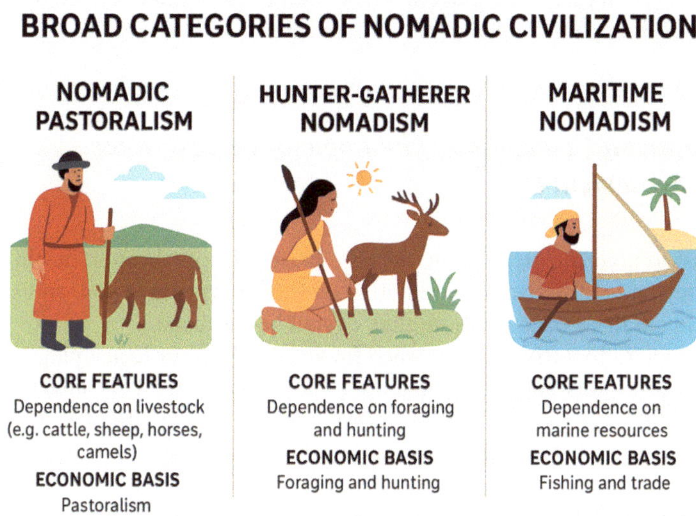


**Fig. 2** Typical forms of nomadic civilization: nomadic pastoralism, hunter-gatherer nomadism, and maritime nomadism

changes, the tribe must move on in search of new resources. Remaining in place would lead to depletion and eventual extinction.

Such environments naturally create a reward-and-punishment mechanism: conservative tribes that choose to stay behind often perish when resources run out, while adventurous ones—those who take the risk of distant expeditions—may find richer pastures and, with them, survival. Through centuries of natural selection, nomadic societies internalized this lesson into a simple yet powerful truth: to survive is to dare. Over time, this principle became embedded not only in their way of life but also in their approaches to war, expansion, and governance.

The Mongol Empire stands as the most vivid example. Genghis Khan's armies swept across Eurasia with astonishing speed—not through the refined productivity of agrarian economies, but through the unparalleled mobility and daring born of nomadic culture. The steppe cavalry had no fixed homeland; their "home" was on horseback, and wherever the pastures were rich, that land became their base.

This spirit of adventure persists in the modern world. Silicon Valley's entrepreneurial culture can be seen as a contemporary expression of the "nomadic logic": rapid experimentation, fearless iteration, and a relentless search for the next fertile "pasture." Many startups knowingly embark on a near-impossible journey—with a high likelihood of failure—yet they persist, much like nomadic tribes who continually migrate in pursuit of survival.

Even Spencer Johnson's best-selling book *Who Moved My Cheese?* inherits this nomadic narrative at its core. The book's central message—that change is the only constant, and that those who courageously adapt to shifting environments are the ones who thrive—is, in essence, a modern articulation of the wisdom forged by nomadic civilizations through millennia of natural selection.

## *3.2 Agrarian Civilization: The Logic of Perseverance in Settlement (Fig. 3)*

In contrast to nomadic civilization, the core of agrarian civilization lies in its deep dependency on land. Agriculture requires stable territory, fertile soil, and sufficient water. Without these conditions, farming cannot be sustained.

In China's Yellow River Basin, when floods, droughts, or locust plagues struck, farmers' instinct was not to migrate but to endure and wait. They understood that the land would not lose its fertility forever—that the next seasonal cycle might restore balance. Rather than risk moving elsewhere, it was wiser to stay and cultivate patience.

This environment also forged its own reward-and-punishment mechanism. Those who migrated rashly left behind fertile and well-watered lands, only to find barren or inhospitable soil elsewhere—and thus perished. Those who stayed, though they might endure hunger in the short term, were rewarded when the climate normalized and the land yielded crops again. Over millennia, agrarian civilizations distilled this logic into a worldview opposite to that of the nomads: "to survive is to endure." From this emerged a culture that valued order, tradition, and stability.

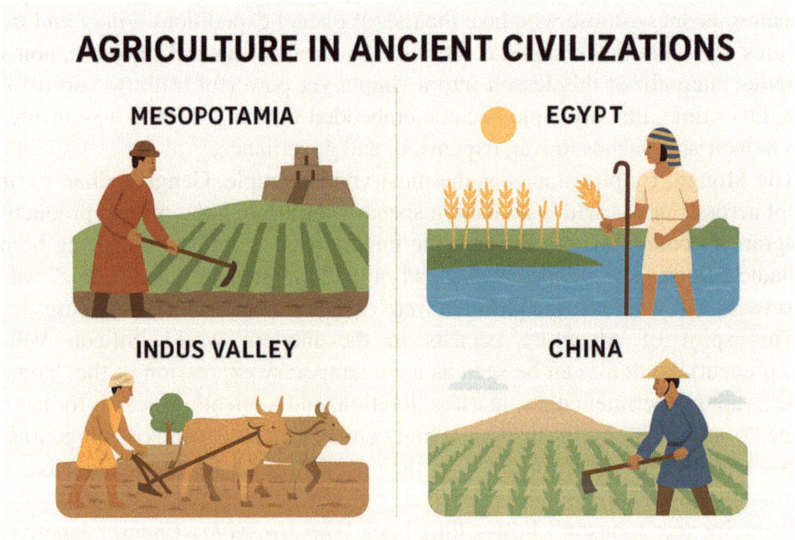


**Fig. 3** The agrarian civilizations of the four ancient cradles of civilization

It is no coincidence that Confucianism emphasizes "the laws of the ancestors must not be changed." This principle is not merely philosophical—it is the natural outcome of thousands of years of agrarian adaptation to environmental realities.

Thus, we see how nomadic and agrarian civilizations, confronted with the same natural phenomena, evolved completely different mentalities through long-term natural selection. We cannot simply declare that one should "adapt through change" (the nomadic way) or "respond through constancy" (the agrarian way)—the right answer depends on the nature of the challenge itself: is it a nomadic-type crisis or an agrarian-type crisis?

The same logic held true in the Nile River Valley. The Nile's annual flooding deposited fertile silt upon its banks. History taught the Egyptians that leaving this land in search of better habitat was futile—there was no comparable alternative nearby. Even when floods were too great or too small, abandoning the land was unwise; in the long run, it remained the most suitable ground for cultivation. Those who stayed through hardship were ultimately rewarded, while those who fled often faced punishment from nature for their impatience.

In the modern world, this spirit of perseverance still holds immense value. Many traditional enterprises thrive not through rapid iteration but through long-term accumulation and stable operation. Coca-Cola has maintained its formula for over a century; Moutai has preserved its craft for generations—both embodying the agrarian ethos of patient endurance and faith in continuity.

## *3.3 Reward Mechanisms and Cultural Genetic Differences*

In summary, the environments of these two civilizations shaped opposite moral economies:

- Nomadic civilizations punished conservatism and rewarded adventure, cultivating values of flexibility, courage, and opportunity-seeking.
- Agrarian civilizations punished recklessness and rewarded endurance, nurturing values of prudence, restraint, and continuity.

These divergent cultural genes profoundly influenced the course of history. Steppe peoples often possessed immense short-term dynamism—capable of rapid expansion—yet struggled to maintain stability over time. Agrarian societies, in contrast, demonstrated enduring resilience, sustaining their civilizations across millennia.

In today's world, when we map this ancient logic onto entrepreneurship and personal growth, we discover that the real question is not whether to "change" or to "persist," but rather: what kind of environment are you in—nomadic or agrarian?

## 4 The Cultural and Behavioral Extensions

Civilization is not merely a matter of survival strategy—over time, it crystallizes into values and modes of thought that shape social institutions, personal behavior, and even psychological traits. The contrast between agrarian and nomadic life eventually evolved into a set of deep "cultural genes," defining humanity's varied understandings of risk, time, order, and invention.

### *4.1 The Extensions of Nomadic Culture: Invention and Expansion*

The nomadic environment made risk-taking not optional, but essential. Gradually, the survival instinct to venture forth became elevated to a cultural ideal. Nomadic civilization, by its very nature, involved rejecting ancestral patterns—leaving behind ancestral lands that could no longer sustain life and seeking new, fertile ground. This process of leaving, rejecting, and rediscovering is, in essence, one of creative renewal.

Nomadic cultures, therefore, naturally exhibit several defining traits:

- Immediacy: Nomadic peoples are accustomed to rapid decision-making. In the face of enemies or natural disasters, hesitation could mean extinction.
- Mobility: Nomadic societies tend to have fluid social structures. Authority often concentrates in charismatic leaders whose legitimacy stems not from inheritance but from valor and achievement. This fosters leadership rather than bureaucracy.
- Opportunism: Living in unpredictable environments makes nomadic peoples highly sensitive to opportunity—whether discovering new pastures or detecting an enemy's weakness, they act swiftly.

These same traits resonate strongly with modern invention and entrepreneurship. Silicon Valley is often described as the "technological steppe," where startups rise and fall in a volatile ecosystem. The failure rate is extraordinarily high, yet this high-risk environment has produced giants like Google, Facebook, and Tesla.

Venture capital, too, embodies a nomadic logic: investors know that 90% of projects will fail, yet they keep investing—because one successful "new pasture" can more than compensate for all losses. The "high-risk, high-reward" mindset mirrors the adventurous ethos of steppe tribes.

### *4.2 The Extensions of Agrarian Culture: Stability and Order*

Agrarian civilization is fundamentally different. The nature of land dictates that stability matters more than change. Embedded in agrarian DNA is a reverence for ancestors and lineage, since staying on ancestral soil and farming according to inherited wisdom was the surest way to survive. Migration—leaving the fields of one's forebears—was a path to ruin.

Thus, agrarian societies evolved complex systems emphasizing order and continuity, characterized by:

- Long-termism: Agriculture requires waiting between sowing and harvest, cultivating patience and foresight.
- Family and Clan Systems: Land ownership tied families to place, and property often passed down generations, strengthening kinship and local cohesion.
- Conservation and Inheritance: Agrarian knowledge retains long-term value; respect for ancestral experience became cultural consensus.

In the modern world, this manifests as a preference for stability and sustainable growth. Japan's lifetime employment system, for instance, reflects agrarian logic—the company-employee relationship mirrors long-term cultivation rather than short-term exchange. This steady mindset is deeply rooted in Confucian order and endurance.

China's century-old enterprises—such as Tongrentang and Changyu Winery—exemplify this tradition of accumulation through perseverance, preserving craftsmanship and values across generations.

## 4.3 Cultural Conflict and Complementarity

Nomadic and agrarian cultures are not strictly divided; they often collide and intertwine, producing both tension and creativity. Historically, nomadic invasions repeatedly challenged agrarian empires—the Xiongnu, Turks, and Mongols all left their marks. Yet such nomadic empires often burned bright and brief, lacking the institutional stability for longevity.

At the same time, the two civilizations complemented each other. The Tang Dynasty of China exemplified this synthesis—its openness and dynamism owed much to interaction with northern nomadic tribes.

In today's world, this dynamic persists. In corporate governance, nomadic thinking promotes rapid iteration and seizing opportunities, but risks impulsiveness and short-termism. Agrarian thinking emphasizes long-term accumulation and order, but can become rigid and conservative.

The most successful organizations balance both. Huawei, for example, embodies nomadic adventurousness in its strategy—venturing into 5G, semiconductors, and cloud computing—yet practices agrarian patience in execution, through heavy investment in R&D and long-term planning. This dual cultural DNA enables it to thrive amid global competition.

### *4.4 The Shaping of Individual Behavior*

Culture not only influences nations and enterprises but also deeply permeates individual values. Those nurtured within nomadic cultures tend to pursue speed, adventure, and novelty—exemplified by the young innovators of Silicon Valley. In contrast, those raised within agrarian cultures value stability, accumulation, and respect for experience—traits often found among young people in East Asian societies.

However, in today's globalized world, no young person can avoid the blending of these two cultural logics. One must both dare to break through like the nomads and know how to persevere like the farmers.

## 5 Cases from History and Reality

The persuasiveness of theory often rests on the support of facts. The distinctions between agrarian and nomadic civilizations are not confined to ancient modes of production; their underlying logics have been repeatedly validated throughout history and modern reality. Whether in the rise and fall of empires or the success and failure of enterprises, the same truth prevails—the environment determines the optimal strategy.

### *5.1 Successful Cases of "Nomadic Thinking"*

In 2007, the iPhone was launched, completely reshaping the mobile phone industry. At the time, Nokia held a dominant 50% market share, seemingly unassailable. Yet Nokia chose to "hold fast" to its feature phones and Symbian system, believing consumers would not easily abandon traditional keyboards or durable batteries. Within just five years, Nokia fell from industry leader to near irrelevance, eventually being acquired by Microsoft.

Apple, on the other hand, made the bold choice to "migrate" to smartphones—even when the iPod was still selling strongly. This decisive shift mirrored the nomads' willingness to abandon depleted pastures in search of new, fertile ones. Ultimately, Apple secured the future of the entire industry. This case illustrates that in fast-evolving technological environments, persistence is often the most dangerous choice, while adaptability ensures survival. In the battle between Apple and Nokia, the nomadic logic triumphed over the agrarian logic.

Amazon began as an online bookstore, yet Jeff Bezos was never content with a single domain. He continually explored new frontiers—expanding from e-commerce into cloud computing (AWS), smart devices (Kindle, Echo), and entertainment (Prime Video). Each expansion appeared risky, but every move represented a nomadic-style "search for new pastures." Today, AWS stands as the world's largest cloud service provider, contributing over 60% of Amazon's profits. Without this nomadic spirit, Amazon might have remained merely an e-commerce giant rather than evolving into a global technology empire.

Looking further back, the American westward expansion in the nineteenth century epitomized the modern expression of nomadic culture. With the population doubling and land in the East growing scarce, thousands of pioneers ventured into the unknown West seeking opportunity. Despite immense risks, their migration expanded the nation's power and laid the foundation for America's modernization.

Together, these cases demonstrate that in nomadic environments, risk-taking and migration are essential. Only those willing to "abandon the old pastures" can find new vitality.

## *5.2 Successful Cases of "Agrarian Thinking"*

Coca-Cola, founded in 1886, has maintained nearly the same formula for over a century. Although the company once attempted to introduce "New Coke," it faced strong consumer backlash and soon returned to the classic recipe. This experience proved that staying true to core products and brand values generates more sustainable returns than blind invention. Today, Coca-Cola's market capitalization exceeds $250 billion, making it one of the most stable giants in the beverage industry. Its success exemplifies the agrarian principle of "holding the foundation."

Imagine if Coca-Cola had aggressively diversified—expanding into multiple soda flavors or venturing into fast food. It might have lost focus and been overtaken by more specialized competitors. Thus, in this case, the agrarian mindset decisively outperformed the nomadic one.

In China, Moutai derives its value not from marketing campaigns but from its commitment to craftsmanship, terroir, and tradition. Producing Moutai requires a rigorous process that takes at least five years before a batch is ready. More importantly, Moutai is deeply intertwined with Chinese culture and social etiquette. This steadfast dedication has translated into extraordinary long-term value—as of 2025, Moutai's market capitalization remains above 2 trillion RMB, making it the world's most valuable liquor brand. Here, the agrarian mentality reveals its enduring resilience.

Similarly, when Samsung entered the semiconductor industry in the 1990s, the market was dominated by Japan and the U.S. The massive investments and long payback periods deterred most competitors. Yet Samsung adopted an agrarian-style perseverance, investing heavily in R&D and production year after year, refusing to retreat even through extended losses. Two decades later, Samsung became the world's largest memory chip manufacturer. Its success was built not on short-term opportunism but on persistence and long-term commitment.

These cases demonstrate that in agrarian environments, reckless migration can lead to rootlessness, while steadfast perseverance builds enduring moats over time.

## *5.3 The Cost of Wrong Choices*

When the environment changes, wrong choices are often punished harshly. Consider the tragedy of several Native American tribes who, as game grew scarce, chose to stay put rather than move. Many perished from famine, while those who ventured farther or embraced trade survived. In the modern business world, Kodak offers a striking parallel. As early as 1975, Kodak invented the digital camera but chose to protect its film business instead of adapting. When the digital wave hit, Kodak collapsed entirely.

Conversely, excessive risk-taking in agrarian contexts can also be disastrous. In Chinese history, farming communities that migrated too frequently often failed to establish stable livelihoods. During the mass migration waves of the Ming and Qing dynasties, many settlers unfamiliar with new climates and soils fell into poverty—and countless died.

In the corporate world, Ofo's downfall illustrates the same principle. In the early days of the bike-sharing boom, rapid expansion was indeed necessary—a "nomadic" phase. But Ofo expanded recklessly before securing stable financing or a sustainable model, ultimately burning through capital and losing its foundation for survival.

These lessons remind us that failure rarely stems from lack of effort, but rather from choosing the wrong strategy for the wrong environment. Both perseverance and change can be virtues—the key lies in knowing when to hold fast and when to move on.

## *5.4 Lessons from the Cases*

Looking across history and the present, two iron rules emerge:

- In nomadic environments, rapid action and an adventurous spirit are essential. Otherwise, one risks being swept away like Nokia or Kodak.
- In agrarian environments, patience, perseverance, and long-term accumulation are crucial. Otherwise, one risks collapse, as with Ofo or farmers who failed in migration.

Ultimately, true wisdom does not lie in blindly advocating "hold" or "change," but in recognizing the environment: Is the situation you face more like a grassland or more like farmland?

## 6 Implications for Contemporary Entrepreneurs and Young People

If the contrast between agrarian and nomadic civilizations reveals two extreme survival logics, their greatest value for today's youth is not to tell us whether to hold or change, but to remind us that the environment determines the answer.

Imagine a startup operating in an environment more like a grassland than farmland. Market demand is unclear, technology changes daily, and competitors can emerge at any time. If founders patiently cultivate like farmers, waiting for "next year's harvest," they will often be overtaken by bolder competitors. The stories of Nokia and Kodak exemplify agrarian thinking misplaced in a nomadic environment—overly reliant on past experience, holding on to old pastures while ignoring that the grass has withered.

Conversely, in certain industries, risk-taking can be blind consumption. In energy, pharmaceuticals, or food, the rules are highly stable. A pharmaceutical company that completely overturns its research direction every few years may end up achieving nothing. True value often comes from companies steadfastly focusing on a single direction for decades. Samsung's success in semiconductors is the result of such perseverance. Had it migrated like a nomadic tribe, it would never have become the global memory chip leader.

Today's young people face challenges more complex than at any point in history. We no longer live in purely agrarian societies, nor in purely nomadic worlds. Our reality is a blend of both. The internet sector resembles a grassland—fast-changing, requiring constant pursuit of opportunities. Traditional industries resemble farmland—steady, patient cultivation yields results. To go far, one must learn to seek new pastures like nomads while also learning to hold one's ground like farmers.

This skill first manifests in entrepreneurship. Early-stage entrepreneurs must embrace nomadic thinking: exploring, experimenting, quickly testing the market, and iterating continuously. Silicon Valley entrepreneurs understand this principle, often saying "fail fast, fail often"—rapid, repeated failures are necessary to discover the right path. This is the essence of the nomadic logic: only by constantly migrating can one find truly fertile pastures.

However, once a business discovers its pasture, the story changes. The entrepreneur must shift from nomadic to agrarian thinking, focusing on consolidating foundations and building long-term accumulation. Coca-Cola's success illustrates that a company cannot survive indefinitely by constantly seeking new pastures; real value lies in establishing long-term moats. If one continues to migrate like a nomad at this stage, the result is losing the foundation. Ofo collapsed precisely because it expanded recklessly before solidifying its base, leaving both people and resources exhausted along the way.

The same logic applies to personal growth. Young adults entering the workforce are better suited to nomadic thinking, as they have limited knowledge of the world and their own interests and strengths. At this stage, it is risky to immerse oneself in a single field for decades like a farmer. A wiser approach is to explore and migrate in one's twenties, seeking suitable "pastures" for growth. Only once one identifies the land where their abilities can flourish should they settle and cultivate long-term.

By the time one reaches their thirties or forties, after clarifying core strengths, the most important quality becomes perseverance, not risk-taking. Frequent job-hopping or changing directions at this stage is like a farmer rotating fields every year—never yielding a true harvest. A Harvard Business School study found that people with more than ten years of experience in one domain earned, on average, over 40% more than those who drifted frequently. Long-term career value is the product of agrarian thinking.

Therefore, young people need to cultivate not a fixed trait, but the ability to switch between nomadic and agrarian mindsets. They must embrace long-termism like farmers while remaining capable of decisive transformation like nomads when necessary. Integrating these two modes of thinking is the most competitive survival strategy in modern society.

## 7 Conclusion: The Environment Determines the Answer

The stories of agrarian and nomadic civilizations serve as a metaphor. They remind us that there is no single correct answer in the world. Change is not always right, and perseverance is not always wrong. What truly matters is the environment.

On the grasslands, waiting for a harvest is foolish. On the farmland, frequent migration is equally foolish. Nature has encoded this principle into human civilization through a system of rewards and punishments. The courage and adventure of nomads are forced by their environment; the resilience and perseverance of farmers are forged by theirs.

Today's youth and entrepreneurs are often caught between two competing voices:

- "You must bravely change and innovate, or be left behind."
- "You must stick to long-term focus and specialize, or never accumulate value."

Both voices are correct—but only halfway. The real answer lies not in "hold" or "change," but in judging the environment.

If your environment resembles a grassland, have the courage to abandon old pastures. If it resembles farmland, have the patience to wait for next year's harvest. Only when your actions align with the logic of the environment can you truly succeed (Fig. 4).

Historical lessons and contemporary examples all confirm this truth. The sweeping victories of Mongol cavalry and the enduring legacy of Chinese civilization, the success of Apple versus the decline of Nokia, the steady accumulation of value by Moutai versus the collapse of oFo—all these stories, spanning millennia, illustrate the same principle: the environment is the primary determinant of success or failure.

For today's young people, the greatest wisdom is not simply to choose between "change" or "persist," but to learn to assess the environment: Is it more like farmland

**Fig. 4** Decisions depend on the environment: Choosing the appropriate strategy according to the environment is the correct choice

or more like a grassland? This seemingly simple question is profoundly important—it determines whether you should hold your ground or pivot, be patient or bold.

The world is increasingly complex, and change comes faster than ever, yet some truths remain constant. Human civilization has already provided countless experiments and outcomes. By learning from them, we can avoid unnecessary detours.

So, when you hesitate at the crossroads of entrepreneurship, or waver in career choices, ask yourself: Is this a grassland, or is it farmland? The answer is often hidden in this very question.

## Further Reading


1. X. Cao, *Strategic Management and Organizational Development*, Springer, 2025.
2. J. Diamond, *Guns, Germs, and Steel: The Fates of Human Societies.* W. W. Norton, 1997.
3. M. T. Hansen, *Collaboration: How Leaders Avoid the Traps, Create Unity, and Reap Big Results*, Harvard Business Review Press, 2009.
4. X. Cao, *Modern Business Management*, Palgrave Macmillan, 2025.

5. P. Frankopan, *The Silk Roads: A New History of the World*, Bloomsbury, 2015.
6. C. M. Christensen, *The Innovator's Dilemma*, Harvard Business School Press, 1997.
7. R. Kaplan and D. Norton, *The Strategy-Focused Organization*, Harvard Business School Press, 2001.
8. S. Covey, *The 7 Habits of Highly Effective People*, Free Press, 2004.
9. H. Mintzberg, *Strategy Safari*, Free Press, 2005.
10. E. Rogers, *Diffusion of Inventions*, 5th ed., Free Press, 2003.

# Chapter 23
# Respecting the Weak, Embracing Diversity: Long-Term Survival Principles in an Uncertain World

## 1 Introduction

Human civilization's pursuit of the "optimal solution" has never ceased. Within the ivory towers of engineering, industrial processes, and even economics, efficiency and a single best choice are often regarded as symbols of rationality and progress. Yet, when we broaden our perspective to the wider domain of survival—from biological species diversity, to pluralism in political decision-making, to asset portfolios in the business world—we find that all systems capable of long-term viability deliberately allow for "suboptimal" or even "mediocre" choices, forsaking extreme efficiency.

This seemingly paradoxical phenomenon reveals a profound survival philosophy: in a real, dynamic world with incomplete information, diversity is not the opposite of optimality, but rather a necessary strategy for achieving superior outcomes over longer time horizons. It serves as an early warning against system fragility, provides strategic tolerance for unknown risks, and represents the ultimate safeguard of systemic resilience (Fig. 23.1).

## 2 Cognitive Limitations: The Trap of Local Optima

Our obsession with a single optimal solution is based on an idealized assumption: that we have precise, comprehensive knowledge of the problem. If the world could be fully modeled like a mathematical optimization problem, a single optimal solution would certainly exist and merit our full commitment. Yet the complexity of reality lies in the fact that our understanding of most business, social, and ecological problems is always limited, partial, and often entangled with path dependencies and biases.

These cognitive limitations mean that we can only construct "suboptimal models" based on local information, from which we may derive misleading "local optima." For example, if you ask a technical manager how to achieve the greatest progress

 
S. Li, *Bridging the Innovation Gap*, Innovation, Technology, and Knowledge Management, https://doi.org/10.1007/978-3-032-22652-5_23

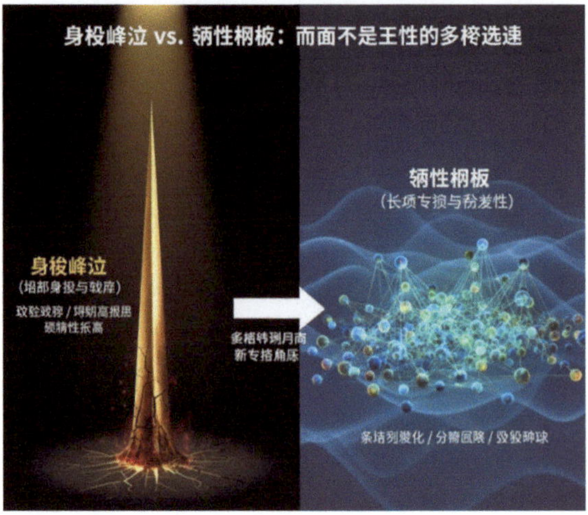


**Fig. 23.1** Diversity is not a compromise on efficiency; it is the only strategic safeguard in an uncertain world. Organizations need to shift their focus from an obsession with a single, fragile "optimal peak" toward building a broad and stable "resilient network"

for the company, their answer might be "technology upgrades." This represents a local optimum from their professional perspective. However, if the same question is posed to the CEO, the answer could be entirely different—perhaps "rapidly expand product sales channels" or "secure the next critical round of financing." Within this broader business model, technology upgrades may be merely a high-cost, low-short-term-return option. The CEO's decision-making framework, encompassing market, financial, and human resource dimensions, helps avoid the pitfalls of seeing only part of the picture (Fig. 23.2).

When information is incomplete, an obsession with a single optimal solution is, in effect, blind trust in our own cognitive blind spots. This "local optimum" trap has

**Fig. 23.2** In a fog of uncertainty, choosing the highest peak you can see within your local environment is obviously a narrow perspective. Prudently preserving diversity and leaving room for alternatives is a wise approach

left deep lessons in business history. For instance, Kodak's "film optimal" trap: at the end of the twentieth century, Kodak was an absolute giant in the photography industry and had even invented digital camera technology early on. However, its management, based on the then-lucrative film and development business, concluded that the optimal decision was to protect and optimize the existing film supply chain. This cognition model, centered on current revenue structures, caused them to perceive the disruptive digital trend as a threat to be avoided. They successfully maximized local profits during the "film era" but completely missed the later industry-wide transition to digital media, ultimately being eliminated by history.

Similarly, the case of Wells Fargo is revealing. In the financial services sector, Wells Fargo once overly emphasized sales metrics, making the "number of new accounts opened" the core local optimization indicator. Frontline employees, in pursuit of the "optimal solution" for this metric, created millions of fake accounts under pressure. While this optimization based on a narrow sales metric made the data look impressive in the short term, it severely damaged the bank's reputation and compliance from a global perspective, ultimately resulting in massive fines and a crisis of trust when the scandal surfaced.

Furthermore, the former video rental giant Blockbuster, once at its peak, optimized its business model to the extreme—charging late fees and occupying prime store locations. This over-optimization of physical rental led its organization and cognition into isolation, blinding it to Netflix's disruptive digital subscription model, and ultimately led to bankruptcy and rapid disappearance.

These cases collectively warn us: diversity is the antidote to cognitive limitations. It means allowing and incorporating "suboptimal suggestions" from different perspectives, thereby building a decision-making system that is closer to global optimality and more adaptive.

## 3 Environmental Dynamism: Today's Optimum, Tomorrow's Poison

If cognitive limitations are internal traps, the dynamism and nonlinear changes of the environment are external black swans. In a stable and predictable environment, a system may evolve toward a highly adaptive single optimal state. However, once this over-specialized efficiency encounters drastic environmental changes, it can become a fatal flaw for an organization or species.

Take biological evolution as an example. In the age of dinosaurs, favorable conditions made "muscular and large-bodied" the optimal solution for survival and competition. Yet when an asteroid struck the Earth, causing massive environmental upheaval, this "optimal solution" instantly became a deadly constraint—the large bodies, requiring enormous energy when the food chain collapsed, were the first to perish. In contrast, those previously considered "weak," small-bodied, and more adaptable mammals survived.

This illustrates the deeper strategic significance of "respecting the weak, respecting diversity." Diversity is not a waste of efficiency but a necessary investment in system resilience. When the environment undergoes dramatic shifts, it is precisely those species, technologies, or ideas deemed "redundant" or "suboptimal" during stable periods that carry the hope of survival for the entire system. A system based on a single optimal solution is efficient but fragile; any external shock can lead to complete collapse.

In business, the fragility caused by over-optimization is even harsher. Swiss mechanical watches, once the pinnacle of craftsmanship with precisely engineered gears, represented the optimal solution for timekeeping. The entire Swiss industry ecosystem revolved around handcrafting and high pricing. Yet when Japanese and American companies introduced low-cost, high-precision quartz technology, this became a disruptive environmental shock. Swiss firms, overly attached to the "optimal" status of mechanical watches and lacking diverse strategies in electronics, lost a substantial market share within a few years.

Similarly, Nokia, once dominant due to excellent hardware manufacturing, supply chain management, and its highly optimized yet closed Symbian OS, held the market throne. Symbian was then the optimal solution for low power consumption and mass production efficiency. However, when Apple and Google introduced smartphones and app store ecosystems, the market shifted rapidly from "hardware efficiency" to "software diversity." Nokia's highly optimized single system lacked evolutionary diversity and flexibility, failing to adapt to this open, multi-platform demand, ultimately proving itself a rigid "dinosaur" that quickly became extinct in the new ecosystem.

These cases clearly show that any "optimal solution" based on past experience may collapse in the face of dynamic environmental changes. Enterprises and individuals must reserve diversity as a strategic buffer, treating efficiency and resilience diversity as a dynamic balance.

## 4 Implications for Entrepreneurship and the Future: Strategic Portfolios

At this point, the necessity of diversity is clear: it counterbalances cognitive limitations and insures against environmental dynamism. How, then, should we balance optimality and diversity in actual operations and entrepreneurial activities? This is not a binary choice but a strategic trade-off based on the degree of uncertainty.

For precisely controllable tasks—such as driving a car from start to finish in the shortest time—the optimal solution is clear and unique: floor the accelerator. Pursuing diversity here only adds inefficiency. However, for long-term strategies and entrepreneurial activities full of unknowns and volatility, diversity is the "insurance policy" that must be purchased.

In entrepreneurship and organizational strategy, diversity as a strategic portfolio manifests across three core dimensions:

1. Product and Market Portfolio (Portfolio Approach): Successful entrepreneurs refuse to invest all resources into a single "perfect" feature or product. They often maintain multiple "suboptimal" product lines or technological paths, ready to pivot based on market feedback. This "multi-pronged attack" strategy ensures that even if one main initiative fails, the enterprise retains backup capabilities and learning experience.
2. Team Composition: Ensure team members come from diverse backgrounds, thought patterns, and professional domains. A team comprised solely of top-tier technical personnel may achieve high local optimality but lack commercial sensitivity and innovative breadth in the face of market changes. Including employees who are not "perfect" in certain areas but bring complementary perspectives significantly expands the company's cognitive boundaries and reduces the risk of major decision-making errors.
3. Core Capabilities and Exploratory Investment (Exploration): While cultivating core competencies, maintain diversified exploration of future trends. A retail giant, while optimizing physical stores, must invest resources in e-commerce, logistics, and even virtual reality "suboptimal" experiments. Most of these experiments may fail, but if the environment shifts, one "suboptimal" seed could become the lifeline that leads the enterprise through a crisis (Fig. 23.3).

In summary, the pursuit of optimality seeks efficiency and short-term gains, whereas diversity ensures survival and long-term resilience. Diversity is the strategic premium we pay to account for our cognitive limitations and the unpredictability of the environment. In predictable and stable local contexts, we can pursue extreme optimization; but in unpredictable, dynamic global contexts, we must embrace diversity. Viewing diversity as part of long-term optimality, rather than as an obstacle, is the fundamental principle for enterprises and individuals to achieve sustained success in a complex world.

## 5 Conclusion

The trade-off between optimality and diversity is not a simple opposition between efficiency and waste, but a strategic choice between maximizing short-term gains and ensuring long-term systemic resilience. In a complex world full of black swan events and cognitive blind spots, a singular optimal solution brings only fragility and rigidity. Enterprises and individuals must recognize that redundancies deemed "suboptimal" and perspectives of the "weak" are in fact invaluable strategic buffers when facing the unknown. Embracing diversity fundamentally means accepting the uncertainty of the world, integrating survival insurance into the pursuit of efficiency. Ultimately, organizations capable of weathering cycles and evolving continuously

**Fig. 23.3** In a complex and ever-changing world, diversity builds a solid foundation for enterprises to withstand risks and achieve long-term success across three dimensions: products, teams, and exploration

will be those that not only pursue excellence but also reserve options and respect all possibilities—a truly wise system.

## Further Reading


[1] X. Cao, *Modern Business Management*, Palgrave Macmillan, 2025.

[2] F. L. Coolidge and T. Wynn, *Cognitive Archaeology and Human Evolution*, Cambridge University Press, 2009.

[3] E. O. Wilson, *The Social Conquest of Earth*, Liveright, 2012.

[4] R. Boyd and P. J. Richerson, *Not By Genes Alone: How Culture Transformed Human Evolution*, University of Chicago Press, 2005.

[5] X. Cao, *Strategic Management and Organizational Development*, Springer, 2025.

[6] J. Surowiecki, *The Wisdom of Crowds*, Doubleday, 2004.

[7] M. Ridley, *The Evolution of Everything*, Harper Collins, 2015.

[8] P. Holland, *Hidden Order: How Adaptation Builds Complexity*, Addison-Wesley, 1995.

[9] H. Thomas, *Diversity in Organizations: New Perspectives*, Routledge, 2014.

[10] D. Kahneman, *Thinking, Fast and Slow*, Farrar, Straus and Giroux, 2011.

# Chapter 24
# The Cognitive Dilemma of Entrepreneurship—Why Grand Visions Often Stall at the Details

## 1 Introduction

In the business world, every entrepreneur harbors grand visions. They perceive unmet market needs and imagine an innovative product capable of changing the world. Yet, the journey from vision to reality is often blocked by innumerable intricate details and complexities. This phenomenon is not accidental; its root lies in a cognitive bottleneck overlooked by most people.

As demonstrated by the "Magical Number Seven" theory in cognitive psychology, human short-term memory has a limited capacity, typically able to handle only $7 \pm 2$ "chunks" of information simultaneously. This seemingly simple rule becomes an iron law when managing complex tasks, both individually and within teams. When a project contains more independent details or critical issues than this threshold, the decision-maker's cognitive load instantly exceeds capacity, leading to a sharp decline in efficiency, and in some cases, total decision paralysis.

We can liken a project to a system that needs to be conquered, where each function or technical point within the system represents a "node". A seemingly simple project may contain dozens or even hundreds of nodes, with intricate dependencies so complex that even the most outstanding teams struggle to make progress (Fig. 1).

From this perspective, the essence of entrepreneurship is not merely about spotting opportunities; it is the art of managing complexity. Grand visions that fail do not falter due to a lack of creativity, but rather because they cannot decompose massive, systemic tasks into controllable, executable sub-tasks. This is the core issue that must be addressed when making business decisions.



S. Li, *Bridging the Innovation Gap*, Innovation, Technology, and Knowledge Management, https://doi.org/10.1007/978-3-032-22652-5_24

**Fig. 1** The journey from vision to reality is often blocked by countless intricate details and complexities. Distilling clear solutions from this complexity is frequently one of the key challenges faced in entrepreneurship

## 2 Modularity Thinking—The Key to Managing Complexity

Faced with exponentially growing complexity, the only way to break through is to apply the concept of modularity derived from computer science. At its core is hierarchical decomposition: a massive, unmanageable problem is systematically divided into several independent, manageable submodules, each of which can in turn be further decomposed into smaller submodules in the same manner. The golden rule of this decomposition is to ensure that at any level, the number of submodules remains within the limits of human cognitive capacity (Fig. 2).

We categorize the nodes within a project by different "granularities": high-level nodes are considered "large-granularity nodes," while the sub-nodes they decompose into are "small-granularity nodes." A project is deemed complete only when all its lowest-level nodes have been fully addressed. This tree-like topology provides a clear project roadmap. If a "large-granularity node" is broken down into more than seven "small-granularity nodes," it indicates that the management complexity of this node has exceeded an effective range and requires further modular decomposition until each branch contains a controllable number of nodes.

In this way, an ostensibly insurmountable task can be transformed into a series of clear, manageable sub-tasks. Teams can work on different modules in parallel, with each module leader focusing solely on the details within their module, free from the complexity of the entire system.

Modularity is not merely task decomposition; it is a rigorous design principle. In computer science, a successful module must adhere to the principles of high cohesion and low coupling. High cohesion means that all elements within a module tightly serve a core function—for example, a "user login" module contains only

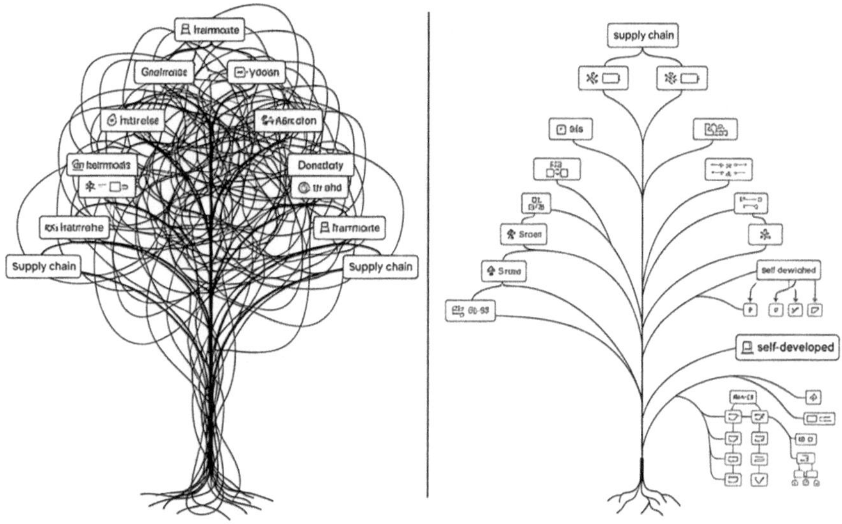


**Fig. 2** Combining a tree-structured project management approach with modularity thinking is a powerful method for handling complex systems

the logic for account verification, password encryption, and related processes. Low coupling requires minimal and straightforward dependencies between modules, so that changes in one module do not broadly affect others. This design philosophy is equally critical in business practice. For instance, in developing a smart speaker, designing "voice recognition" and "audio output" as two independent modules allows optimization of the voice recognition algorithm without altering the hardware or software interface of audio output.

This layered, high-cohesion, low-coupling modular structure not only significantly reduces the cognitive load of individual tasks but also greatly enhances organizational efficiency. It enables large teams to operate like multiple independent, high-performing small teams. Project managers can clearly assign tasks, track progress, and designate responsible individuals for each module. When a module encounters issues, the team can quickly pinpoint the problem and perform precise fixes without halting the entire project. Fundamentally, this transforms the traditional linear, sequential project management model, making parallel development and rapid iteration possible—a critical breakthrough for managing modern business complexity.

## 3 The Choice Between "Build" and "Buy"

After completing modular decomposition, entrepreneurs face a crucial strategic decision: for each node, should we develop it in-house ("Build"), or leverage existing supply chain solutions ("Buy")? (Fig. 3).

The answer to this question directly determines a project's success and its risk level. We must clearly understand that, whether at the atomic scale of micro-modules or the galactic scale of macro-modules, if a module lacks a mature supply chain solution and must be developed in-house, the effort, resources, and risks involved are essentially the same. Each self-developed module represents an exploration from scratch, with a success rate that is highly uncertain. This uncertainty is unrelated to the module's scale but is proportional to its level of invention.

The overall success probability of a project can be seen as the product of the success probabilities of all the "atomic nodes" that must be developed in-house. This means that the more nodes requiring self-development, the lower the project's overall chance of success. Therefore, prioritizing the resolution of sub-module issues through mature supply chains is the primary strategy for project success. Modules sourced from the supply chain have usually undergone extensive market validation, offering higher reliability and serving as solid "building blocks" that provide a high-certainty foundation for the project.

This "buy" strategy is not as simple as just spending money; it requires the entrepreneur to have a deep understanding of the entire industry ecosystem and the technology supply chain. Like an experienced architect, they must know which components (e.g., steel, cement) can be procured directly from the market, and which unique artistic designs (e.g., specific architectural curves) must be created in-house. Blindly choosing to develop everything internally not only incurs high trial-and-error

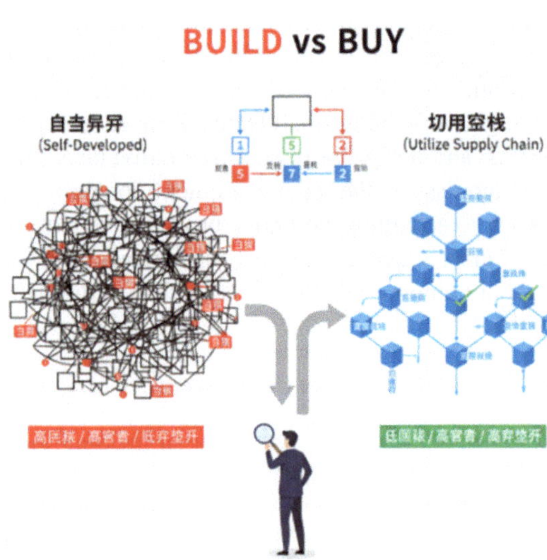


**Fig. 3** Fully leveraging existing elements that can be reliably sourced through the supply chain as core components, and focusing in-house development efforts only on the remaining parts that cannot be addressed by the supply chain, is the key to ensuring the success of a complex system by minimizing the number of modules that require self-development

costs and delays but also risks dragging down the stability of the entire project due to low-reliability modules.

A typical example is a company focused on developing new smart home products. If it chooses to self-develop all chips, sensors, and operating systems instead of adopting mature solutions, the likelihood of failure is extremely high. Chip design, sensor manufacturing, and OS development are themselves extremely complex projects, each containing hundreds of "self-developed nodes," any one of which failing could collapse the entire project.

This theory also perfectly explains why making a lighter entirely from scratch is not necessarily harder than developing Musk's spacecraft. The reason the lighter is easier in reality is that there is sufficient supply chain coverage, meaning very few nodes require self-development, whereas Musk's spacecraft contains a large number of nodes that must be developed internally. If company leadership lacks understanding of or sensitivity to the supply chain and blindly chooses full self-development even for a simple lighter, failure is almost guaranteed.

## 4 The Essence of the Supply Chain—Humanity's Collective Wisdom Across Time and Space

Before deeply understanding the strategic value of the supply chain, we must recognize its sociological essence. The supply chain is fundamentally about leveraging the wisdom of predecessors; it is not merely a system of buying and selling goods. Humans are a society, not isolated individuals. The success of modern science is not the achievement of a single person but the cumulative result of generations of people—historical actors and contemporaries alike. Contributions from past humans to today's technologies are embodied through the supply chain. In other words, socialized mass production and historical collective effort are concretized via the supply chain. Only by fully leveraging the supply chain can we harness the collective capabilities of humanity to solve problems.

Consider, for example, the skill of making fire by friction—it is a "technology" provided by the supply chain. If early humans did not learn from or build upon the experience of predecessors, each person would have had to endure hundreds or even thousands of years of iterative trial and error to master the technique. Fully utilizing the supply chain is essentially taking advantage of the "high-reliability building blocks" accumulated by human civilization over millennia.

This "collective wisdom" effect of the supply chain is vividly evident in any mature industry. For instance, a modern smartphone developer does not need to design CPU transistors from scratch, create display technologies independently, or mine rare earth elements personally. These sophisticated and high-difficulty "self-developed nodes" have already been transformed by giants like TSMC, Samsung, LG, and Qualcomm, through decades of technological accumulation and massive investments, into high-reliability "building blocks" available on the market. These building blocks, as part

**Fig. 4** The essence of the supply chain lies in the collective wisdom of humanity across time and space—people from different regions and different historical periods coming together to form a cumulative force. Leveraging the outputs of the supply chain is, in effect, harnessing the collective intelligence of all humanity throughout history

of the supply chain, allow anyone who masters software integration and product definition to launch a competitive smartphone in a remarkably short time (Fig. 4).

If we view human history as a single, continuous R&D project, then the supply chain functions as its core version control system and knowledge-sharing platform. It consolidates the wisdom and labor of countless individuals into standardized, reusable components. This system of sharing allows every successor to stand on the shoulders of giants, rather than reinventing the wheel from scratch. Such efficient resource allocation and knowledge inheritance form the foundation for continuous progress and invention in any society, and indeed, within any company. Therefore, a successful entrepreneur's foremost capability lies in recognizing and leveraging this omnipresent "collective wisdom of humanity across time and space."

## 5 The Pioneer's Dilemma and the Later Entrant's Opportunity—Lessons from History

Looking back, countless examples highlight the tension between "pioneers' dilemmas" and "later entrants' opportunities." For instance, Japan began developing its robotics industry decades ago, yet its influence has waned even as humanoid robots boom today. Similarly, Boston Dynamics spent decades advancing legged robotics, achieving technical supremacy, but struggled to achieve large-scale commercial success.

The underlying reason is that these pioneers faced a landscape in which almost every module lacked a mature supply chain in the early stages of technological development. From hardware joints and sensors to control algorithms and operating systems, they had to develop nearly every module from scratch, dramatically increasing project risk and hindering large-scale commercialization.

## *5.1 Pioneering Alone in a Technological Wasteland*

Pioneers often tread in a technological wasteland. They must solve not only the core product problems but also countless foundational technical issues. It's akin to building a skyscraper while having to manufacture bricks, forge steel, and invent cement formulas yourself. Each step represents a massive, uncertain self-developed node. This exponentially lengthens project timelines, increases resource investment, and multiplies the probability of failure. Boston Dynamics exemplifies this dilemma: while their technology is impressive, in the early stages critical modules—like high-precision servo motors and complex motion control algorithms—were unavailable externally and had to be developed in-house.

## *5.2 Supply Chain Integration of Core Modules: From "Build" to "Commodity"*

However, the pioneers' efforts were not in vain. The technical breakthroughs they achieved often became foundational infrastructure for the entire industry. When their R&D outcomes (e.g., Boston Dynamics' high-dynamic balance algorithms) were abstracted, standardized, and open-sourced or commercialized, these technologies transitioned from high-risk "self-developed nodes" into high-reliability "supply-chain building blocks." These blocks allow later entrants to avoid reinventing the wheel, focusing instead on higher-level invention. For example, many contemporary humanoid robot companies can leverage mature open-source motion libraries and mass-produced servo motors, directing more effort toward application scenarios, human–machine interaction, and business model invention.

## *5.3 The Later Entrant's "Aggregated Advantage"*

Consequently, modern entrepreneurs can leverage modular thinking to enjoy unprecedented "aggregated advantages." They can source top-tier sensors, chips, batteries, and other modules globally, rapidly assembling them into fully functional prototypes. This drastically shortens R&D cycles, reduces trial-and-error costs, and crucially transforms overall project risk from the "product of all self-developed nodes' success probabilities"—a high-risk model—into the "product of a few core self-developed nodes' success probabilities," a lower-risk model. This explains why humanoid robots have recently surged after decades of Boston Dynamics' groundwork: many core modules have already been "supply-chained."

## 6 Profound Lessons for Entrepreneurs

From an in-depth analysis of modular thinking, supply chain strategy, and industry history, several core insights emerge as guiding "North Stars" for today's entrepreneurs:

### *6.1 The Primary Imperative of Risk Management: Survival*

The ultimate goal of entrepreneurship is not merely to "change the world," but to survive. A highly ambitious project with too many self-developed nodes has an almost negligible chance of success. Wise entrepreneurs recognize that the first priority is not achieving 100% disruptive invention but minimizing risk through mature supply chains. Like skilled system architects, they prioritize identifying and integrating high-reliability "building blocks," ensuring the product's core functions operate stably. Only once survival is secured can higher-dimensional invention occur.

### *6.2 Timing of Entrepreneurship: Beyond Market Trends to Supply Chain Maturity*

Successful entrepreneurs are often said to have "caught the wave," but the underlying factor is usually the maturity of foundational technology supply chains. Apple, for instance, was not the first to invent the smartphone, but it was the first to perfectly integrate touchscreens, mobile processors, battery technology, and other critical nodes and bring them to market. This is the power of being an "aggregator." Therefore, entrepreneurs should focus not just on macro market trends but also scrutinize the maturity of each critical module. The true entrepreneurial window opens when previously "technological black holes" become commercialized, standardized, and accessible at a manageable cost.

### *6.3 The Essence of Teams: Modular Organizational Structure*

A successful team is more than just a division of labor—it is a modular organization. Team leaders are no longer omniscient problem solvers but exceptional "system integrators" or "chief architects." Their core capability lies in identifying key project modules and finding the most suitable "collective intelligence" for each—encompassing both specialized team members and external suppliers or partners. Efficient leaders focus internal efforts on a few truly critical self-developed nodes while boldly outsourcing other generic modules to the supply chain.

### *6.4 The Golden Rule for Launching Projects: Map Module Risks*

Before starting any new project, conduct a rigorous self-assessment. Break your product or service into a clear "module tree." Examine each node and ask: "Should this node be self-developed (Build) or procured from the supply chain (Buy)?" Mark every "Build" node as a potential risk point. Then, evaluate the number and complexity of all "Build" nodes. If this exceeds your team's cognitive limits or if the cumulative success probability is too low, the project may lack commercial viability at this stage. This rational and rigorous evaluation serves as a strategic guide for pragmatic entrepreneurs.

## 7 Conclusion: Evaluating Projects Means Evaluating the Number of "Self-Developed" Modules

In summary, entrepreneurs and project managers should abandon blind technological heroism. Before launching any project, the most crucial homework is not the breadth of the market but the depth and maturity of technology. A pragmatic entrepreneur must first assess how many core modules of a product or project still require self-development. Only when this number is compressed to a controllable range within cognitive limits does the project enter a viable industrialization window. Choosing the right timing and leveraging accumulated "building blocks" to rapidly construct products, rather than pioneering alone in a technological desert, is the core logic of modern business success.

## Further Reading

[1] X. Cao, *Modern Business Management*, Palgrave Macmillan, 2025.
[2] H. A. Simon, *The Sciences of the Artificial*, 3rd ed., MIT Press, 1996.
[3] M. Malone, *The Future of Work*, Harvard Business Review Press, 2004.
[4] X. Cao, *Strategic Management and Organizational Development*, Springer, 2025.
[5] R. L. Ackoff, *Creating the Corporate Future*, Wiley, 1981.
[6] E. Ries, *The Lean Startup*, Crown Business, 2011.
[7] P. Drucker, *Management Challenges for the 21st Century*, HarperBusiness, 1999.
[8] S. Johnson, *Where Good Ideas Come From*, Riverhead Books, 2010.
[9] J. Dean, *Modular Design in Complex Systems*, MIT Press, 2012.
[10] A. Edmondson, *Teaming*, Jossey-Bass, 2012.

# Chapter 25
# End-State Thinking: Foreseeing the Inevitable, Strategizing the Present

## 1 Introduction

In today's complex and ever-changing world, a strategic concept that has increasingly gained attention is *end-state thinking*. This is not merely about envisioning the future; its deeper implication lies in the ability to anticipate, *today*, the inevitable state that something will take when it reaches stability or completion. Such insight allows one to use this end-state as a reference point to work backward and determine the most rational layout and courses of action in the present. Although such a strategy may not represent the most obvious or fastest optimization in the short term, it ensures the eventual attainment of global optimality and long-term victory.

The essence of this way of thinking is that it transcends the subjective expectation of "what we hope the future will look like" and instead focuses on the objective inevitability of "what the future will ultimately be based on existing conditions and intrinsic laws." Whether in the construction of scientific theories, the orchestration of military strategies, or the performance analysis of computer algorithms, end-state thinking demonstrates remarkable insight and practical guidance. It requires us to pierce through the immediate fog and grasp the essence of things, understanding their fundamental laws of development and ultimate trajectory.

## 2 Darwin and Malthus: Revealing the Inevitable of Natural Selection

Throughout the history of human thought, major leaps have often stemmed from ultimate inquiries into the essence of the world and the profound revelation of its core contradictions. When Charles Darwin was developing his groundbreaking theory of evolution, he grappled with how to precisely explain the mechanism of natural selection. He introduced the concept of the "struggle for existence," yet the driving



S. Li, *Bridging the Innovation Gap*, Innovation, Technology, and Knowledge Management, https://doi.org/10.1007/978-3-032-22652-5_25

force behind this struggle and its universality in the biological world remained a perplexing question. It was not until he read Thomas Robert Malthus's *An Essay on the Principle of Population*, published in 1798, that he experienced a moment of clarity (Fig. 1).

Malthus's *Essay on Population* itself represents a profound "terminal forecast" regarding the conflict between societal resources and population growth. His core ideas are clear and unsettling:

1. Without external constraints, human population grows geometrically (i.e., exponentially), exhibiting the potential for explosive expansion.

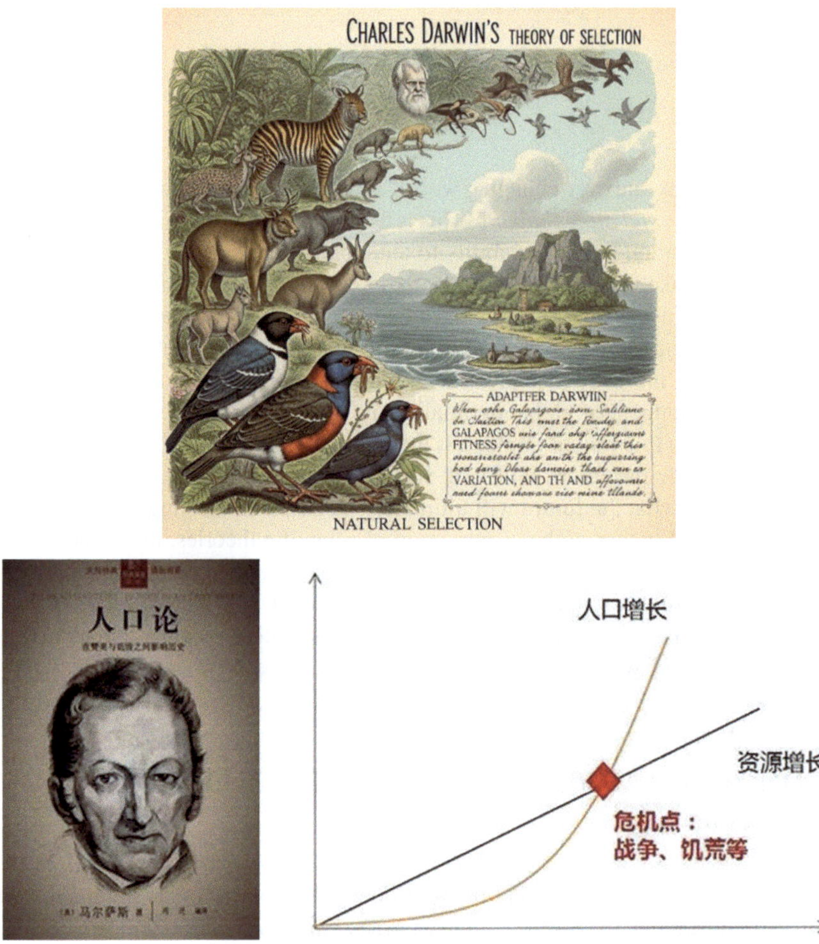


**Fig. 1** Darwin's theory of evolution and Malthus's principle of population

2. However, the material resources essential for human survival—particularly food and land—are constrained by natural endowments, land area, and technological progress, and tend to increase only arithmetically (i.e., linearly) and slowly.

From this, Malthus derived an unavoidable "terminal outcome": over time, the exponential growth of population will inevitably outpace the linear growth of resources, ultimately leading to a societal demand for materials far exceeding their supply. This vast gap between supply and demand will inevitably trigger intense competition among people for limited survival resources, resulting in famines, epidemics, and wars, which in turn forcibly reduce population back to levels compatible with available resources. This societal "end state" under extreme scarcity and survival pressure is precisely the inevitability that Malthus foresaw and emphasized. He was not predicting when a specific famine would occur, but rather revealing a macro-level, irreversible trend.

Darwin's extraordinary insight lay in his ability to creatively transplant and generalize Malthus's understanding of the "terminal outcome" in human society to the entire biological world. He realized that if human societies face fierce competition due to resource scarcity under certain end states, then all biological populations in the vast natural world confront a similar predicament: organisms' inherent reproductive potential far exceeds the carrying capacity of their environment. This means that in any ecosystem, the total amount of resources necessary for survival and reproduction—food, space, water, mates—is always limited, while reproductive potential can drive dramatic population growth. This inherent, irreconcilable contradiction inevitably leads to a "terminal state": among the infinite reproductive potential and finite resources, the vast majority of individuals cannot survive and reproduce successfully; only a few with stronger adaptability in the struggle for survival endure and leave offspring.

From this, Darwin gained a profound understanding of the essence of the "struggle for existence": it is neither random nor accidental, but a necessary and ongoing phenomenon arising from the inherent contradiction between unlimited reproductive potential and finite environmental resources. It is precisely this ruthless struggle, rooted in inevitability, that continuously selects traits better suited to the environment, forming the core mechanism driving natural selection and species evolution.

In this landmark case, Malthus provided society with a "terminal model" based on its intrinsic laws, anticipating the inevitable competition arising from the irreconcilable conflict between population and resources. Darwin, applying this cross-disciplinary "end-state thinking," cleverly extended the model to biology, explaining the mechanism of natural selection and laying a solid theoretical foundation for his theory of evolution. What they foresaw was not specific details, but a profound grasp of the underlying laws of development and the state that would inevitably manifest under those laws.

# 3 Mao Zedong's *on Protracted War*: Insights into the Terminal Victory of War

During the turbulent period of the Chinese War of Resistance against Japanese Aggression, facing the overwhelming military advances of the Japanese forces and widespread domestic and international pessimism, Mao Zedong published the famous essay *On Protracted War* in 1938. The core idea of this work is grounded in a profound insight into the "terminal outcome" of the Sino-Japanese War, providing a strategic direction for the Chinese nation to ultimately achieve victory. It stands as a paradigm of applying end-state thinking in military strategy (Fig. 2).

At the early stage of the Anti-Japanese War, the Japanese army, leveraging its overwhelming advantage in weaponry and well-trained troops, quickly occupied vast areas of Chinese territory. This rapid advance left many people feeling uncertain about the war's prospects and even gave rise to notions of "quick defeat" or unrealistic "quick victory" theories. However, Mao Zedong was not misled by immediate tactical gains or apparent setbacks. Employing end-state thinking, he fundamentally analyzed the war potential, resource endowments, and international strategic landscape of both China and Japan, making a broad yet precise prediction about the ultimate trajectory of the conflict.

The core conclusions of *On Protracted War* are based on a thorough end-state assessment of the balance of forces and the intrinsic laws of warfare:

1. Japan, as a small country, had relatively limited human and material resources. As the Japanese frontlines extended deeper into China, the demands for strategic supplies, troop deployment, maintenance of transportation lines, and occupation costs grew in direct proportion to the area under control. This demand for

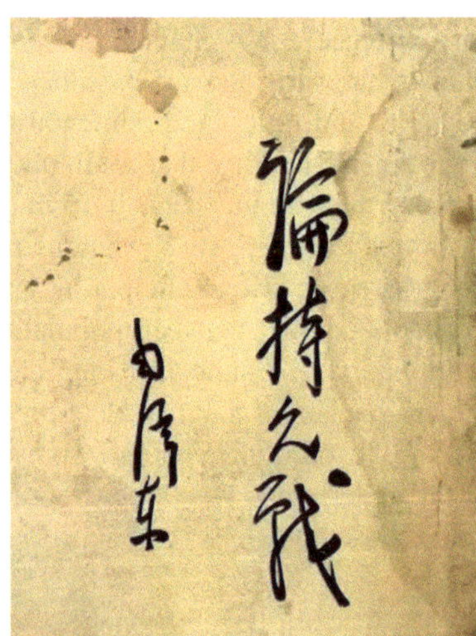

Fig. 2 On protracted war

resources and manpower escalated continuously as the invasion expanded both in area and duration.
2. China, a large country, possessed vast strategic depth and enormous population potential. Although China's military strength was relatively weaker in the short term, its abundant human and material resources could not be matched by Japan domestically or replenished in the short term. More critically, Japan's domestic resource supply and manpower reinforcement capabilities were limited and could not increase infinitely with the expansion of its invasion lines.

From this, Mao foresaw an irreversible "end-state": as the war prolonged and the frontlines stretched, Japan's total strategic supply requirements and troop consumption would increase linearly with the occupied area, eventually surpassing its maximum domestic supply capacity and sustainable limit. When the gap between supply and demand reached a critical point, Japan would be unable to continue, and its war machinery would inevitably stall and eventually collapse. Meanwhile, China, leveraging its vast strategic depth, large population base, and the determination of its people to resist, could sustain the conflict long-term, gradually dragging Japan into a war of attrition until it exhausted itself and brought about its own demise.

Based on this end-state assessment of the war, Mao proposed the strategy of "protracted war," dividing the resistance into three stages: strategic defense, strategic stalemate, and strategic counteroffensive. He emphasized that China should not seek quick victories but instead fully utilize its territorial advantages and population size, combining guerrilla and mobile warfare to engage the enemy across a vast land, continuously depleting Japan's active forces and resources while accumulating its own strength. Although this strategy implied that the Chinese people would endure greater hardships and sacrifices in the short term, it was the only path that could lead to ultimate victory.

The successful practice of *On Protracted War* fully demonstrates the immense value of end-state thinking in military strategy. It is not a prediction of the outcome of a specific battle but a macroscopic judgment of the war's overall trajectory. It revealed the inevitable victory scenario under specific force comparisons and development trends, guiding the Chinese people to adopt the most appropriate strategies and ultimately achieve the great victory of the Anti-Japanese War.

## 4 Computational Algorithm Complexity: Anticipating End-State Performance with Large-Scale Data

In the field of computer science, particularly in algorithm design and analysis, the concept of algorithmic complexity embodies end-state thinking in technical evaluation. It does not merely focus on the exact runtime for small data sets but emphasizes the ultimate performance and trends of an algorithm when the input data size (usually denoted as $n$) becomes extremely large.

When analyzing algorithm efficiency, we typically use Big O notation to describe time complexity or space complexity, such as O(n), O($n^2$), O(log n), O(n!). These notations reveal the growth rate of an algorithm's runtime or memory requirement relative to *n* as *n* approaches infinity.

To illustrate more concretely, consider an algorithm with an exact runtime function: $T(n) = 5n^2+100n+500$.

- When n is small, for example $n = 10$, the contributions of each term are: $5 \times 10^2 = 500$, $100 \times 10 = 1000$, and the constant term 500. Here, the 100n term is even larger than $5n^2$, and the constant term also has a noticeable effect.
- However, when n becomes very large, for example $n = 10^4$ (10,000):

  $5n^2 = 5 \times (10^4)^2 = 5 \times 1^8$ (500 million)
  $100n = 100 \times 10^4 = 10^6$ (1 million)
  Constant term 500 is negligible at this scale
  Constant term 500 is negligible at this scale

In this "end-state" scenario (as n approaches infinity), the growth rate and magnitude of $5n^2$ far exceed those of 100n and 500. Therefore, we describe the algorithm's time complexity as O($n^2$), because for sufficiently large n, the $n^2$ term dominates the runtime, and the contributions of the other terms can be ignored (Fig. 3).

This method of analysis is a quintessential example of end-state thinking:

- Anticipating the dominant factors at the "end state": It does not concern itself with the specific impact of constant factors or lower-order terms at small data scales, but directly predicts which component will become the sole determinant of algorithm performance when the data scale reaches its extreme ("end state"). This "dominance" is a mathematical inevitability, unaffected by specific machine performance or programming language.
- Guiding algorithm selection and system design: Such predictions of "end-state" performance are crucial for developers choosing the appropriate algorithms. For

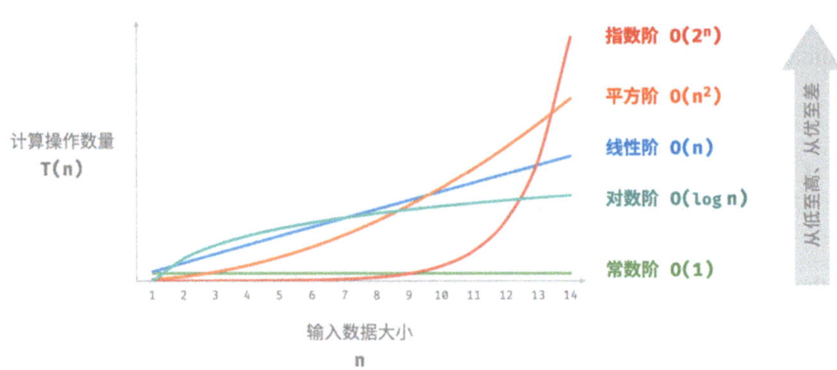


**Fig. 3** The essence of algorithm complexity analysis is also a form of end-state thinking

instance, in an application that must handle massive datasets, an O(nlogn) algorithm might underperform compared to an O(n) or O($n^2$) algorithm in small-scale testing due to larger implementation constants. However, from the perspective of end-state thinking, we would still steadfastly choose O(nlogn), even if it requires upfront optimization and implementation costs. We understand that when the data truly reaches the "end-state" scale, the efficiency advantage of O(nlogn) will be overwhelming, and no constant factor can compensate for the magnitude difference. This allows software engineers to strategically plan in advance, building systems that remain efficient at future data scales, avoiding the enormous cost of redesign caused by suboptimal early choices.

Algorithm complexity analysis is a mathematical prediction of a system's performance limits and final behavior under large-scale input. It represents a quantitative understanding of the "end-state" of technological development, guiding the construction of scalable and robust software systems that maintain efficiency and stability even as data volumes grow.

# 5 The Essence and Practical Value of End-State Thinking

Through Darwin and Malthus' revelations of natural selection, Mao Zedong's assessment of the course of war in *On Protracted War*, and the foresight of performance bottlenecks via algorithm complexity analysis, we can gain a deeper understanding of the essence of "end-state thinking" and its tremendous practical value.

## *5.1 The Essence of End-State Thinking: Insight from Inevitability*

The core of end-state thinking is not rooted in imagination or idealistic visions, but in a deep understanding of the inherent laws, core contradictions, and developmental trends of a system, from which one can deduce the inevitable outcomes when it reaches stability or its limit. It requires stepping beyond immediate details and distractions, elevating one's perspective to identify the key variables and dominant forces that ultimately determine success or failure.

- Revealing the inevitable eruption of latent contradictions: Malthus highlighted the irreconcilable tension between geometric population growth and arithmetic growth of subsistence resources. While this contradiction may be imperceptible in the short term, it inevitably erupts as a survival competition in the long-term "end-state."
- Grasping the ultimate impact of power differentials: Mao observed the fundamental disparities in national scale, war potential, and resource capacity between

China and Japan. This ultimate imbalance dictates that the aggressor will inevitably weaken in a prolonged war of attrition, while the defender can endure to achieve the victorious "end-state."
- Predicting the absolute dominance of key factors: Algorithm complexity analysis shows that for massive datasets, the term with the highest order of growth will mathematically become the decisive "dominant factor" in performance. Its effect may be subtle at smaller scales, but at the end-state, it is irreplaceable.

These examples collectively illustrate that end-state thinking is concerned not with "what might happen," but with predicting, based on objective analysis, "what will inevitably happen." It emphasizes insight into unavoidable trends and the final stable state.

## 5.2 The Practical Value of End-State Thinking: Begin with the End, Strategize the Present

The practical value of end-state thinking lies in its powerful guidance of "starting from the end." Once the end-state is clearly understood, even when faced with immediate challenges or decisions that seem suboptimal in the short term, decision-makers can steadfastly advance toward the ultimate goal, knowing that each step is a necessary accumulation toward achieving that final state.

- Avoiding short-term temptations and superficial distractions: End-state thinking helps decision-makers resist short-term gains, tactical wins or losses, and surface-level illusions. For example, in the early stages of the Anti-Japanese War, focusing only on Japanese territorial gains could easily lead to pessimism. *On Protracted War* transcends these short-term phenomena, focusing on the strategic goal of gradually exhausting the enemy's overall strength.
- Formulating fundamental and forward-looking strategies: End-state thinking fosters strategies that are truly forward-looking, address fundamental issues, and guide the overall situation, rather than merely applying tactical band-aids. It prompts deep strategic-level thinking and planning.
- Optimizing resource allocation efficiency: Predicting the end-state allows resources to be allocated more rationally and efficiently. It guides us to invest limited energy, time, and capital in areas that accumulate long-term advantages and ultimately lead to success, avoiding wasteful expenditure.
- Enhancing strategic resilience and adaptability: Even if the path to the end-state is winding and external conditions change, understanding the core trends and ultimate goal ensures that strategies remain resilient. Decision-makers can adjust tactics quickly without losing direction or deviating from core objectives.

# 6 Implications for Entrepreneurs

End-state thinking is not limited to grand historical events or scientific theories; it serves as a guiding North Star for entrepreneurs navigating the rapidly changing business environment. The entrepreneurial journey is full of uncertainty and temptations; short-term gains and superficial prosperity often obscure long-term strategic objectives. End-state thinking helps entrepreneurs maintain clarity and make decisions that are both insightful and sustainable.

1. Anticipate the industry end-state rather than blindly chasing trends: True innovators do not merely follow current trends; they foresee the ultimate shape of their industry. For example, when electric vehicle technology was immature, those who anticipated its eventual replacement of combustion vehicles and the end-state standards for energy efficiency and intelligence could strategically plan technology choices, product positioning, and business models, instead of scrambling to adapt after trends peak. Just as Malthus and Darwin saw the end-state contradictions between population and resources, and between reproduction and environmental capacity, entrepreneurs must see the ultimate balance between market supply and demand, technology, and user experience.
2. Build core competencies rather than pursue short-term gains: In the short term, startups may face funding pressures and survival challenges, making them susceptible to chasing rapid monetization opportunities, which often undermines long-term core competence development. End-state thinking requires entrepreneurs to consider: in the industry's mature "end-state," what will sustain your company? Unique technological barriers? Exceptional user experience? Irreplaceable brand value? Efficient cost structure? By defining the core competencies of the "end-state," entrepreneurs can invest early, even at the cost of short-term revenue or profit, to lay a solid foundation for long-term growth. This mirrors *On Protracted War*, where short-term sacrifices were necessary to gradually exhaust the enemy.
3. Understand the end-state evolution of user needs: User needs are not static but evolve with technological progress and societal development. Entrepreneurs must ask: when all technological bottlenecks are overcome and services are instantly available, what will be users' "ultimate" needs? For instance, the ultimate requirement for transportation is "point-to-point, safe, efficient, environmentally friendly, personalized mobility," not merely "owning a car." Understanding this end-state need enables the design of forward-looking products and services, such as autonomous driving and shared mobility, rather than only improving existing transportation methods.
4. Identify resource constraints and growth bottlenecks: No startup grows indefinitely; limits in resources, talent, and market capacity inevitably emerge. End-state thinking requires entrepreneurs, like algorithm complexity analysts, to identify which factor will ultimately constrain company growth as scale increases. Is it R&D speed, market expansion, organizational efficiency, or supply chain

stability? Anticipating these ultimate bottlenecks allows proactive planning and resolution, preventing critical failures when constraints arise.

5. Start with the end in mind and maintain strategic determination: Entrepreneurs face countless challenges, setbacks, and external noise. Without a clear perception of the end-state, it is easy to waver under pressure, frequently adjust strategies, and achieve nothing. End-state thinking provides strong strategic determination, enabling entrepreneurs to execute long-term plans with confidence, even in adversity, knowing that every step taken is necessary on the path to the ultimate goal (Fig. 4).

**Fig. 4** Applying end-state thinking in entrepreneurship

**Fig. 5** End-state thinking: Navigating uncertainty, anchoring the future

## 7 Conclusion: Anchoring Certainty Amid Uncertainty

In a world full of dynamism and uncertainty, "end-state thinking" provides a powerful cognitive framework and practical tool, helping us anchor those future trends that are relatively certain amid apparent chaos. It reminds us that true wisdom does not lie in predicting every moment with precision, but in deeply understanding the ultimate trajectory of developments, and using this as a foundation to build, step by step, a path toward final victory and long-term success.

Whether exploring the ultimate expressions of natural laws in scientific research, forecasting the final balance of power in strategic competitions, or predicting the ultimate performance bottlenecks in technological development, end-state thinking guides us to transcend short-sightedness, to view problems with broader perspectives and longer-term vision. It enables us, amid apparent disorder, to outline a clear picture of the future and, guided by this vision, make the wisest and most effective choices—thereby gaining initiative in intense competition and achieving ultimate victory. This mode of thinking is not only an advanced strategic tool but also a philosophy of life grounded in wisdom (Fig. 5).

## Further Reading

[1] X. Cao, *Strategic Management and Organizational Development*, Springer, 2025.
[2] C. Darwin, *On the Origin of Species*, John Murray, 1859.
[3] T. Malthus, *An Essay on the Principle of Population*, 6th ed., 1826.
[4] X. Cao, *Modern Business Management*, Palgrave Macmillan, 2025.

[5] M. Zedong, *On Protracted War*, Foreign Languages Press, 1938.
[6] R. Axelrod, *The Evolution of Cooperation*, Basic Books, 1984.
[7] H. Simon, *Models of Bounded Rationality*, MIT Press, 1982.
[8] D. Kahneman, *Thinking, Fast and Slow*, Farrar, Straus and Giroux, 2011.
[9] R. Kaplan and D. Norton, *The Strategy-Focused Organization*, Harvard Business School Press, 2001.
[10] N. Taleb, *The Black Swan*, Random House, 2007.

# Chapter 26
# Terminal Cost—Understanding the Evolutionary Logic of Business

## 1 Introduction

Inspired by the core philosophy of *The Almanack of Naval Ravikant*, this chapter defines and systematizes the concept of **terminal cost** as a framework for analyzing the essence and evolution of business models.

Terminal cost refers to how a company's total cost grows as the number of units sold, denoted by $n$, approaches infinity. Using this lens, we can categorize business models into several types:

- Traditional goods models with terminal cost **O(n)**,
- Information or infrastructure models with terminal cost **O(1)**, and
- Platform models with terminal cost **O(1)** and **spatial replicability**.

Through rigorous definition, mathematical derivation, and economic interpretation, this chapter aims to provide decision-makers with a **practical compass** for choosing business arenas, designing organizations, and formulating expansion strategies.

## 2 Your Business Compass: What is Terminal Cost?

In the grand chessboard of business, we often focus only on the visible pieces—gross margin, net profit, market share. These are the scenery before our eyes. But the true determinant of victory is your ability to see the end-state.

You must ask yourself one profound question:

> When my business reaches the entire world, when my product serves a billion users, what will my cost curve look like?

The answer to that question leads us to the core concept—terminal cost.



S. Li, *Bridging the Innovation Gap*, Innovation, Technology, and Knowledge Management, https://doi.org/10.1007/978-3-032-22652-5_26

Terminal cost is not an accounting term meant to balance your books. It is a strategic lens that reveals the underlying logic of a business. It describes how your total cost behaves as your business scales infinitely—when your product or service is consumed by countless people.

We use mathematical asymptotics to capture this trend. Like an X-ray for business models, it penetrates the surface and reveals the genetic code of your enterprise.

Let C(n) denote the total cost when $n$ units are sold. We define terminal cost as the growth trend of C(n) as $n \to \infty$, and simplify it into three common forms:

- Linear terminal cost (O(n))—Each additional unit sold increases your cost in fixed proportion. This is the "work more, earn more" model—the oldest and most pervasive business law.
- Constant terminal cost (O(1))—Your total cost remains essentially fixed, barely increasing with sales. This is the "one effort, infinite use" model—your initial work can be leveraged endlessly into the future.
- Constant and spatially replicable—The *super-evolved* version of O(1). Not only can you serve more users at a fixed cost, but you can replicate the same business system across the world almost effortlessly.

To visualize these three types, imagine three roads: one that must keep expanding as traffic grows; another, a tunnel built once and used indefinitely; and the last, a network of tunnels that can be instantly replicated anywhere on earth.

The road your business chooses determines both your ultimate destination and your speed.

## 3 Act I: The Endless Linear Trap (O(N))

This is the first principle of the business world. From a stone axe to a smartphone, from a small workshop to a multinational factory, such businesses share the same essence: they transform inputs (materials, labor) into products, and then extract value through sales.

We can express this cost structure mathematically as:

$C(n) = \alpha^{*}n + \beta$.

Here, $\alpha$ represents the variable cost—directly tied to production volume—while $\beta$ is the fixed cost. When your sales volume $n$ becomes large enough, the fixed cost $\beta$ becomes negligible, and your total cost grows linearly with $n$. This is the core of a terminal cost that scales as O(n).

It's a never-ending treadmill—a "business running machine." To increase revenue, you must continually increase input. Each product sold requires another unit of cost. Produce 100 million smartphones, and your total cost will be vastly higher than if you produced 10 million.

Take Foxconn, the world's largest electronics manufacturer, as an example. Each time Apple releases a new iPhone, Foxconn must invest heavily in new or upgraded production lines and hire tens of thousands of workers. Even though mass production

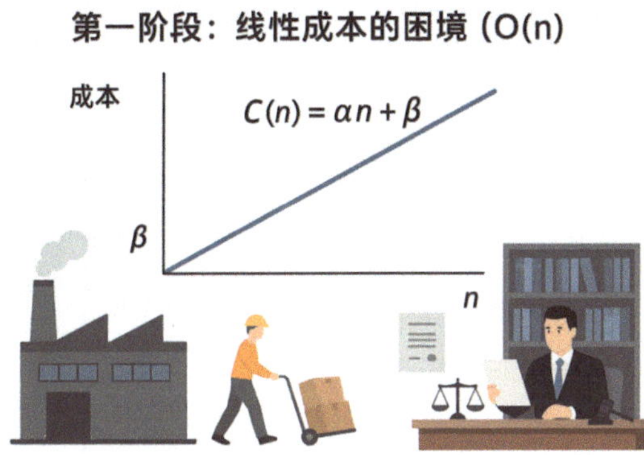


**Fig. 1** Linear terminal cost

drives down per-unit costs, those costs can never reach zero. No matter how large Foxconn becomes, its cost structure remains bound by the linear O(n) law—it must endlessly replicate its labor-intensive process. Its ceiling lies in the inescapable fate of "the bigger you get, the harder you work."

Another classic example of the O(n) model is a law firm or consulting company. Their core product is human expertise and time. To serve more clients, they must hire more partners and consultants. Each new client requires the allocation of one or more professionals' time. Even if a top lawyer charges a fortune per hour, his time is finite. The terminal cost of such a firm ultimately scales with the number of lawyers it employs (Fig. 1).

## 4 Act II: The Magical Leap to Zero Marginal Cost (O(1))

Yet the evolution of business has never stopped. As humanity entered the Information Age, a revolutionary concept began to emerge—marginal cost approaching zero.

In the language of our terminal cost framework, this corresponds to a total cost that scales as O(1). This means that no matter how many units you sell, your total cost barely increases (Fig. 2).

This represents a nonlinear growth pattern that completely breaks the linear bond between cost and sales volume. Within this category, we can identify two major types of business models:

### *4.1 Virtual Information Products: The Miracle of Replication*

At the heart of these businesses lies the digitization of knowledge, information, and creativity. The reason their terminal cost is O(1) is that the cost of replication for virtual products is almost zero.

**Fig. 2** Constant terminal cost—The case of marginal cost approaching zero

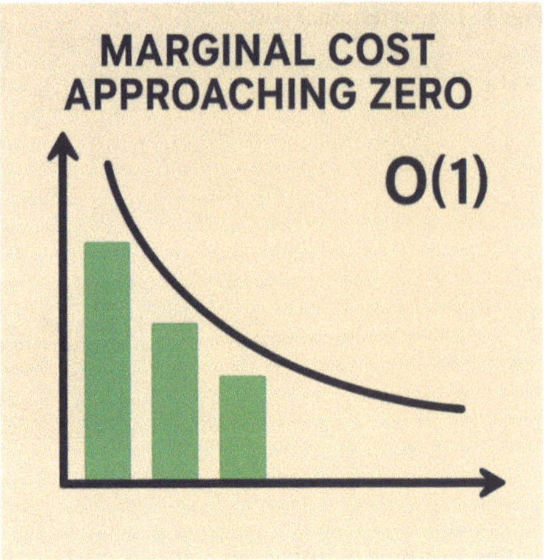


- Knowledge and Content: Writing a book, producing a video, or developing an online course all require significant upfront investment—but that investment happens only once. Take the online education platform *Coursera* as an example: creating a course demands substantial resources, yet once it is launched, adding another student consumes only a negligible amount of server bandwidth and storage—costs so small they can be ignored. This "one effort, infinite leverage" effect forms the foundation of industries such as knowledge monetization and digital content creation. Similarly, when *Netflix* produces an original series or film, the production cost may reach tens of millions of dollars. However, that fixed investment can be distributed among hundreds of millions of global viewers. Each additional viewer adds virtually no extra cost, making the marginal cost per user close to zero.
- Software and Patents: Developing software is an intensive intellectual endeavor, requiring substantial upfront labor and expertise. But once the code is written, replicating and distributing it to millions of users incurs almost no additional cost. That's why software giants like *Adobe* enjoy exceptionally high profit margins. After building applications like *Photoshop* and *Illustrator*, they can sell them to millions of users worldwide—revenue scales upward, while cost remains nearly flat.

## *4.2 Shared Infrastructure: The Power of One-Time Investment*

In this second category, the terminal cost remains O(1) because the business relies on a massive one-time investment that possesses strong shared utility.

- Large-Scale Infrastructure: Constructing a highway or a Disney theme park requires astronomical funding, but such investment is largely fixed. Once completed, whether it serves a thousand visitors or a hundred thousand, the core operational and maintenance costs remain nearly the same. Take *Shanghai Disneyland* as an example: most of its expenses occur before opening day. For each additional visitor, apart from a trivial increase in electricity and water consumption, virtually no new costs arise. As attendance grows, average cost per visitor plummets—creating immense room for profit expansion.
- Software-as-a-Service (SaaS): Many B2B software companies, such as *Salesforce*, provide customer relationship management solutions via the cloud. They invest heavily in building a robust software platform and hosting it on cloud infrastructure. When a new enterprise subscribes, the incremental cost to *Salesforce* is merely assigning an account—negligible compared to the client's annual subscription fee. This enables SaaS businesses to rapidly scale their customer base and achieve nonlinear revenue growth.

Both types of O(1) models share a common essence: they decouple the input of time, creativity, or capital assets from the number of units sold, unlocking the potential for exponential, non-linear growth.

## 5 Act III: The Ultimate Evolution of Platforms and the "Winner-Takes-All" Dynamic

Building upon the O(1) model, the rise of the internet gave birth to the most explosive business form of our time—the platform economy. It not only inherits the advantage of near-zero marginal cost but also possesses two additional superpowers: spatial replicability and network effects.

At its core, a platform does not directly produce goods or services. Instead, it serves as a bridge—or more precisely, an infrastructure—that connects the supply and demand sides, generating profit by facilitating transactions. For instance, *DiDi* connects drivers with passengers, while *Meituan* links merchants with consumers.

The primary costs of a platform lie in the construction of its technological infrastructure, algorithmic development, and marketing for user acquisition. Due to the infrastructural nature of these elements, most of these investments are one-time costs.

More importantly, the platform's core codebase and business logic can be replicated across the globe at virtually zero additional cost. This frictionless spatial expansion enables platforms to capture markets at extraordinary speed, fueling exponential growth on a global scale (Fig. 3).

Even more importantly, platform models possess network effects. This means that as the number of users on one side increases, users on the other side are naturally drawn in, creating a positive feedback loop. Such effects cause a platform's value to grow exponentially with its user base, while its operating costs remain relatively stable.

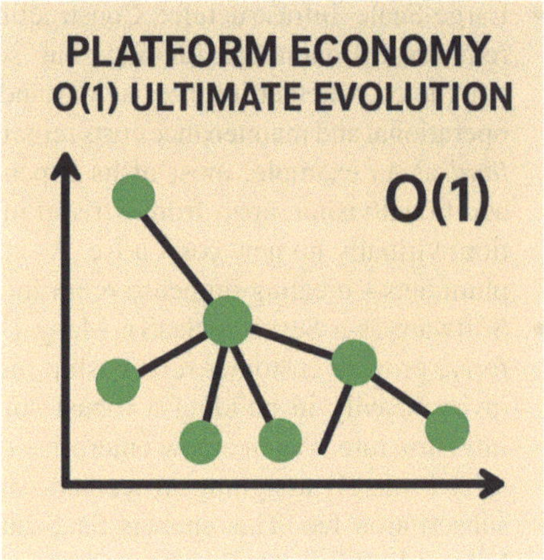


**Fig. 3** The platform economy: Constant terminal cost with massive spatial replicability

Within the terminal cost framework, the platform economy not only maintains an O(1) terminal cost, but its revenue model grows exponentially. This is the most explosive form of business evolution—a perfect embodiment of the "winner-takes-all" law.

## 6 Seeing Beyond the Numbers: The Ultimate Link Between Terminal Cost and Profit

To understand this concept more rigorously, let's reveal its logic with simple mathematics. Let the product price be p, total revenue $R(n) \approx p\, n$, and profit $\pi(n) = R(n) - C(n)$.

Why is the O(1) model so irresistible?

Because when your terminal cost is O(1), as sales $n \to \infty$, your total cost C(n) approaches a fixed value. This means your average unit cost $c_{avg}(n) = C(n)/n$ approaches zero.

When n becomes very large, profit $\pi(n) \approx p{*}n$—it scales linearly with sales. By the time you sell your millionth unit, your incremental profit is nearly equal to the product's full price.

By contrast, in O(n) models, your unit profit is perpetually constrained by marginal cost c, and profit growth is capped by that ceiling. This explains why O(1) businesses can achieve such astonishing profit margins.

## 7 Your Business Compass: Applying Terminal Cost Thinking

Terminal cost is not an abstract mathematical construct. It is a foundational logic for understanding the essence and evolution of business. It helps you break free from linear thinking and instead adopt an end-state perspective—allowing you to chart your path toward exponential growth.

Prioritize lower terminal cost industries: In the early, resource-constrained stages of a startup, choosing businesses whose long-term marginal costs approach zero can dramatically improve your capital efficiency. Examples include information products, software tools, and scalable course systems.

Distinguish "near-zero" from "zero" cost: In reality, there's no such thing as absolute zero cost. Cloud hosting, bandwidth, local compliance, and customer service will all increase with scale. When evaluating, estimate both the rate of marginal cost decline and any persistent long-term components.

Build an uncopyable moat: When terminal cost is O(1), competition shifts from price and efficiency to platform, brand, data, and habit. Your company must transform its low-cost advantage into sustainable profitability through network effects, data barriers, API ecosystems, brand loyalty, and legal protections.

Design replicability into the product itself: Where possible, architect your product as a modular, easily replicable system across geographies and contexts.

Technically, this means adopting cloud-native infrastructure, microservices, and parameterized configurations; commercially, it means enabling franchising, white-label partnerships, or channel alliances.

But beware the end-state traps:

- The platform trap: Low terminal cost and high replicability attract competitors. Without strong network effects or regulatory protection, your profits will erode over time.
- Regulatory and compliance risks: Cross-border replication introduces compliance costs, tax complexity, and political risk, which can abruptly elevate your originally O(1) cost structure.
- Marginal cost misjudgment: Ignoring ongoing costs—maintenance, customer support, content updates—can lead you to mistake an O(n) business for an O(1) one, resulting in major capital misallocation.

## 8 Conclusion

The asymptotic behavior of terminal cost is a crucial indicator for assessing the long-term value and scalability potential of any business model. It teaches us that the most efficient businesses don't just lower costs through scale—they eliminate marginal cost altogether, transforming time and creativity into infinitely replicable, infinitely leveraged assets. By embracing the terminal cost perspective, you can transcend linear thinking and strategically design a business that follows the golden path to exponential growth.

## Further Reading


[1] X. Cao, *Modern Business Management*, Palgrave Macmillan, 2025.
[2] A. Shapiro and H. Varian, *Information Rules: A Strategic Guide to the Network Economy*, Harvard Business School Press, 1999.
[3] X. Cao, *Strategic Management and Organizational Development*, Springer, 2025.
[4] C. W. Clark, *Mathematical Bioeconomics*, 3rd ed., Wiley, 2010.
[5] J. Rifkin, *The Zero Marginal Cost Society*, Palgrave Macmillan, 2014.
[6] E. Brynjolfsson and A. McAfee, *The Second Machine Age*, W. W. Norton, 2014.
[7] P. Hagel, *Net Gain: Expanding Markets Through Virtual Communities*, Harvard Business School Press, 1997.
[8] M. Porter, *Competitive Strategy*, Free Press, 1980.
[9] D. Teece, *Dynamic Capabilities and Strategic Management*, Oxford University Press, 2009.
[10] S. Varian, *Intermediate Microeconomics*, 9th ed., W. W. Norton, 2014.

# Chapter 27
# The Secret to Longevity Is "Petrification": Survival Strategies from the Horseshoe Crab

## 1 Introduction

In the vast epic of biological evolution, species on Earth have risen and fallen like the tides, with the overwhelming majority ultimately swept away by the currents of time and driven to extinction. Yet, one ancient marine creature has stood firm like an anchor amid these waves of change: the horseshoe crab, celebrated as a "living fossil." This remarkable arthropod has thrived on Earth for over 400 million years, surviving multiple mass extinction events, while its form and lifestyle have remained largely unchanged. The astonishing resilience of this creature can perhaps be encapsulated in a profound concept we term "petrification" (Fig. 1).

"Petrification" here does not literally mean turning into an inanimate stone; rather, it is a highly distilled metaphor representing extreme conservatism, remarkable stability, and indestructible defense. Just as solid rock can withstand billions of years of weathering and geological change, the horseshoe crab has, through a "petrified" survival strategy, skillfully avoided nature's ruthless selection pressures, becoming an exemplary model of longevity. By closely analyzing the survival strategy of the horseshoe crab, we can extract many valuable lessons applicable to human society, particularly in entrepreneurship and development.

## 2 The "Petrified" Survival Rules of the Horseshoe Crab: The Underlying Logic of Longevity

The horseshoe crab's status as one of Earth's oldest surviving species is rooted in unique biological traits that bear a remarkable resemblance to what we understand as "stone":

 
S. Li, *Bridging the Innovation Gap*, Innovation, Technology, and Knowledge Management, https://doi.org/10.1007/978-3-032-22652-5_27

**Fig. 1** Minimal appetite and strong defenses have enabled the horseshoe crab to endure across hundreds of millions of years of temporal and environmental change

## *2.1 The Life Philosophy of "Minimal Appetite": Low-Cost Survival through Minimalism*

Imagine a rock—it does not need to eat; it exists silently in the world, taking nothing and demanding nothing. In a similar way, the horseshoe crab embodies a "low-desire" survival philosophy. Its metabolic rate is extremely low, meaning its energy requirements are relatively small. Horseshoe crabs primarily feed on small benthic invertebrates, such as sand worms and bivalves. This relatively simple and easily accessible food source minimizes their dependency on environmental resources. They do not need to traverse mountains and seas in search of scarce resources, nor do they need to battle stronger competitors for food. This "minimal appetite" lifestyle drastically reduces their "operational costs" for survival, allowing them to be self-sufficient within a relatively stable ecological niche and avoiding risky expansions driven by overconsumption. We can understand this strategy as ecological minimalism—a life wisdom of non-contention with the world (Fig. 2).

In stark contrast, organisms that require "more food and more energy" must continuously expand their activity ranges to meet their high physiological demands, sometimes even traversing different geographic regions and ecosystems. This relentless expansion inevitably pushes them into broader yet more complex living spaces, where they unavoidably compete with more species for resources and territory. Every conflict carries substantial risk, and each expansion stretches their front lines indefinitely, causing management costs and uncontrollable factors to surge. This kind of expansion is akin to the unchecked proliferation of cancer cells: it may grow rapidly in the short term, but eventually it exhausts the host's resources, leading to its own

**Fig. 2** The horseshoe crab's minimal appetite and low-desire lifestyle

demise. Ultimately, this scenario of "too many enemies" or "overextended front lines" often becomes the deep-rooted reason for decline or extinction.

## 2.2 *"Indestructible" Defense System: The Wisdom of Stability amid Change*

A rock, with its extraordinary hardness and weight, is not easily destroyed by external forces. Similarly, the horseshoe crab takes its defensive capabilities to the extreme. It possesses a sturdy and thick exoskeleton, a natural "armor" that effectively repels attacks from the vast majority of predators—whether fierce fish or cunning birds, few can penetrate this physical barrier. This provides the horseshoe crab with unparalleled physical protection, shielding it from direct harm (Fig. 3).

Even more astonishing is that the horseshoe crab's defense system is not limited to the physical realm. Its blue blood contains a unique protein—Limulus Amebocyte Lysate (LAL)—which is extremely sensitive to bacterial endotoxins, toxins produced by Gram-negative bacteria. Upon detecting these endotoxins, the protein rapidly coagulates, forming a gel-like substance that encapsulates and immobilizes invading bacteria. This unique immune mechanism grants the horseshoe crab remarkable resistance to pathogens, significantly reducing the risk of infection. Such formidable internal defenses allow it to remain healthy even in oceans teeming with bacteria and viruses.

It is precisely this combination of physical and biochemical defense that enables the horseshoe crab to survive without frequently relying on genetic mutations to adapt to rapidly changing external threats. When a species can effectively protect itself from

**Fig. 3** Horseshoe crab defense mechanisms

predators, disease, and other environmental pressures, it does not need to undergo large-scale, disruptive adaptive changes. This survival wisdom—"staying unchanged to handle change"—allows the horseshoe crab to faithfully retain its form and lifestyle from hundreds of millions of years ago, achieving extraordinary longevity through geological time. Rather than passively changing to fit the environment, it actively defends itself to maintain stability, embodying the essence of "petrification"—like an impenetrable fortress, standing firm against the winds and rains of time.

## 3 The Universality of "Petrification" Wisdom: Comparing Lifespans of Living and Non-living Entities

When we step beyond the biological domain, we are struck by how this "petrification" logic also illuminates truths in many areas of human society. Moreover, when observing different categories of existence on Earth, an intriguing pattern emerges: animals generally have shorter lifespans than plants, and plants in turn generally live shorter than non-living entities such as rocks or mountains. This phenomenon can be perfectly explained by the core concept of "petrification."

## *3.1 Animals: High Activity and High Consumption Lead to Shorter Lifespans*

Most animals must move frequently, hunt, evade predators, and compete for mates to survive. Such high-intensity "offensive" and "expansive" behaviors entail tremendous energy expenditure and physical wear. They require substantial food intake to sustain metabolism and frequently interact with their environment and other organisms, increasing the risk of injury, disease, and predation. Every sprint, fight, and migration consumes life energy and exposes them to greater dangers. Their lives are defined by constant activity and consumption, burning like a fleeting flame—brilliant, yet short-lived. This high-investment, high-risk survival strategy determines their relatively brief lifespans.

## *3.2 Plants: Relatively Stationary and Self-Sufficient, Living Longer than Animals*

Compared to animals, plants adopt a more "petrified" survival strategy. They are generally immobile, rooted in a fixed location, and self-sufficient through photosynthesis, relying minimally on external resources (only sunlight, water, $CO_2$, and soil nutrients). Although plants face threats such as pests, diseases, and drought, many long-lived species (e.g., the African baobab tree, North American bristlecone pine) have developed robust defenses: tough bark, antimicrobial compounds, deep roots to withstand extreme weather, and strong regenerative abilities. This relatively stationary, low-consumption, and highly defensive survival strategy allows them to accumulate many growth cycles, achieving longer lifespans. They are akin to "living stones," existing quietly and steadily, silently resisting the erosion of time (Fig. 4).

## *3.3 Non-living Entities Have the Longest Lifespans: The Ultimate Manifestation of "Petrification"*

Ultimately, when we turn our attention to non-living entities—such as mountains, rocks, and planets—their lifespan is measured in geological epochs, far surpassing that of any living organism. They represent the ultimate embodiment of the "petrification" concept: they do not require sustenance, have no metabolism, exhibit no proactive expansion, and possess extreme physical stability and defensive capacity (resistance to weathering and erosion). They exist in a completely passive yet remarkably resilient manner, largely unconstrained by the concept of time, only undergoing significant change during extreme geological events such as tectonic upheavals or volcanic eruptions. Their existence perfectly illustrates the philosophy of "less is more, stillness is longevity."

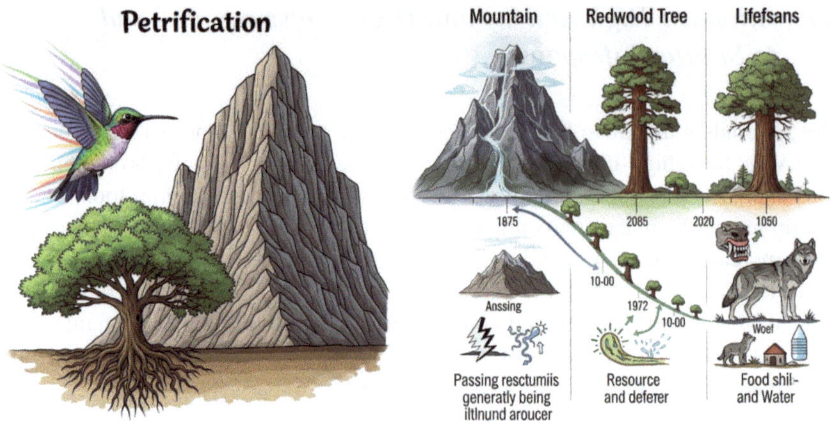


**Fig. 4** Animals, plants, and non-living entities exhibit varying degrees of "petrification," which correspond to differences in lifespan and relative stability over the course of long-term evolution

Thus, from the uniquely enduring horseshoe crab, through the general kingdoms of animals and plants, to non-living entities, the length of life appears to correlate strongly with the degree of "petrification"—that is, their resource demands, proactivity (expansion), and defensive capacity. The closer an entity is to the attributes of a "stone," the stronger its continuity of life (or existence).

The rules of corporate survival: In fierce market competition, many startups in their early stages are often seduced by slogans of "grow bigger, grow stronger," blindly pursuing scale and market share at the cost of burning cash or engaging in low-price competition for short-term growth. However, such relentless "offense" and "consumption" strategies often lead to collapse due to overextended operations, loss of managerial control, or broken financial chains. These enterprises resemble highly active, frequently expanding animals, rapidly depleting their vitality in the process.

In contrast, century-old businesses or industry leaders that endure over time rarely rely on endless expansion. Instead, they depend on their indestructible "core competencies" (such as unique technologies, inimitable brand culture, or exceptional user experiences) along with robust "risk resilience" (including healthy cash flow, stable financial structures, and efficient crisis management). These elements collectively form the company's "defense system," allowing it to withstand market turbulence and remain unassailable. Such enterprises prefer to cultivate their areas of advantage and fortify their protective moats rather than recklessly venturing into unfamiliar domains. This is the practical business application of "petrification" wisdom—focus and defense trump blind expansion.

## 4 The Boundaries of Expansion and the Reevaluation of Defense Value

From the extraordinary survival of the horseshoe crab and the comparative study of lifespans among animals, plants, and non-living entities, we can draw a profound and universal lesson: the longevity of a life form (or an enterprise) is determined less by its offensive or expansion capabilities and more by the solidity and stability of its defensive capacity.

Unlimited expansion, while potentially delivering short-term prosperity and influence, simultaneously entails higher operational risk, longer management lines, and more potential competitors. It is a high-stakes game where a single misstep can lead to total loss. True wisdom lies in exercising measured expansion and focusing resources on the continuous cultivation and reinforcement of core "defensive power." This defensive strength includes resistance to external threats, control of internal depletion, and preservation of core value.

Just as the horseshoe crab, through its "petrified" conservatism, stability, and resilience, has endured the vast span of Earth's history, so too in life and business, controlling desires, deepening protective moats, and strengthening defensive walls remain timeless secrets to longevity and success. In today's rapidly changing and uncertain world, revisiting and applying this "petrification" wisdom may be more critical than ever.

## 5 Balancing Offense and Defense in Invention and Development: Practicing "Petrification" Wisdom

Understanding the profound impact of "petrification" on longevity raises a practical question: in today's fast-paced, competitive environment, how can we pursue invention and development while skillfully balancing the seemingly opposing forces of "offense" and "defense" to achieve sustained success? This is not a binary choice but a strategic art of fine balance.

### *5.1 Strategic Defense: Building the Foundation for Survival*

First and foremost, strategic defense should always take priority, serving as the prerequisite and safeguard for all "offensive" actions. This includes:

1. Consolidating core capabilities and deepening the "moat": A company's "petrified" defensive strength is first reflected in its core competencies. These may include unique technologies, hard-to-replicate brand value, highly loyal customer bases, or efficient operational models. Rather than chasing every trend, resources

should be concentrated on areas of advantage, continually honing and reinforcing "hardcore" strengths. Just like the horseshoe crab's sturdy shell and unique blood, these are its survival fundamentals. For individuals, this means continuous learning and skill enhancement to become indispensable in one's field.
2. Building robust risk resilience: Facing uncertainty requires a sound risk management system, including healthy finances (adequate cash flow, reasonable debt levels), diversified revenue streams, flexible organizational structures, and effective crisis response plans. When market volatility or unexpected events arise, strong resilience allows stability, like a rock, preventing easy toppling. Startups must particularly avoid over-financing or reckless spending and maintain healthy "self-sustaining" capabilities.
3. Maintaining moderate "low desire" and efficient utilization: Inspired by the horseshoe crab's "low appetite," enterprises should avoid unrealistic dreams of "big and all-encompassing" expansion. This entails rational resource planning, investing funds, talent, and energy into areas that truly generate value and reinforce defense, preventing resource dispersion, overextended operations, and inefficiency. For individuals, it involves examining personal desires, avoiding being swept up by consumerism or endless material pursuits, thereby reducing survival pressure and maintaining inner stability.

## *5.2 Precision Offense: Expanding Boundaries Judiciously*

On a solid defensive foundation, effective "offense" and invention can be pursued. This type of offense should be precise and purposeful, not blind expansion:

1. Focused invention rather than broad attacks: Invention drives development, but not every invention warrants massive resource allocation. Companies should select strategically significant inventions that reinforce defense or create new barriers, based on core competencies and market demand. Examples include developing technologies that synergize with existing products or entering closely related, low-risk new markets. Every "offensive" move should have clear objectives and measurable returns.
2. Small steps, rapid validation: In unfamiliar domains, rather than investing heavily in a "grand battle," adopt a small-step, rapid iteration approach. Use MVPs (minimum viable products) or limited trial-and-error testing to quickly validate market responses and adjust directions promptly. This is akin to scouts probing ahead rather than sending the main force recklessly into enemy territory, greatly reducing offensive risk.
3. Vertical or horizontal integration along the value chain: Expansion can be vertical—integrating upstream or downstream to increase control over the value chain, thereby reducing costs or increasing bargaining power—essentially an extension of defense. It can also be horizontal but within strongly related areas, creating scale effects and enhancing market position. This expansion is not for its own sake but to consolidate existing advantages and build a stronger ecosystem.

### 5.3 *Continuous Learning and Adaptation: The Art of Dynamic Balance*

Ultimately, the balance between "offense" and "defense" is not static but requires continuous adjustment:

1. Embrace change and maintain alertness: While emphasizing defense and stability, "petrification" does not mean rigidity. The horseshoe crab's survival over hundreds of millions of years also stems from its extreme adaptation to specific environments. This necessitates constant attention to external changes, including technological invention, market trends, and competitive dynamics, enabling swift responses and strategic adjustments when potential threats or opportunities arise.
2. Build learning-oriented organizations/individuals: Continuous learning and reflection are crucial for dynamic balance. By reviewing successes and failures, offensive and defensive strategies can be optimized. For companies, fostering invention, tolerating reasonable trial-and-error, and establishing knowledge-sharing mechanisms are essential; for individuals, lifelong learning and updating knowledge and thought frameworks are key.
3. Culture shaping: balancing values: Within organizations, it is important to cultivate a culture that encourages invention and breakthrough while emphasizing prudence and risk control. Such a culture helps employees understand the dialectic between "offense" and "defense" and consciously balance both in daily work.

## 6 Conclusion

The secret to longevity does not lie in relentless forward charging, nor in complete stagnation. It is a profound art of balance: under a solid defensive system, carefully choose the direction and intensity of offense. Just as the horseshoe crab, over hundreds of millions of years, has exemplified life's continuity through its "petrified" stability and defense, so too should we, in personal growth, business development, and societal progress, draw inspiration from it—learning to advance strategically while fortifying our foundations, navigating storms with stability, and achieving enduring success.

## Further Reading

[1] X. Cao, *Strategic Management and Organizational Development*, Springer, 2025.
[2] E. O. Wilson, *The Diversity of Life*, Harvard University Press, 1992.
[3] R. Dawkins, *The Selfish Gene*, 40th Anniversary ed., Oxford University Press, 2016.
[4] X. Cao, *Modern Business Management*, Palgrave Macmillan, 2025.
[5] F. L. Coolidge, *Cognitive Archaeology and Human Evolution*, Cambridge University Press, 2009.

[6] J. Diamond, *Collapse: How Societies Choose to Fail or Succeed*, Viking, 2005.
[7] M. Ridley, *The Origins of Virtue*, Penguin, 1996.
[8] P. Holland, *Hidden Order*, Addison-Wesley, 1995.
[9] H. Thomas, *Long-Lived Species and Business Lessons*, Routledge, 2014.
[10] A. Edmondson, *Teaming*, Jossey-Bass, 2012.

# Chapter 28
# Constancy in Evolution: The Survival Wisdom of Living Fossils

## 1 Introduction

The evolutionary history of life on Earth, spanning over four billion years, is a grand and often unpredictable epic. At the heart of this epic lies Darwin's principle of "natural selection and the survival of the fittest," acting like an invisible hand that shapes the complex and diverse forms of life across the planet. We tend to assume that only through continuous variation and adaptation can species that best fit their environments survive the relentless pressures of natural selection and successfully reproduce. We are accustomed to seeing iterative changes in biological forms, accustomed to witnessing life display astonishing adaptive capabilities and evolutionary paths after each geological shift or climatic upheaval. It seems as though "change" is the eternal truth of the biological world—that only by actively embracing change and rapidly iterating traits and strategies can a species secure its foothold, or even rise to dominance, on the stage of life (Fig. 1).

However, upon closer examination of this vast timeline, a paradoxical phenomenon emerges: some "maverick" life forms, as if forgotten by time, have maintained nearly unchanged morphologies and core characteristics over hundreds of millions of years, yet have miraculously withstood countless environmental upheavals and survived to the present day. These ancient and stable organisms are what we call "living fossils." Notable examples include the coelacanth, horseshoe crab, and nautilus. Their life stories read like living history textbooks, challenging our conventional understanding of evolutionary patterns. The existence of living fossils raises a fundamental question: in an era that universally pursues "change," how should we understand and learn from the wisdom of "constancy"? This is not only a biological mystery but also offers profoundly valuable insights for modern entrepreneurs navigating a rapidly changing world.

 
S. Li, *Bridging the Innovation Gap*, Innovation, Technology, and Knowledge Management, https://doi.org/10.1007/978-3-032-22652-5_28

**Fig. 1** Living fossils spanning time and space

## 2 Universal Traits: The Conservative Beauty and Extreme Efficiency at Life's Core

The story of evolution is not only one of radical change and invention. Behind the sweeping transformations of species, there exists a deeper conservative beauty—traits that persist across vast geological periods and fluctuating environmental conditions, maintaining their effectiveness. These are the universal traits, which serve as the solid foundation of life's edifice. No matter how the upper structures change, the foundation remains steadfast, providing the underlying support for life's continuity and reproduction, and representing the core capabilities that enable life to withstand any challenge.

We can illustrate this universality and efficiency with a few examples. First, the vertebral column of vertebrates. This axial skeleton, composed of a series of interconnected vertebrae, has remained remarkably consistent through hundreds of millions of years of evolution—from primitive fish swaying through oceans, to amphibians laboriously crawling onto land, to massive dinosaurs ruling terrestrial realms, to birds soaring through the sky, and finally to humans walking upright. The vertebral column serves as the structural support and protector of the central nervous system, and its core function has been preserved astonishingly well. While details differ—the vertebrae of fish adapt to buoyancy in water, those of snakes allow for flexible twisting, and bird vertebrae fuse in places to facilitate flight and reduce weight—the structural and functional conservatism of the vertebral column remains high. It efficiently addresses universal challenges for large multicellular animals in movement, weight support, and spinal cord protection, making it a long-lasting evolutionary success preserved by natural selection.

Second, the bilateral symmetry found in nearly all animals. This is not a coincidental case of convergent evolution but a highly optimized result of natural selection. Such body organization allows efficient forward movement and concentrates major sensory organs (eyes, olfactory, auditory organs) and neural centers at the front, forming a centralized head. This "cephalization" trend enables animals to perceive the environment ahead more quickly and accurately, offering significant advantages in both food acquisition and predator avoidance. The efficiency and universality of this layout are widespread across animals—from insects to fish to mammals—playing a key role in directional movement and information processing in complex environments.

A deeper, more fundamental universality exists at the molecular level: all known life (excluding viruses) uses DNA as its genetic material. The double-helix structure of DNA, base-pairing rules, and semi-conservative replication mechanism ensure the stable storage and precise transmission of genetic information, forming the basis for life's continuity and trait expression. This molecular universality reveals the operational logic at life's core, and its efficiency and stability in encoding and replicating information have remained unsurpassed for billions of years, serving as the shared "source code" and cornerstone of life on Earth.

The presence of these universal traits demonstrates that life has already found nearly perfect and highly efficient solutions to fundamental survival problems, eliminating the need for frequent alterations. For living fossils, the traits they carry are precisely these time-tested universal characteristics, providing a solid biological foundation for maintaining "constancy" over eons. These foundational advantages enable them to withstand countless environmental changes, large and small, and remain resilient through the ages.

## 3 The Art of Survival for Living Fossils: Responding to Change Through Constancy

Living fossils did not survive to the present merely by chance. Each has evolved a refined and unique set of survival strategies, allowing it to face environmental variability with a relatively unchanging posture, becoming long-lived members of their respective ecosystems. These strategies are not rigid but highly optimized, demonstrating profound adaptability.

### *3.1 Coelacanth: A Time Refuge in the Deep Sea and a Conservative Life Philosophy*

The coelacanth, a "Lazarus species" once thought extinct for tens of millions of years, astonished the scientific world when rediscovered in 1938. Its fossils date

**Fig. 2** Coelacanth

back to approximately 400 million years ago in the Devonian, and its morphology is strikingly similar to that of its ancient ancestors, almost as if it stepped straight out of the geological past. The survival strategy of the coelacanth can be summarized as "finding and remaining in a stable ecological niche while adopting a conservative life strategy" (Fig. 2).

They primarily inhabit specific deep-sea regions, usually dwelling in dark, cold environments at depths ranging from 200 meters to several thousand meters. The deep sea is a relatively isolated world, where variations in light, temperature, currents, and food supply are far less pronounced than in sunlit shallow waters or on land. This extreme environmental stability greatly reduces external selective pressures, allowing coelacanths to survive without undergoing dramatic morphological changes. In essence, they have chosen the slowest-changing "safe harbor" on Earth.

At the same time, coelacanths adopt a conservative life strategy characterized by low metabolic rates, exceptional longevity, and relatively low reproductive output. Their metabolism is exceedingly slow, maximizing adaptation to the cold, nutrient-scarce deep-sea environment and minimizing energy expenditure. They can live for decades, even over a century, ensuring that individuals have sufficient time to reproduce; even if a reproductive cycle encounters difficulties, the individuals can survive until the next opportunity. Their low reproductive rate—producing relatively few but large eggs, with embryonic development lasting up to three years within the mother—means they do not rely on rapid generational turnover to adapt. Instead, they maintain population numbers through individual resilience and the accumulation of time.

This "act by stillness" strategy represents a profound risk-avoidance wisdom: rather than struggling to change in the fiercely competitive, unpredictable "Red Sea," it is wiser to dwell in the relatively stable, low-competition "Blue Sea" of the deep, moving at a composed pace and relying on inherent strong adaptability to minimize the impact of external environmental fluctuations over millennia. This survival philosophy perfectly embodies the deeper meaning of "slow is fast."

## *3.2 Horseshoe Crab: Multi-Layered "Biological Insurance" and Robust Defense*

The horseshoe crab (pronounced *hòu*), an ancient marine arthropod, dates back approximately 450 million years to the Ordovician, predating dinosaurs and even many modern insects. Its survival strategy resembles a form of "multi-layered biological insurance": risks are dispersed, and strong defensive mechanisms are built in, ensuring that it remains unvanquished in ever-changing environments (Fig. 3).

They exhibit remarkable environmental tolerance. Horseshoe crabs primarily inhabit intertidal zones and shallow sandy or muddy seabeds, areas subjected to drastic fluctuations in tides, salinity, temperature, and oxygen levels—conditions that are harsh for many other organisms. Yet, horseshoe crabs navigate these challenges with ease, even surviving in sulfur-rich, low-oxygen environments for several hours. This can be seen as a physiological form of "diversified investment," enabling them to thrive under multiple, sometimes harsh, environmental conditions rather than relying on a single stable habitat.

Additionally, they possess a broad diet: detritus from algae, shell fragments, and other organic matter, as well as small invertebrates like worms and mollusks. This dietary flexibility ensures energy intake even when certain food sources are scarce, significantly reducing starvation risk and allowing continuous survival despite fluctuations in the food chain.

Their most striking feature—the rigid, semi-circular carapace—provides exceptional physical protection. This thick exoskeleton effectively shields them from predators, such as seabirds and large fish, as well as from physical impacts caused by tides, waves, or even human activity, such as being stepped on or run over, without sustaining fatal damage. The tail spine, although sharp in appearance, primarily aids in movement within the sediment and allows the animal to right itself if flipped, rather than serving as an offensive weapon. This illustrates a survival philosophy where defensive strength outweighs offensive capability: by building a formidable self-protection system, they minimize exposure to danger and avoid unnecessary conflict.

**Fig. 3** Horseshoe crab

In terms of reproduction, horseshoe crabs gather in large numbers on beaches to spawn annually. Females can lay tens of thousands or even hundreds of thousands of eggs at a time. Although the survival rate of individual eggs and larvae is low, the sheer number ensures species continuity—a strategy of "risk dispersion through quantity."

This combination of multi-layered protection, robust defense, and risk-spreading resilience has allowed horseshoe crabs to reproduce steadily over hundreds of millions of years, becoming an indispensable part of shallow marine ecosystems.

### *3.3 Nautilus: The "Technological Monopoly" and Niche Competition in the Deep Sea*

The nautilus, the only extant shelled cephalopod and a distant relative of octopuses and squids, has a fossil record dating back approximately 500 million years to the late Cambrian. Its survival secret lies in its successful execution of "niche differentiation" within a specific deep-sea "raceway," combined with the establishment of a "core technological barrier," allowing it to maintain a stable position amid evolutionary tides and become a de facto "monopolist" within its unique ecological niche (Fig. 4).

They inhabit the deep-water regions along the continental slope, typically between 100 and 500 meters below the surface. This zone allows them to avoid direct confrontation with the sunlit, highly competitive, and species-rich shallow waters—home to fast-swimming fish and more advanced shell-less cephalopods—while also avoiding the extreme scarcity of true abyssal zones. In doing so, they have cleverly found a relatively stable and resource-sufficient "blue ocean market," a niche with few competitors yet adequate resources for survival.

The nautilus' "core technology" is its perfect buoyancy regulation system: its spiral shell contains multiple precisely partitioned chambers. By adjusting the ratio

**Fig. 4** Nautilus

of gas to liquid within these chambers (via siphuncle filtration), the nautilus can effortlessly ascend or descend, hovering or moving at precise depths. This enables it to seek prey, such as small fish and crustaceans, while evading predators. Coupled with its strong, pressure-resistant shell, it can withstand the immense pressure of the deep sea, protecting its soft body and allowing it to move freely in and out of deep-water habitats—something many shell-less cephalopods and shallow-water species cannot achieve.

These "core technologies" prevent other animals from easily competing within the nautilus' ecological niche. Octopuses and squids, while agile, lack pressure-resistant shells and precise buoyancy control, limiting their ability to stay at specific depths for extended periods or endure deep-water pressures. Most deep-sea fish lack the same predatory flexibility. As a result, the nautilus has effectively achieved near-monopoly status within its "technical lane." Even if macro-environmental conditions shift slightly, as long as the fundamental deep-sea characteristics it relies on—pressure, temperature, and buoyancy requirements—remain stable, the nautilus can continue to survive using its unique capabilities. Additionally, it employs nocturnal feeding, taking advantage of temporal "displacement" to avoid predators and competitors active during the day, increasing hunting efficiency and reducing risk. This strategy demonstrates that it does not adapt to all environments indiscriminately, but rather leverages its specialized "technological" advantages to secure an irreplaceable position in a selected, stable "blue ocean" niche.

## 4 The Wisdom of "Living Fossils": Profound Lessons for Modern Entrepreneurship

The survival strategies of living fossils provide valuable insights for navigating today's unpredictable business environment. Their stories illustrate that success does not depend solely on disruptive invention; sometimes, the wisdom of "constancy" can build enduring enterprises and grant deeper vitality.

1. Find and cultivate your "deep-sea blue ocean": Like the coelacanth, modern entrepreneurs should avoid blindly chasing crowded, popular "red ocean" markets dominated by powerful incumbents. Instead, they should identify neglected niches with slow change but steady demand. By leveraging expertise and patience, a business can become a specialist and leader in these areas, building defensible advantages that are difficult to dislodge. This requires sharp market insight, the ability to identify genuine gaps and long-tail opportunities, and a long-term vision with the perseverance to wait for results. Rather than exhausting resources in cutthroat competition, it is wiser to secure a leading position in a uniquely suited niche and build deep industry moats.
2. Build resilience, not fragility: Drawing inspiration from the horseshoe crab, modern enterprises should construct multidimensional, highly resilient business models—like purchasing "biological insurance"—to withstand unpredictable

external shocks. This involves diversifying revenue sources, avoiding over-reliance on a single-product, service, or client; enhancing risk management through healthy cash flow, controlled debt, and sufficient emergency reserves; and reducing supply chain dependency to ensure critical stability. Equally important is strengthening the company's foundational defenses—loyalty-building brands, excellent customer service, robust legal compliance, and cohesive corporate culture and workforce. These "shell-like" internal strengths help the enterprise endure market volatility, economic downturns, or crises, ensuring core business stability. This approach offers more sustainable long-term growth than simply chasing rapid expansion.

3. Forge core technology barriers and leverage strategic displacement: Learning from the nautilus, entrepreneurs should invest in genuinely unique, hard-to-replicate core technologies, patents, or business models. Such "special skills" create strong competitive barriers and enable "displaced competition," avoiding direct confrontations in commoditized markets. This may involve highly differentiated product features, service experiences, or cost structures, or providing highly customized solutions for specific vertical user groups. By exploiting temporal advantages—such as capturing early gains from emerging trends or acting during competitors' dormant periods—or spatial advantages, like expanding into new regions or cross-industry applications, companies can maintain dominance in their exclusive "deep-sea lane," building formidable moats that competitors cannot easily breach. This strategy is not rigid adherence but a precise, innovative deployment on a stable foundation.

In summary, the survival wisdom of living fossils is a masterpiece of natural selection. Their extraordinary "constancy" demonstrates that, beyond rapid adaptation and change, there exists a path to success grounded in profound environmental understanding, meticulous honing of core strengths, and clever risk avoidance. For modern entrepreneurs, studying these ancient life forms can reveal a steadier, more enduring path in a rapidly changing world—one that enables sustainable development and allows enterprises to become enduring "business living fossils" within their domains.

## 5 Conclusion: The Enduring Wisdom of Living Fossils and the Future of Entrepreneurship

The existence of living fossils provides a fresh perspective on the evolution of life and business. They are not biological anomalies but extreme adapters selected by natural selection over vast timescales. Their "constancy" clearly demonstrates that success is not solely achieved through disruptive invention; sometimes, steadfast adherence to core strengths, deep cultivation, and defensive strategies can produce achievements that withstand the test of time.

For modern entrepreneurs, the philosophy of living fossils offers profound guidance. In an increasingly chaotic and fast-changing business environment, blindly

**Fig. 5** The enduring wisdom of living fossils offers profound insights for entrepreneurship

chasing trends or over-expanding can cause enterprises to fall like shooting stars. In contrast, companies that identify and defend unique niches (like the coelacanth's secluded deep-sea habitat), build multidimensional, resilient risk defenses (like the horseshoe crab's robust shell), and forge hard-to-replicate core technologies (like the nautilus' buoyancy system) are truly equipped to weather market storms and endure.

Ultimately, the stories of living fossils teach us that true wisdom lies in understanding the dialectic between change and constancy. While the external world evolves, recognizing and firmly holding core competencies of universal value, building irreplaceable advantages, and managing with a stable, long-term mindset may be the key for enterprises to achieve sustainable development and become enduring "business living fossils" in their respective fields (Fig. 5).

## Further Reading

[1] X. Cao, *Modern Business Management*, Palgrave Macmillan, 2025.
[2] E. O. Wilson, *The Social Conquest of Earth*, Liveright, 2012.
[3] R. Dawkins, *Climbing Mount Improbable*, W. W. Norton, 1996.
[4] X. Cao, *Strategic Management and Organizational Development*, Springer, 2025.
[5] J. Gould, *Wonderful Life: The Burgess Shale and the Nature of History*, W. W. Norton, 1989.
[6] F. L. Coolidge and T. Wynn, *Cognitive Archaeology and Human Evolution*, Cambridge University Press, 2009.
[7] M. Ridley, *The Evolution of Everything*, HarperCollins, 2015.
[8] P. Holland, *Hidden Order*, Addison-Wesley, 1995.
[9] C. Darwin, *On the Origin of Species*, John Murray, 1859.
[10] N. Tufekci, *Twitter and Tear Gas*, Yale University Press, 2017.

MIX
Papier aus verantwortungsvollen Quellen
Paper from responsible sources
FSC® C105338

If you have any concerns about our products,
you can contact us on
**ProductSafety@springernature.com**

In case Publisher is established outside the EU,
the EU authorized representative is:
**Springer Nature Customer Service Center GmbH**
**Europaplatz 3, 69115 Heidelberg, Germany**

Printed by Libri Plureos GmbH
in Hamburg, Germany